TO THE ENDS OF THE EARTH

To the Ends of the Earth

Norman McLeod and the Highlanders' migration to Nova Scotia and New Zealand

Neil Robinson

HarperCollins*Publishers New Zealand*

Author's note

MacLeod, McLeod or Macleod: These are some of the variations in the spelling of the surname, typical of many Scottish names. I once thought that "Mac" was the Scottish choice, with "Mc" favoured in New Zealand and no clear preference in Nova Scotia. But now I find there is no firm rule, no consistency even with the Rev. Norman MacLeod/McLeod, so I have made no attempt to follow one spelling or the other. — N.C.R.

By the same author:
Lion of Scotland (1952, 1972)
James Fletcher: Builder (1970)
Not as Strangers (1967)

First published in 1997 by
HarperCollins*Publishers (New Zealand)* Limited
P.O. Box 1, Auckland

ISBN 1 86950 265 5

Neil Robinson asserts the moral right to be identified as the author of this work.

Cover: "The Final Farewell" by Nova Scotian artist Barrie Fraser (courtesy Gaelic College Foundation, St Ann's).
Designed by Pages Literary Pursuits
Printed by Wright & Carman (N.Z.) Ltd, Wellington

Contents

Acknowledgements

"History and songs and literature and folklore and memory and stories all swing around in their habitual untidy magic inside my head."

That is how Frank Delaney, whimsically but with a measure of truth, sets the scene for his delightful book, *Walk to the Western Isles (after Boswell and Johnson)*, recently published by HarperCollins. Much the same mixture swims around in my head as I attempt to list those, alive and dead, who have helped me with this book. Many people, now living in different lands but sharing the same interests, have come forward with letters, anecdotes, records of events in danger of being forgotten, tales that, handed down from one generation to another, still have freshness and vitality.

So many have helped me that I can mention only some of those to whom my debt is greatest. A few years ago when we were in Nova Scotia, Bonnie and Roland Thornhill, friends since their visit to New Zealand when he was Minister for Tourism and Culture in the Nova Scotian government, suggested that I should write some more about the people involved in the McLeod migration, about their descendants and the way life has gone in the lands the people had known. The infectious Thornhill enthusiasm, and that of others spoken to since then, kept my hand to the task. Betty Powell, building up a great store of material at the House of Memories, Waipu, and using her computer-like brain to answer wide-ranging questions, will always have me in her debt. Barbara Weiskrantz, descendant of a first cousin of Norman McLeod, brought Assynt and the Sutherland "Clearance" country to life when she and Larry, her husband, escorted us to the far North-West. She also introduced us to Norman MacAskill, OBE, fisherman, musician, custodian of the history and folklore of his piece of the Highlands; the man who, with a talented band of helpers, made the unveiling of the Norman McLeod memorial at Clachtoll a memorable occasion. Sam MacPhee, executive director of the Gaelic College of Celtic Arts and Crafts at St Ann's, Nova Scotia, has assisted me in many ways, as have many other Nova Scotian folk with an interest in the Scottish migration. The debt that I gratefully acknowledge to many others is implicit in the story: Ian Lang, who died at 97, and Hector Lang; the late John "Sam" Nicholson, and Barbara; Belle Matheson and the late Captain Keith Matheson; the late Norrie and Alex MacLeod; Les Meiklejohn; Anne Finlayson; Colin McGregor who died at 100; Angus Campbell; Doris Ewen;

Anne Picketts, Barley McKay, Ted and Sheryl at the House of Memories; Trevor McKenzie; Dan Lewis; McLeans living in Cape Breton and New Zealand; and a special mention for two women, Isobel Macaulay Jones, who will be long remembered in Cape Breton, and my aunt, Beulah (Campbell) Williamson who, in the years before her death at 95, could show me Waipu before the First World War as seen through the eyes of a lively girl. Finally, my grateful thanks to Bob Campbell, Cape Breton-born professor of English at Prince Edward Island University who, while visiting New Zealand, read my manuscript, made some thoughtful suggestions and wrote the foreword, and to Ray Richards, friend over many years and a wise counsellor.

NEIL ROBINSON
Campbells Bay, Auckland

Foreword

By Robert L. Campbell
Dean of Arts, University of Prince Edward Island

Having been born and raised in Cape Breton, I had heard of the Rev. Norman McLeod when I was quite young, but it was not until I read Neil Robinson's *Lion of Scotland* that I came to realise the great drama of the McLeod story. It was a genuine pleasure, therefore, to meet Neil and Flora Robinson on the occasion of the 1995 Waipu Caledonian Games, and an equal pleasure to learn that Neil was preparing a further work on the subject of McLeod and his people, and on the way life has gone since McLeod's time in the Western Highlands where the story began, and in Nova Scotia and New Zealand where the migrants made their homes.

The migration of over eight hundred Highlanders from Scotland to Nova Scotia and then, more than thirty years later, to New Zealand is a fascinating enough saga to have attracted the attention of a number of writers. In New Zealand, for instance, works on the subject have included a major play and an award-winning novel, as well as a number of factual studies. Unfortunately, most of these works have overplayed the autocratic nature of McLeod's leadership and the austerity of the Calvinism practised by his people. In *Lion of Scotland*, and now in this present volume, Neil Robinson has provided an alternative view. And well he might for, as he reveals for us, the St Ann's/Waipu story is overwhelmingly one of good humour, courage and resourcefulness, not of tyranny.

Since he is of "Novie" stock on one side of his family, Robinson has known the Waipu district from an early age, and enjoys an easy familiarity with its people, which has been reinforced by several visits to Nova Scotia, to the Highlands and to Skye, the home of his mother's people. He is thus able to present an insider's view of the subject, one laced with his own memories as well as with those of countless others in the community. He has been given access to family journals and to numerous letters, and incorporates this material very effectively.

Readers in Scotland, in Nova Scotia and in New Zealand will find here a timeless and a universal story of pioneering, one to which the enigmatic character of Norman McLeod adds a special flavour.

Approximate area from which the migrants came

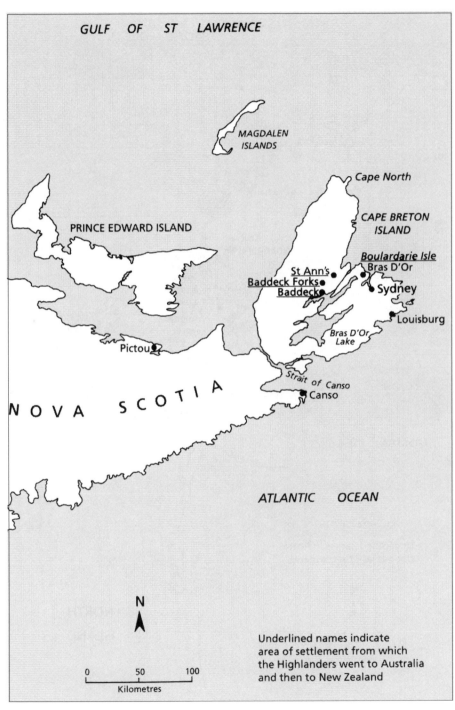

GULF OF ST LAWRENCE

MAGDALEN
ISLANDS

Cape North

PRINCE EDWARD ISLAND

CAPE BRETON
ISLAND

Boulardarie Isle
Bras D'Or

St Ann's
Baddeck Forks
Baddeck

Sydney

Louisburg

Bras D'Or
Lake

Pictou

N O V A   S C O T I A

Strait of Canso

Canso

ATLANTIC   OCEAN

N

0   50   100

Kilometres

Underlined names indicate
area of settlement from which
the Highlanders went to Australia
and then to New Zealand

Areas of migrant settlement

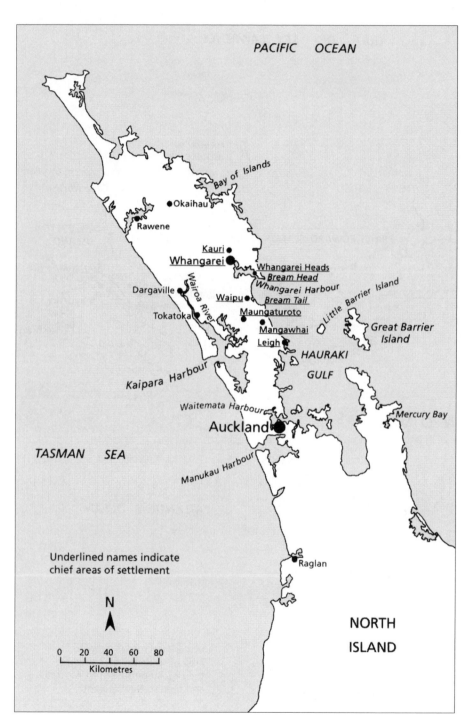

PACIFIC OCEAN

Bay of Islands

●Okaihau

Rawene

Kauri
Whangarei ●
Whangarei Heads
Bream Head
Whangarei Harbour
Dargaville
Waipu ● Bream Tail
Tokatoka
Maungaturoto

Wairoa River

Mangawhai
Leigh ●

Little Barrier Island

Great Barrier Island

HAURAKI

GULF

Kaipara Harbour

Waitemata Harbour
Mercury Bay

Auckland ●

TASMAN SEA

Manukau Harbour

Underlined names indicate
chief areas of settlement

N

0 20 40 60 80
Kilometres

Raglan

NORTH

ISLAND

Areas of migrant settlement

Preface

This is not a formal history, a regular progression through the years that saw Norman McLeod, that formidable, arrogant and very lively man, and many others who loved or rejected him, leave their Highland and Hebridean homes for Nova Scotia, and later for New Zealand. The history is there, in many good books that tell the story of the Clearances, and the thinning-out of the Highland population in various other ways.

What I have attempted to do is to show the migrants as they were, their descendants as they were — and are — and, in an informal way, show that they are still one people.

It is episodic, it goes backwards and forward in time. I kept hoping that, when I was going back to another age as I wrote, I wouldn't meet myself coming forward! But this book will, I hope, make readers feel that today and 150 years ago are not so very far apart, basically, in the way people think and act.

In case some readers are not familiar with the history behind my stories, I shall set out some of the hard facts of the migration. Norman McLeod, born in 1780 at Clachtoll, Assynt, grew up as a rebel against entrenched privilege. It was a tough battle and he decided to seek what he wanted in the New World. In 1817, he went to Pictou, Nova Scotia, with a loyal band of followers; in 1820, to St Ann's, on Cape Breton Island, and there he stayed for over thirty years, his following reinforced by other arrivals from Pictou and Scotland. In the 1850s, six ships, mostly built by their own craftsmen, took 800 men, women and children to New Zealand, after a tentative look at Australia. And there many of their descendants still live. They have lived varied and, at times, exciting lives.

Their story, as one Scottish newspaper has said, is an important contribution to the history of the Scottish people. The links grow stronger all the time and I hope that strength, which fortifies so many people in the Highlands, in Nova Scotia and in New Zealand, shows through to some degree in this book.

Chapter One

New Year's Day at Waipu:
A Harvest of Memories

To THE BEMUSED BOY standing alone in the crowd, the day seemed like a great wheel, revolving slowly and implacably, throwing up light, voices, laughter, the skirling of pipes, the beating of drums. It was, he knew, the first day of the year, the day for the games, but nothing had prepared him for this. Waipu was a quiet village where no-one seemed to hurry, where there was always time for a friendly word or two when people met in the street. What had happened now? He stood silent while the day moved on to its peak.

He remembered all this, in a sudden flash, many years later. Everything had changed, but everything remained the same: bagpipes and drums, voices and laughter, a warmth and stability were still there, although many of the faces were no longer familiar. Waipu, on New Year's Day at the Highland games, was a stimulating place. No unseemly haste among the spectators, greetings among old friends, talk that still allowed an occasional look at a caber-tossing, a hammer-throw, the twinkling feet of young dancers.

Once again he stood among a flowing, orderly crowd. The mid-summer sky was a clear blue, holding its colour to where it met the sharp crests of the inland ranges. The stream ran down to the sea, not visible from where he stood, but which he knew would be even bluer than the sky, right out to the fantastic, tortured islands of Bream Bay and the raw peaks of Whangarei Heads. The scatter of buildings in the village spread a little further now along tarsealed roads, but for the most part they were cosmetic changes; and further out, trees had grown taller, the grass on dairy farms, after rain, was a deeper green. The land, a rich loam, had a steadfast, enduring look.

Was this scene something that, with minor differences, could be found in a hundred other parts of New Zealand? Peaceful, bland, pleasant without perhaps being exciting. What could he uncover beneath the surface?

Modesty that is not deliberate, an ingrown reticence, can affect a community as well as a person. Successes, not just failures, can be concealed in silence. As he allowed himself to be carried along in the crowd, his thoughts went in this direction. He could see at the centre of Waipu not only the church and the House of Memories but two monuments — one to those who had come from Nova Scotia in six ships in the 1850s, the other to

15

Ian Lang at the gate of the family homestead on Langs Beach. Sand and cliff continue in a great arc to Bream Tail, on the horizon. Ian died at the grand age of 97.

those who had died in two major wars. A veil of silence did not mean things were forgotten, or that pride did not exist.

At that moment he saw a familiar face, known to him for many years. Ian Lang, a vigorous 95-year-old, with lively eyes, a long, lean body, sat comfortably in a shaded spot in a small court of his own while the crowd went by. One man in the group was listening with some perplexity as Ian, leaning forward cordially, addressed him: "You've come all the way from Nova Scotia to meet your kinsfolk. Have you enjoyed our Waipu beef?"

Waipu beef proved to be a dish which the Nova Scotian had known and enjoyed at home under the name of curds.

Food habits, Ian suggested, had not changed in the move from Nova Scotia, in one other respect at least. When two Waipu men went fishing they took some potatoes with them — nothing else, as they didn't plan to be out long. The weather turned bad, they pulled their boat up on a rocky little island, and were stuck there for a week when the weather got worse. They lived on potatoes boiled with the fish they caught. When at last they got home, the first question was what they wanted to eat. Just name it, they were told, and it will be made ready. The older man replied promptly, "Just give me some fish and potatoes!"

Ian enjoyed telling the story. An interesting man, the Nova Scotian said later to a friend. Was he a fisherman himself perhaps, or a farmer?

He was an engineer. You'd have to know him a long time before he would tell you, but he set out the road through the gorges and ridges of the Brynderwyns, coming down to Waipu. However, his great secret pride was the lighthouse at Cape Reinga, at the northern tip of New Zealand, remote and storm lashed, a true test for an engineer.

Engineers may be a reticent breed, especially Scottish ones born in New Zealand, and Lockie Campbell's relatives had to wait until after his death, many years later, to learn of his part in one of the most remarkable events in the First World War: the tunnelling under the German lines at Messines, on the Western Front. And it was only a diary kept by his comrade, Peter Keller, that told something of what was involved, in human terms, in building a railway track through one of the most difficult parts of New Zealand seven years before that war. Plenty of tunnelling there, too!

Lockie, joined later by his younger brother Owen, surveyed in high mountain bushland in the heart of the North Island, seeking the best route for the final section of the Main Trunk Railway that would link Auckland to Wellington, the capital. The celebrated Raurimu Spiral, still one of the marvels of the railway world, turns a complete circle in a stretch of 11.5 kilometres travelling through two tunnels and three horseshoe bends while it climbs a height of 215 metres. Vivid impressions from Peter Keller's diary, but not from the down-to-earth Lockie Campbell: "Winter roads deep in mud; monthly pay brought in on horseback with a rifle over the saddle; excavating done by pick and shovel, the spoil from tunnels and cuttings moved to fillings by wheelbarrow on running planks, by handcarts or horse-drawn trucks on rails for the longer distances. A pleasure to see an intelligent horse working underground, under lighting from candles and later, acetylene lamps," Peter wrote. "Putting in the centre pegs in the filthy mud on the tunnel floor was a slow and unpleasant job, not improved in any way by the horse droppings and the stench left after months of working..."

After all that, Lockie must have found similarities, as well as differences, tunnelling ten years later in the mud of Flanders, to create a huge underground area, sufficient to hold hundreds of fighting men. The sudden emergence of these men, fully armed, behind the German lines, made Messines one of the few decisive battles of the deadly trench war.

A long way from Waipu on New Year's Day, from Ian Lang and his friends sitting companionably in the shade on a summer afternoon. It was a day to rouse old memories, stimulated by the reviving of near-forgotten associations and friendships. No matter how far a young man or woman had been taken by the demands of work or changing circumstances, New Year's Day would sooner or later draw each one of them back. And now, as Ian and his friends sat together, a voice broke into their wide-ranging memories.

"Just listen to that noise, that music! One thing's for sure. *He* wouldn't have approved of all this frivolity!"

No one needed to ask who "he" might be. It is a measure of Norman McLeod's vitality that, born more than two hundred years ago, dead for over a century, mention of his name can still arouse keen discussion and powerful argument.

"Why was he so much against things? So much of what could so naturally be part of his people's life? The pipes, singing in church, clothes that had some colour and style in them, men who wore beards?"

Answers are still being found to that question, none of them conclusive, all of them keenly argued over. Here is one view of the man: "In the year 1817 Norman McLeod — fisherman, farmer, philosopher, preacher, active protester against the privileged in church and state — left the Scottish Highlands, never to return. Craggy, tough, with the presence of a chieftain of old, he drew people to him even more easily than he repelled others with his harsh, aggressive style. With him on the *Frances Ann* as it left the Assynt coast behind was a tight little band of followers, drawn to him by the strength of his personality, the fervour and logic of his denunciation of the decadent established church."

All of that is true, but not necessarily conclusive; there are so many fringe arguments that carry some weight. Highlanders, rooted for generations to the family croft, to the one piece of ground, would not necessarily move halfway across the world for religious reasons. A harsh life enhanced the appeal of the unknown, of the romantic. Culloden was in the past, its romance quenched in butchery, but the Highlander could still look around for colour and a measure of excitement. Those who went with McLeod were no dumb oxen, driven by a dominating master, yet stories of McLeod confronting the powerful ones became part of their folklore: McLeod the student, arguing against the entrenched power of the university; McLeod the young father, carrying his baby across moor and mountain to find a proper minister to christen his child, only to be thwarted by his local priest. Some remarkable events on the *Frances Ann*, almost overwhelmed by days of storm in mid-Atlantic, added another page to the McLeod story.

As the years passed, other events would gain the magic gloss of folk legend. Right through to Australia when Norman, after a journey to the interior of Victoria, where the law was frail, was confronted by bushrangers who demanded money and threatened his life. McLeod was not intimidated. Forcefully, he made them see the error of their ways and, before bidding them farewell, led them in prayer begging for their salvation.

And so Norman McLeod was more than the minister to his followers. He was a formidable man they could take pride in. And, just to make matters even less simple, those close to him could tell stories that seemed to

Norman McLeod: a fascinating, highly complex character. Born in 1780,
he died at Waipu in 1866, strong to the end.

contradict much of what they saw—his willingness to live on human terms
with leaders in, for example, the Catholic church, as long as they earned his
approval; his gentle affection for little children, recalled often by grizzled
old men remembering their youthful contacts with the minister.

Norman McLeod was a fascinating, highly complex character; the one
sure thing about him was his absolute faith in God. In other ways a man of
contrasts — harsh and kindly, dogmatic, but listening to reason when he
was inclined. And around him he gathered, through a long life, men and
women with strongly developed, highly varied personalities, which at times
would defer to the leader. Significantly, he was known to many simply as
the Man. The study of Norman would certainly be incomplete if it did not
include those who travelled the long sea-road from Scotland, to Nova Scotia,
to New Zealand. And also those whose kinsfolk still remain in the Highlands and in the quiet valleys of Cape Breton Island.

Thousands of Highlanders had already crossed the Atlantic when the
Frances Ann sailed. Others would follow, leaving crofts that would become
the haunt of ghosts and of sheep. Some of these already knew McLeod and
joined him in Nova Scotia. Others, early settlers as well as new arrivals,
heard him preach and became his followers. At St Ann's, a remote and

*Captain Duncan "Prince" McKenzie who, with his brother Murdoch "Captain",
was a strong supporter of McLeod for over forty years.*

lonely bay on Cape Breton Island, he established what others would call his
kingdom. And so the first stage in the journey was completed.

Remarkably, another thirty years would pass before the next, most ambitious part of the migration began — 14,000 miles across two oceans to
Australia and, finally, New Zealand. Men of varied and formidable talents
had gathered around McLeod and most were still there. Donald "Squire"
McLeod was connected with Norman by marriage. Norman McDonald
had grown up close to him and probably knew him better than any other
man. There were the Munro brothers, Alexander and John, well educated,
capable and highly independent. Young John taught school at Pictou in
Nova Scotia, but later became a shipowner, merchant and politician. Then
there were two more brothers, sea captains both, Duncan "Prince" and
Murdoch "Captain" McKenzie, whose knowledge of the world became
increasingly valuable over the next forty years. And John McKay, a man of
many parts who never lost his loyalty to his minister.

These were some of the leaders, but there were many others, men and
women, about whom little might be known but who were the unsung

heroes of the migration. If someone had told them, when they first reached Nova Scotia, what journeys they would make over the next forty years, the reaction would have been utter disbelief. Meanwhile, the routine of daily living would keep them in thrall. In Nova Scotia, in Waipu, and wherever else they might settle, the chief tasks had a basic similarity: building homes, clearing land, growing crops and tending their sheep or cattle. And, when they rested, there was God's Word to ponder and discuss. It is not surprising that, under these conditions, few written records survive to give a picture of the daily routine. The occasional journals and letters that still exist have a special value. They help to fill "the teasing gap separating a lived event and the subsequent narration", as the historian Simon Schama puts it. Perhaps letters are the most valuable. Most of those I have seen were designed to pass on news or elicit information. And in almost every case there is a picture of the writer, more revealing than he might imagine or desire. There could also be a touch of dry humour, a subtlety hinting at unexplored depths in the writer's personality.

Here as an illustration is a letter from one who signs himself plainly as R. Matheson who, thirty years after leaving Nova Scotia, had established himself as a roading contractor in Gippsland; he was one of the few who stayed in Australia when the first wave of Nova Scotian migrants arrived there, instead of going on to New Zealand. Now he was writing to his old friend Annie, back in North Gut St Anns.

He had just learned that Annie's father was blind and her mother had died.

> Are you living in the old place yet? You should try and come out to this country. It is the best country in the world, the trees and grass is green all the year round. When we are on the roads contracting we live in calico tents winter and summer. Before coming to Gippsland twenty-five years ago I was following the goldfields for about ten years and did no good. I am settled down here now. I suppose I will be here till I go to my long home.
>
> About four years ago I sent for my brother Donald. I am giving him 120 pounds a year and his wife 52 pounds per annum to keep the two boys and look after them. I give them a good house to live in, a horse and buggy to drive out when they like and as many cows as they like to milk so they have no reason to grumble. He is looking after one contract, I have three contracts in hand now. I have 21 men working for me this winter and ten horses. But the horses is all my own.

And at last, after this impressive build-up, comes the crunch:

> Dear Annie, I would like to see you very much. I remember you so well. Angus says in his letter if I wanted to get married again you would give me one of your daughters. Perhaps she would not be willing if I was — I

think you and I would be more equal match — don't you forget to send your likeness and the two daughters so I can send for the best-looking one... I hope you will excuse me for calling you Annie because I don't know what your husband's name was. Remember me kindly to your father and all inquiring friends. I remain, dear Annie, your appreciative old friend, R. Matheson, Contractor, Gippsland.

I do not know if dear Annie ever yielded to Matheson's pleas and went to Australia, but after reading his letter, I feel I know much more about Mr Matheson himself and, incidentally, about the lifestyle of his times.

Abe McMillan, precentor at the Waipu church at a time of change, was a rock standing against flowing tides. When, under the new order, the congregation rose to sing, he sat; when they sat to pray, he stood. Abe (short for Ebenezer) would not remain in church when it was announced that a woman would sing a solo; didn't the Bible say "join in song"? When the first organ was introduced to his church — until then, the psalms had been sung unaccompanied — Abe showed his disapproval by thumping the floor with his stick.

Leaders could rise and fall, but most of the people went more or less serenely on with their lives; particularly in the practice of religion, as the Abe McMillan anecdote would suggest. Interest in religious matters remained intense after Norman McLeod's death. Faith within the community was essentially conservative as is shown in letters, some of them published in local newspapers, written by members of the congregation. There were rebels, active and passive, and the ties weakened when family members went away. But well within living memory there were households following the tight discipline that had ruled earlier generations.

Someone once remarked to Dr Adam MacFarlan, founding headmaster of St Kentigern College in Auckland, that a certain Nova Scotian family was very religious. He replied: "Very religious? No. But deeply Calvinistic. Some might go to church once a year, but their word always stood. With them, black is black and white is white." Adam MacFarlan, an urbane and warm-hearted man, shared some of the qualities that made Norman McLeod so remarkable. He once referred to a fellow-minister at a Presbytery meeting as "my ignorant brother". Asked to apologise, he did so — in Gaelic.

Essentially conservative though the migrants may have been in matters of religion, as in their social attitudes, they left behind them in Britain much of the harshness prevailing there. McLeod himself had moved a long way from the rather bleak prospect offered by Saint Augustine a thousand years before: "He who puts himself outside the authority of the church will be damned to eternal torture, even though he allow himself to be burned alive for the sake of Christ." Making comparisons with what went on elsewhere in the civilised world during the first half of the nineteenth century, I am inclined to feel that the St Ann's settlement, under McLeod's rule — like other Canadian settlements of the same vintage — was a gentler place. For example: while Norman and his associates were debating whether a nick out of his ear was a suitable punishment for a lad found guilty of theft, teenage boys were being hanged on the public gallows in England, or transported as convicts on suspicion of setting fire to a hayfield.

St Ann's might be a gentler place, and Waipu too, in religious beliefs; but the Waipu congregation to which Abe McMillan belonged would expect and demand sermons that had some meat in them, no less than was the case in St Ann's. Norman McLeod seemed more concerned with the moral welfare of his people during their lives on earth than their place in the hereafter; working perhaps on the realistic principle that, if they did the right thing here, the hereafter would look after itself.

It wasn't like that everywhere. Describing a minister back in Scotland, preaching at about the same time as McLeod, Neil Gunn told how he had fallen out of favour: "There wasn't enough hellfire in his treatment of the Word to warm his breath." And another writer said about an English preacher and his congregation in the 1830s: "These were the people he saw before him on most Sundays. They came to hear him shout at them, to be told how wicked they were, and of how, without God's grace, they would roast forever in the nethermost pit of Hell."

St Augustine had his followers right through to the nineteenth century. But to most of the Nova Scotian followers of McLeod, and to their children, to be denied the warm community of their church was a more potent threat than what might happen in the hereafter.

One of the most important things was the sanctity of Sunday. A day devoted to worship. No extravagant clothing, no food to be prepared, no water to be drawn from the stream; no idle chatter or careless laughter. Rather than desecrate the Sabbath, one of the Urquhart family at Whangarei Heads who was an elder at the Waipu church would leave home on Saturday, row across the harbour entrance to Marsden Point and then walk seven miles to Waipu, reversing his long journey on Monday after a day of worship with his friends.

These stories show the respectable public face of a McLeod community. Against them can be set anecdotes which display a certain irreverence as well as humour. There was the St Ann's citizen who became a bosom friend of a German visitor, under the influence of a dram or two. His guest, a cheerful and convivial man, enjoyed teaching him a few of the songs that a German sailor would know. Their voices carried a long way, disturbing the peace of a St Ann's Sunday morning. When he was taken to task later in the day, the Cape Bretoner had a ready answer. "We were singing our favourite psalms in German," he explained.

Music, especially in Nova Scotia among McLeod's followers, was something of a problem. Norman had banned the bagpipes, just as the English did after Culloden. But, the year after he left Nova Scotia on the *Margaret*, the *Highland Lass* was launched at Big Harbour to the sound of the pipes. Norman apparently felt less strongly about the piano and the fiddle and, in a community that inherited traditional folk songs as well as psalms, it would have been impossible to prohibit singing, even if an effort was made to diminish the secular side. The *ceilidh*, in which song and story featured, was deeply implanted in community life, as were the milling and other frolics, with their centuries-old chants — with improvisations — that made the tedium of many communal domestic tasks easier to bear.

Another tradition that continued to flourish through the generations was the holding, during the week, of Bible readings and discussions in the home. The talk could range widely, straying more often than not away from set texts and topics for the night. Most of the people, as is usually the case in isolated and closely knit communities, were hungry for knowledge. Books were read, digested, commented on and passed from one person to another.

And Norman's people were not all of the kind to accept passively whatever came from the pulpit. They reserved the right, within bounds, to approve or reject, sometimes openly, more often within themselves. His direct utterances, rarely tactful, offended some of his listeners sufficiently for them to vote with their feet. Splinter groups from St Ann's moved to other parts of Canada and the United States. In New Zealand, a secondary migration continued with families such as the Sutherlands, affronted by the minister's habit of giving his victims a public dressing-down that didn't spare personal feelings, moving elsewhere. Kinship ties were still strong. They still kept in touch with friends and relatives in Waipu, and in many cases continued to worship just as their forefathers had done.

Storytelling is one of the most potent ways of keeping the past alive. All the way from the Highlands to Nova Scotia and on to New Zealand, every family kept its own modest treasury of heroes, men and women remembered for personal qualities or deeds that caught the imagination. There were wanderers, adventurers, daring but matter-of-fact seamen whose way of life hadn't varied greatly as they moved from the stormy seas battering the Scottish coast to Nova Scotia with its fogs and iron-bound cliffs, and on to the waters of the Pacific, an ocean blandly smiling and treacherous enough to trap ships and men with gales that belied its name. There were men who encountered pirates in the Far East, some who tried to make their fortunes from gold in Alaska, in California, in the deserts of Central Australia. Some succeeded. Others of the Nova Scotian line are remembered

Doris Ewen at 90: eight McKenzies out of twelve immediate ancestors.

for their strength and skill in the forests and on the sports field; more for their academic brilliance, leading to high posts in universities across the world.

But most of the stories deal not with the great or the famous but with men and women who could easily be one's next door neighbours. Hidden behind a straight face there can be a outrageous sense of humour, an innocent and beguiling way, perhaps, of putting it across anyone with an obsessive pride in his power or authority.

I hope the stories show something of the communities I have come to know — whether in Scotland, Nova Scotia or New Zealand; communities vibrating with energy, gaining strength from the diversity of their parts.

Not long ago we were on a quick visit to Waipu and on impulse called in to see an old friend, Doris Ewen, in her home near the little township. It was nearly five o'clock on a winter afternoon and darkness was thickening. But Doris was out in the chilly air, weeding her garden.

"What on earth are you doing out there?" I asked.

"I've just slipped out for a few minutes while the dinner's cooking. I broke my arm not long ago, and the weeds have all got away. But the doctor's very pleased with the way it mended, and now I can do something again." She grinned cheerfully. "There's still something strange in

25

my shoulder that grinds away if I move it, but that will get better no doubt."

For a woman who was over ninety, Doris had certainly done well, but she didn't spare any time looking for sympathy. "Now come on in and we'll have a cup of tea. And I've even done a little baking. Now doesn't that smell beautiful?" She opened the oven door to show us. "Pork pieces, courgettes, other vegetables too, all together in a bag where they'll cook themselves." Her eyes twinkled. "So easy, isn't it?"

We talked for half an hour over our tea while the evening quietly gathered outside, the only sounds an occasional passing car and the calm voice of a dairy cow as it settled for the night.

Doris could count eight McKenzies out of twelve immediate ancestors. They were proud of their clan and of their heritage. All through the Highlands and Hebrides, in Nova Scotia and in New Zealand, there are women who take their place in family memories: the women who survived early death from many causes — consumption, heavy domestic and farming toil, premature or complicated births. Passing through these hazards they lived on, often to a great age, and afterwards in the minds of their families. Doris typifies for me the women who have become, in their own way, part of a common heritage: serene, indomitable, and often, because of their faith, full of the wonder and joy of living. They never die.

Chapter Two

Return to the Highlands

LIKE MANY A SCOT before and since, Ian Lang could hide humour or whimsy under a deep mask of solemnity. Now, leaning forward in his chair, he fixed me with earnest eyes. A pronouncement was due. There was a telltale crinkling at the corner of his mouth but his eyes were still serious.

"Most stories about Waipu," he said, "have some truth; and if something can be added to make a better story, that becomes the truth too."

I laughed, and he held up a hand to check me.

"Now Neil, I've told you a lot of stories and answered a lot of questions. May I ask one for myself? What's the weather going to be like for the big game tomorrow?"

Ian eased himself from his chair and stood erect, a commanding figure in spite of his nearly ninety-five years. "I'll see you at the sports next New Year. Look after yourself." And he waved goodbye.

I stood there for a long time, looking at the sea and reliving old memories. More than forty years before, I had talked in that same room with Ian's mother Willina. She too had been a story-teller; with a lilting voice that would break effortlessly into Gaelic — anecdote, folksong or both. One talked to her without realising that her eyes were sightless. She had a merry laugh, and her knitting needles clicked as she talked.

For many years the beach below the Lang home had been the sole preserve of the family; now summer cottages and more pretentious houses lined most of the foreshore. But nothing could diminish the beauty of the scene before me. A flawless light-blue sky, the sea, dark blue where it was not glittering in the morning sun, contained within an arc of nearly 180 degrees. A curving beach of clean white sand on which waves sparkled as they broke. Unseen beyond a rocky point to the left, the beach swept smoothly past the Cove with its sheltering trees, past the Waipu rivermouth and round to Marsden Point, where a great inlet ran through to the town of Whangarei. And out to sea the wide horizon held the eye, its sharp blue line broken by the fantastic fairy-world profiles of the Hen and Chicken Islands, Manaia rising to the north on a mountain range that ran to the ragged peaks of the Whangarei Heads.

This is Bream Bay, from Bream Head in the north to Bream Tail in the south; the final resting place for many of those who had sailed from Scotland to Nova Scotia and, the longest journey of all, down across the world to New Zealand. Each part of the bay has its own stories and memories, some comic, some tragic, but nearly all, as my friend Ian Lang suggested, containing some measure of truth. Not least of these parts is Langs Beach, tranquil now but once ravaged by bush fires; the scene, too, of battles of wits between customs officers and seafaring Nova Scotians who saw no harm and some profit in smuggling rum and other useful articles ashore there. True to their tradition, the nickname "Smuggler" was in no way thought shameful. Anyone delving into the history of the seafaring Nova Scotian McKenzies could justifiably be confused by the way the nickname is used to describe different men, not all of them in the same family. I know of at least three "Smuggler" McKenzies.

Some anecdotes, particularly the more domestic ones, can carry the listener a long way back, to Nova Scotia and a half-century further to the Highlands and Hebrides.

I can remember my mother — and my grandmother — preparing curds for their own special delight: as far as I can remember, skim milk standing on the warm side of the wood-burning stove gradually built up to what might be called a soft cheese. It was usually eaten with a light sprinkling of salt. But curds went back a long way from Waipu, to the times in Scotland when crofters had a few black cattle to graze. They were too valuable to eat. The cow's milk would be shared between calves and the crofter's family. In the hard days of winter and spring, blood might be drawn from the beast to help sustain human life. When the cattle were brought down from the summer grazing in the hills, surplus young stock, usually about two years old, would be assembled and driven south to the fatter lands of England. Even today, long after the last herds travelled that way, the old drove roads can be traced through the glens and over the passes. This was a vital part of the Highland economy, and it survived wars, inter-clan feuds, raids by the MacGregors and others for whom in turn, the lifting of cattle was an essential part of life. In the year 1745, famous in Scotland for other reasons, the diligent English buyers were on the island of Skye organising the next cattle drive.

Anecdotes or stories, oral or written, can help to give us a picture of what life was like in Scotland for our ancestors: ideally, to add a personal touch to the facts of history. It is not easy to find direct links between the Waipu of today and the Scotland left behind nearly two hundred years ago. But for James Sutherland, who would let the neighbour's sheep into his fields through a hole in the fence, "just for the pleasure of dogging them out", memories of the Highland Clearances were still a grim reality. In 1818 he had seen his tenant neighbours evicted from their glen and their cottages put to the torch. The anger does not seem to have persisted in later generations. John Sutherland, the son of James, named his Waipu farm Helmsdale after the village to which the family was moved on the east coast of Scotland. When Neil Sutherland, on holiday from his Clevedon farm, visited Brora, a village not far from Helmsdale, he found to his surprise a memorial to the victims of the Clearances who eventually went to America. In his family there was no tradition of involvement in the Clearances but, ironically, New Zealand Sutherlands had contributed to the memorial.

If they had wanted to nurse a grievance, the Sutherlands could have found plenty of excuses. Between 1810 and 1812, thousands of clansmen were shifted from their homes in the west and settled in fishing villages created for them on the east coast. The materials for the cottages were charged to the tenants at false prices. "In Assynt," writes John Prebble, "the sheep arrived before the people had time to obey the writs of eviction. They pulled down their house timbers and walked with them to the coast where the villages in which they were to live had not yet been built, the boats from which they were expected to fish had not been launched, the nets unspun."

"There was a coal pit at Brora, herring fisheries planned at Goldspie and Helmsdale. Mountain men began to captain and man their own boats," wrote a Strathnaver man. Success was great.

Down the west coast from the Sutherland country, at Lochalsh, were the McKays who, by the time they were settled in New Zealand, had formed what in numbers and in unity could well be called a new clan. The progenitor was Donald McKay, born in 1753 and, for the first fifty years of adult life, fighting a losing battle against his Argyll landlords. The strategy was to raise rents until the tenants were squeezed out and the land could be turned into a pleasure park inhabited by deer and sheep. Family tradition tells the story. In 1820 Donald's eldest son John (Ian Ruadh) was sent to Nova Scotia to see what prospects it offered. He was well fitted for the mission. A man of great physical strength, a classical scholar who had studied for the church, a schoolmaster in Scotland, he was thirty-five years old when he first left Scotland. He died a few months before his ninety-eighth birthday in Waipu, still, it is said, scandalising Norman McLeod by riding a spirited horse to church at a breakneck pace. John found it was possible to acquire a block of several hundred acres — a vast difference from what they had known — and before long he was joined at Middle River, near Baddeck on the Bras d'Or Lakes, by his parents, four brothers, two sisters and numerous grandchildren. There they carved out farms from the forest.

When most of the McKays followed Norman McLeod to New Zealand, some stayed in Nova Scotia where the families have flourished. Memories of Scotland may have grown dim, but the ties between kinsfolk in Nova Scotia and New Zealand have remained strong.

Reunions can help to keep the past alive; early ancestors can become flesh-and-blood people, instead of dusty portraits stowed in a back room. The process depends largely on the enthusiasm and energy of one person; in one recent case, Wallace MacRae, member of a team that, a few years ago, produced an excellent history of Middle River. Donald MacRae and Isabella MacLennan were both born at Applecross, he in 1760, she in 1757. They married and around the year 1803 migrated to Prince Edward Island — 500 Highlanders in all, packed into the *Polly*, a small warship. They stayed there for several years, during which Mary, their eighth child, was born, to a mother who was forty-eight years old. After a short spell at Broad Cove, in Inverness County, they took up land in Middle River, one of the first four families to settle there. And at Middle River they died, Isabella on April 1, 1852, Donald just eight days later. He was ninety-two, she ninety-five. One marvels constantly at the age reached by so many of these pioneer settlers. At the same time in heavily populated, disease-infested parts of England, someone could write: "He's only fifty-two, he could live another ten years yet!"

Within a few years of their death other MacRaes, insatiable for change, had moved on to New Zealand. Among them were descendants to the third and fourth generation. Their youngest daughter Mary, married to Duncan (Ban) MacKay, had ten children. Another daughter, Effie, married to John Campbell, died in Nova Scotia, but her husband and four daughters went to New Zealand. Elizabeth, wife of Captain Murdoch McKenzie of the *Highland Lass*, had a family of nine; and Mary, who died on the voyage, had three children.

The MacRaes and the McKays become inextricably linked, at the same time spreading all over the world. And it all goes back to two husbands and two wives who decided, more than two hundred years ago, to abandon what they knew so well and seek something different in a distant land.

For some of the Campbells who came on to New Zealand there was, for a long time, little to link them back to their island home on Skye. For them, home was Nova Scotia when they were in a nostalgic mood. But when Dick Campbell left New Zealand in the 1920s to study at the London School of Economics, he probed the memory of older kinsfolk and eventually found himself, on a fine summer's day, walking up a quiet country road in Glendale to a cottage tucked comfortably into the hillside. Watching him with some curiosity as he approached was young Mary Campbell, who invited him in, introduced him to her parents and made the impecunious young student feel very much at home. Mary's great-grandfather, Roderick Campbell, had had a brother Neil who had gone away to Nova Scotia and who was vaguely remembered by the descendants of those who had stayed behind. Neil was Dick's great-grandfather. He had found his Scottish kinsfolk; more than that, after what he used to call his Biblical seven years' courtship, he found in Mary a charming wife and companion.

At the height of the bombing of London in the Second World War, Dick, at that time deputy-High Commissioner for New Zealand in Britain, persuaded Mary to take their children back to Glendale and greater security. So, in a strange way, the cycle was completed.

Within the Campbell family there was no memory of why they had gone to Nova Scotia, except for a feeling that, hearing how others had fared across the Atlantic, they also could become landowners and independent of the landlord. They certainly had not been physically evicted, or shipped off like so many cattle. They had been luckier than many.

How is it that there are still Campbells on some of the crofts at Glendale? The answer may be found in events there a century ago. Those who had stayed on Skye, I was told, were less aggressive in the face of harsh treatment than those who had gone away. But when the quiet man is aroused, things begin to happen. Reaction against tyranny may have been a long time coming, but it came at last.

Crofting dated from the start of the eighteenth century; the system was modified after the '45 when bagpipes and the tartan were banned and the chiefs, sucked into the vortex of the nation and lured to the capitals, degenerated from patriarchs and chieftains to landlords. By the nineteenth century there was still no way in which a Skye crofter could pass his croft on to his son. In 1882, however, sixty years after the migrants had left, the crofters rebelled against the system. The British Government sent marines to arrest the ringleaders of the Glendale Land Leaguers, but found themselves face to face with six hundred determined crofters. They had to give way. For four years a desultory conflict was carried on until victory was conceded by the Government forces. And so, as sometimes happens, the quiet ones, those with hidden reserves of strength, came out on top.

Visiting there long after these events, I am tempted to feel it was a gallant effort, a "forlorn hope" too late to achieve social or economic sanity. Between 1750 and 1770, rents had doubled because of the demand for black cattle. Bad seasons followed, and during the next twenty years eight large transports sailed from Skye to America, carrying about 2000 people. The boom during the Napoleonic Wars ended. Once again the crowded ships began to sail away; and even in peacetime the army still attracted Highland recruits. Today Glendale and the great stretch of land to the west seems empty, lonely under the sky. An English family has made Mary Campbell's cottage its home. Down at Loch Pooltiel, near the pier where cattle were once brought from the outer Hebrides on their way to England, and where the derelict mill had once been busy, another English family, opting out of

31

A "black house" on Skye, a reminder of the days when the population of Glendale was much higher than today.

the rat race, has an attractive bed-and-breakfast house and a garden where they grow vegetables for a restaurant a few kilometres away. Down the road not far from Glendale is Dunvegan Castle, where McLeods come every summer from all over the world, but few seemed to find their way to the quiet roads facing the sunset. A pleasant young Campbell family farmed not one croft but three, and even then required the special subsidy the Government provides to keep the land productive. And a few miles further west, near Ramasaig, the bones of a deserted village stood out from the green, close-cropped turf. In 1830 the ten resident families had been given a month's notice to pack up and go.

The personality of Captain John McKenzie gained and still holds a place in family legend. He left Applecross, on the mainland opposite Skye, to make a home on Prince Edward Island at the end of the eighteenth century. There he raised a family and traded energetically — and adventurously enough to earn the nickname of "The Smuggler". It is possible that, like others, he found that goods obtained on the neighbouring French islands could be sold elsewhere at a reasonable profit. He also established contacts in Pictou, the Nova Scotian port of entry for many migrant Highlanders. When his children were still young, he brought his family back to Applecross for their education, including a further taste of the sea which was, for them also, to provide a livelihood. While his sons, Duncan and Murdoch, were growing up, and trading down the Irish Sea with their brother-in-law, Hector McDonald, the Smuggler was back and forth across the Atlantic, taking Highlanders and Hebrideans one way and loading timber for the return. In 1818, the year after Norman McLeod made his hazardous crossing in the shaky old *Frances Ann*, the brig *Perseverance* brought more migrants from Assynt to Pictou, among them Donald McLeod "Squire" and a number of others who would play an important part in establishing the new community. It would have been fitting if the McKenzie who captained the *Perseverance* had been the Smuggler, but not so. However, Captain Hector McKenzie was probably a relative, and he deserves to be remembered as the man who brought, in 1818 and again in 1821, valuable reinforcements to the first settlers when they moved from Pictou to St Ann's, Cape Breton.

On a brilliant day in the short northern summer we drove to Applecross from Lochalsh over what is said to be the highest road in Scotland. The broad uplands were empty of life. Once, on such a summer day, the black cattle belonging to crofters living down below would have been grazing the sparse but succulent native grasses. But now they have all gone, along with most of the people who found a living there. The road curved in great sweeps, with two dizzy hairpin bends, until it came down to the sea. There were campers and picnickers along the sheltered coastal fringe, reminding us of similar days beside beaches in our own New Zealand. Across the water, not far away, resting like an intimate friend was the island of Skye, and to the north, dimmed by distance, was Harris, home also to many of our migrants.

We drove north along the coast past sandy coves and stark granite cliffs, washed by a restless sea. Here, two hundred years ago, had dwelt a community linked not by roads but by little boats — Raasay, Skye, Applecross, other tiny settlements along the deeply indented Ross-shire coastline. Once, it is true, the daily routine would have been enlivened by long-lasting feuds and bloody skirmishes. But the links remained and became stronger with the shared stresses that developed in the late eighteenth century. The interclan fire went out, and MacDonalds, MacLeods, Campbells, MacKenzies would marry and become one people.

Not so many years ago, belief would have been strained by a story told by 83-year-old Mrs Campbell when we stayed at her house at Broadford, on the island of Skye. Unlike most of the local families, she said, Gaelic and only Gaelic was spoken in her house between members of the family. Her son, in due course, went off to university on the mainland. Returning, he passed her his certificates and said: "I'm not going away again"; and he became a teacher at Portree. Then came an unexpected chance. An administrator who spoke Gaelic was wanted at the Clan Donald Centre at Armadale, a little to the south on Skye, and he was chosen. On our second night with the Campbells he came in smiling.

"The MacLeods at Dunvegan had been having their 'parliament'," he said, "and a few hundred of them came over to visit the MacDonalds at Armadale. I had the pleasure of introducing them to the MacDonalds assembled to meet them, and I was able to say that, for the one clan to be introduced in peace to the other might once have seemed a very unlikely thing — especially when it was a Campbell who introduced them!"

The afternoon stretched on endlessly as we followed the coast road north from Applecross, looking for somewhere to stay the night. There were few cottages until we turned sharply east along the lower edge of Torridon, the great sea loch, and came in the evening to Shieldaig. There we found comfortable beds at the home of John and Catherine MacKenzie. Crofting did not provide a sufficient living for John and his family, even though he farmed two crofts and had restricted grazing on the hill. Taking in guests helped in the summer season, and he had also served terms as a commercial fisherman; but, as has always been the case on that coast, the rewards were uncertain and the conditions hard. However, John seemed a contented man, quiet spoken and friendly, happy to be living his life where his people had been for centuries.

Survival outside the reach of the grasping landlord seems to have been easier for a seaman than for a crofter. The Mathesons, most of them seamen and boatbuilders, had migrated from Balmacara, in the Lochalsh area, to Cape Breton, but tradition had it that they, like so many MacLeods and others, had originally come from Assynt. McKenzies and Mathesons both trained their own crewmen and boatbuilders. In their boatyards and at sea they made contacts beyond the reach of the crofter. They developed independence, initiative and, quite frequently, open minds; qualities that made them not only good seamen but men equipped to be leaders in a migration across the world. Captain Hector McKenzie was an active agent in the first stage of the migration, and in the future two seagoing Matheson brothers, Duncan and Angus, and two McKenzie brothers, Duncan and Murdoch — all four of them deep-water captains — would be leaders who helped make the migration a success.

Glimpses of the past come in many ways — from household tools durable enough to last several generations, useful enough not to be discarded on the way; from trinkets and heirlooms; from words and phrases that are still spoken even though their meaning, like the rest of their native Gaelic, is forgotten. Story-tellers enjoyed their greatest days before the reading and writing of English became common. Perhaps the Nova Scotian Highlanders, beset as they were with the problems of survival, did not concern themselves overmuch with tradition, legend and history. Yet it was all there, making them what they were. Many of them, indeed, professed to reject the idea of Scotland. And yet the names of Scottish villages and glens still distinguish farms, houses and roads in the land where they finally rested.

What had happened to the Highlands since the breakdown of the old clan system following Culloden? Before that time, the chiefs had tight control of a host trained to fight for their clan, to raid the cattle of their traditional enemies, to be pawns in the power games of the times. They belonged to their chief just as their chief belonged to them, and there was complete loyalty both ways. But by the end of the eighteenth century little was left of this except pride in the past and in their name. Many of the chiefly families left the Highlands for the delights of London, happy to see their clansmen replaced by sheep, and handing executive power over to the tacksmen, leaseholders often linked with the family, who quickly converted the once free clansmen into tenants scratching an existence from a few rented acres.

"If the function of farming was to enable a generation of Highland crofters to lead the life of their forefathers," writes Rosalind Mitchison, "there would not be much profit for the landowner. And if, as food shortages increasingly made it clear in the early years of the nineteenth century, there were too many of them to be supported in this style of life, there would soon be no profit at all."

Not so many years before the young men would have been fighting for (or against) Prince Charlie. Now, denied their traditional activity at home, they went off to Canada, India or Europe in regiments to fight in England's wars. They would return to find glens emptied by forced migration, crofts reduced to broken walls, sheep feeding where once there had been gardens. Some of the men didn't bother to return. Others who did return did not stay long. John Finlayson, who belonged to the 77th Regiment and was a veteran of the Peninsular War, settled near Baddeck, where he died in 1855. His widow, with four of their children, migrated to New Zealand. John was known as the Soldier. It would have been difficult for a stranger to distinguish him from Alexander Finlayson, another army veteran, like John a native of Lochalsh and a farmer at Middle River. It made things simpler that he was known as Alex the Soldier.

In the Highlands, however, the most urgent problem was what to do about a population that, in spite of everything, continued to increase; a population sustained to a large degree by the humble potato. This had transformed the spartan diet of the crofters, allowing more people to exist on less land, often supported by seaweed gathering until, as still happens today, a limit was reached and starvation loomed again. There was no dole in the Highlands; traditionally it was the chief's responsibility to keep his retainers alive. After the potato blight struck in 1846, MacLeod of MacLeod, at Dunvegan, and other landlords found themselves bankrupt as a result of providing famine relief for their tenants; some estates passed into the hands of trustees who rectified the situation by bringing in more sheep. The words of the Countess of Sutherland, when her clansmen were reluctant recruits for her regiment (the 93rd) would have been echoed by other landlords: "They need no longer be considered a credit to Sutherland, or an advantage over sheep or any useful animal."

For many years the army took into its care thousands of young Highlanders. A stroke of government policy turned potential rebels into one of the most formidable units in the forces fighting Napoleon — clan tartans, kilts, bagpipes and all were there to build up morale and attract the young, the adventurous and the hungry. One of the earliest of those who settled in Nova Scotia after severing from the army was Simon Fraser, who was with the Fraser Highlanders at the capture of Quebec in 1757.

Reproached for being lazy and improvident, living in a state of semi-starvation, the crofters nevertheless produced a breed of men who, in the words of poet and writer Edwin Muir, were the admiration of Europe. Muir quotes a passage about them from Eckermann's *Conversation with Goethe*. In Napoleon's time, Eckermann said, he had seen a Parisian infantry battalion, "all of them so small and thin he could not conceive what they could have done in battle". Wellington's Scottish Highlanders, Goethe replied, "were a different set of heroes, from all accounts." Eckermann answered: "I saw them in Brussels a year before the Battle of Waterloo. They were men! All strong, nimble and free as if they had come straight from the hand of God. They carried their heads so freely and gaily and marched so lightly, swinging along with their bare knees, that you would have thought they never heard of original sin or the primal curse."

Pursued by such overwhelming eulogies, wherever the Highlanders fought, in India, the Far East, the Sudan, all around the globe, their exploits reinforced the romantic picture of Scotland, a region compounded of heather, wild deer, sporting fish and kilted Highlanders. The "ladies from Hades," as they were once called, take part today in more peaceful occasions: Caledonian sports days charged with the challenging sound of Highland music and the sight of the pipe band in full swing; singing and dancing to traditional music; young men never blooded in battle tossing the caber or the oatsheaf with the enthusiasm that their forebears put into a bayonet charge. Colourful pageantry that is now, to many visitors, the essence of their ancestral land; so pervasive, indeed, that in sound and colour, a festival day in St Ann's, Waipu, or a thousand other places across the world can be as Scottish as Scotland itself.

But there is a poignant side to it all. Away from the excitement and the spectacle, a visitor travelling the country may feel a hollow melancholy when he sees that many of the glens from which the crofters were driven so long ago still lie desolate. There is a loneliness peopled with ghosts from the past.

How was this allowed to happen, when the use of new and available agricultural methods could have made the glens happy and productive communities? Edwin Muir suggests that, during the nineteenth century:

> Intelligent men's minds were possessed by a dream of general wealth for society, which would be realised by adhering to the latest economic principles, and by the natural and beneficent growth of Capitalism... They had no understanding of the Highland crofter who, though he lived more poorly than the cotton-spinner in the north of England, lived also with more human satisfaction. They did not care very greatly what happened to the population if wealth could only be increased. It is this particular ideal for progress that has depopulated the Highlands and reduced them to the status of a backward region. They were robbed of their life by exactly the same process that built Glasgow.

The split between town and country is graphically illustrated by an outburst from the great Lord Macaulay, when Southey had the temerity to suggest that the life of a country labourer might be more desirable than that of a factory worker. All Macaulay's invective was brought out to ridicule this absurd notion.

And so visitors today find peace and tranquillity in the Highlands, beauty in the long, shining perspectives of sea, sky and land, and sometimes a melancholy that clutches the heart.

However, at least to those looking back with a certain measure of nostalgia, the picture was not entirely dark. Food was plain, not always easy to come by, but of a kind that encouraged long life among those who escaped the scourges of smallpox, tuberculosis and various respiratory diseases. It is possible, too, though of no great comfort to those on short rations, that periods of abstinence do not harm the human system. What were the chief ingredients of their diet?

Perhaps a little story from Waipu in the 1920s will give a clue. When a party of young folk from Waipu, my aunt Beulah Campbell among them, set out to play a tennis match against a team from Whangarei Heads, they were met at Marsden Point by a dashing young former Mounted Rifleman, Colin McGregor, not long back from fighting the Turks in the deserts of the Middle East. Colin rowed them across the narrow harbour entrance to McGregor territory on the northern side. There, lunch was waiting: a kerosene tin over a fire of driftwood, with fish and potatoes cooking in it. A marvellous meal, Beulah recalled seventy years later. A hundred years before, the same dish was a top favourite on the Highland coast. The potatoes not only added flavour and substance; they also removed any extreme saltiness from the fish.

The Highlander's food almost always had a tang of the sea. Mussels and other shellfish were often used in soup, with oatmeal added. Seaweed might bring in a useful income, but it was even more important to their diet. Children on the Scottish Island, writes Theodore Fitzgibbon in *A Taste of Scotland*, in the old days would eat stalks of raw redware, known also as sea-tangle; or it would be roasted and then put on a buttered bannock. For general use the seaweed would be soaked in cold water, simmered for three or four hours in a covered pot, drained and beaten. It became a tasty soft jelly which could be mixed with a little oatmeal, shaped into small flat cakes and fried. There was no end to its virtues. It you were tired of eating it in these ways, it could be used as a soup, possibly with milk and mashed potatoes beaten together.

As far as I can discover, seaweed did not figure in the diet of the migrants to New Zealand, although tradition was certainly followed in using it as a fertiliser on farm and garden, especially in the potato patch. There was more variety available in New Zealand; in the Highlands, just about everything in the normal diet came from the sea or was grown close at hand. Only in times of famine or crop failure would food be shipped in from more favoured areas. Some old-time recipes make interesting reading. Chickens stewed in a closed pot with shallots and sliced potatoes; oatmeal porridge and oatcakes; harvest broth containing every kind of fresh young vegetable and wild herb that could be found; with hopefully an occasional neck chop. It is enlightening to read the comments of one eighteenth-century observer: "Only a few pounds of meat were eaten in a house in a year, and an egg was a delicacy." In the Hebrides and on St Kilda, another report says, the gannet or Solan goose was a favourite: "Most delicate of fowls which have very good flesh."

Gradually, however, with closer contacts with the outside world, exotic foods became more common. Sugar quickly proved that the Highlander had an unrealised taste for sweetness. Soldiers returning from service abroad were largely responsible. Dick Campbell used to tell the story of a kinsman in Victorian times who returned from army service in India with a very special present for his mother: a packet of tea. Mother accepted it gracefully. When time came to prepare dinner, she poured the tea into a pot, boiled it, drained away the liquid and served the leaves as a vegetable.

We visited Dunvegan Castle on a summer day of gentle rain. I had received a welcoming note from the chief, John MacLeod of MacLeod, in which, however, he said he could not be sure he would be home at the time we expected to arrive. And so we were delighted to see, in a courtyard behind the castle, an athletic young man in jeans, who was trying with no success to open the jammed boot of his Peugeot. We approached, introduced ourselves and our son Alistair succeeded in opening the boot.

"We've had a big clan gathering this week," John explained, "and we're tidying up."

Then he added with a smile: "But having come all the way from New Zealand you won't be wanting to spend your time opening stubborn cars." We talked for a while about the clan gathering, about his grandmother, the celebrated Dame Flora who had done so much to make MacLeods, and the descendants of Highlanders in general throughout the world, conscious of their past.

"They come back to see us from everywhere," he said thoughtfully... John is a modern man. Was it fanciful for me to feel, as we stood silently together, that he was seeing two vastly different pictures in his mind's eye: the clan of today, involved with the world in all its activities, and the way it used to be during a thousand years — a closely knit, single-minded community of no great size, one of the players in the power game of the Highlands, fighting often for its survival, but with a pride and loyalty that was measured and felt by all its members, from the chief to the humblest crofter?

Chapter Three

Picture of a Leader

ONE OF THE MOST REMARKABLE things about Norman McLeod is that, more than two hundred years after he was born, people still talk about him as a flesh and blood person, not as an historic artefact. He remains a vital, formidable personality, but does that make him any easier to know and understand? We study him, we read what he said about himself and others; and what others have written about him. We peel away another layer and think that at last we are getting close to the real Norman. But there is only one thing certain: to categorise exactly a person or place is an impossible task. There is always more hidden than revealed, even to the most diligent seeker. And perhaps that is all for the good. If everything was known, might not the magic disappear?

It would be pretentious to call this chapter a journey into the *terra incognita* of Norman McLeod. All I have done is to gather material from writings all over the place, listen to people telling tales their fathers told, study the changes in life in the Highlands during his early years, and see what comes up. Norman McLeod was the product of forces operating with great vigour in his country. Writing about him, one cannot ignore his setting, and the story would be incomplete if mention was not made, however brief, about the way life went on in the Highlands after he left.

Even now in Assynt, in the Highlands, there can be warm arguments about him, in Nova Scotia where he spent over thirty years and in New Zealand where he died in 1866 in his eighty-sixth year. Not far from Waipu, where he was buried, there was a village where the butcher was also a McLeod. Someone innocently asked him if he was related to the old leader. The butcher drew his big knife from his belt, grabbed his questioner in a massive grip, held the knife-point to his throat and growled: "Say that again and you'll never say another thing!" The fact that throughout the incident there was a glint of humour in his eye did not completely mask his feelings.

Whatever reactions he aroused among the people, however, most would agree that the long, involved journey from the Highlands to Nova Scotia and then to New Zealand, by more than seven hundred men, women and children, would not have taken place if McLeod had not decided to leave sinful Scotland behind him in search of a better world. In his seventies as well as forty years earlier, McLeod was the catalyst, or else the man around whom everything happened. His friends and followers were staunch in their loyalty, at least for most of the time; his adversaries were also strong-minded, but somehow there was no fatal disruption. There were ties in the community, based to a large degree on McLeod's personality and power, that held even disparate elements together.

That feeling of community is still there today, even though members and descendants spread to new places and lands. What happens today is more than just a search for ancestors, although that is there too; more importantly, the warmth, the kinship, the sense of involvement have persisted through the generations, diluted but still potent in a vastly changed world.

What sort of man was Norman McLeod? We can go back to words that he wrote, to words that were written about him, to the few facts that appear in records, but most of all to the stories that grew about him.

The most vivid picture of the country and people among whom young McLeod would have grown up came to me out of the blue. It was a letter from a delectable Oxford address, Jack Straw's Lane, which seemed as far from the Highlands as anything could be. The writer was Barbara Weiskrantz, whose American-born husband, Larry, had been professor of psychology at Oxford for twenty-five years. Barbara's grandmother, daughter of a first cousin of Norman's, had been born at Elphin, in the north-west of Sutherland, and at the age of fourteen, like many another Highland girl before and after, entered service in London. There she married a butler, Edmund Collins. She never returned to her birthplace. Barbara remembers her as a tiny old lady all in black who seemed lost and out of place in the big city. Only one of her family returned to Scotland. That was George Norman MacLeod Collins who, at the age of nine, was taken up to his maternal grandmother, Dolina MacLeod, at Elphin, to recuperate from a childhood illness. George said later that on his first morning there, his uncle made him a fishing rod, his aunt introduced him to scones and oatcakes baked over a peat fire, and his grandmother lovingly began to teach him to speak Gaelic. She lived to the age of 101. At the end of summer George declined to go home and enrolled at the local school.

Barbara wrote: "In spite of his humble background, because of innate ability and the opportunities afforded in that country, George was well educated, ordained and twice became Moderator of the Free Church of Scotland Assembly — a rare distinction. He also guided his people with dedicated paternalism, according to Calvinist principles, and lived to the age of 89." For many people there is an additional interest in the fact that he carried into another generation the name of a man whose memory will stay green. George, whose own memoirs display a gift for words and a delightful sense of humour, described Norman as the vagrant ecclesiastic from Assynt. However, elsewhere he shows a demonstrable kinship with

Lochinver, fishing port and part of a thriving tourist industry.

the old man who, of course, he would never have met. In a letter to his niece Barbara he said: "What a maverick he was! And to think that for no fault of my own, I share his name. [George was named after his uncle who in turn was named after Norman.] Still, I think that we can allow that 'e'n his failings leaned to virtue's side' and I only hope that mine have taken a similar slant!"

Elphin is only a few miles from Clachtoll, near Stoer, where Norman was born. And the whole district has been full of MacLeods for centuries. So much so that two septs of MacLeods in the area were distinguished from each other as the Crawfords and the Browns, two names quite unknown at that time in a West Sutherland community. George Collins, in a letter to his niece, gave the origin of the distinction. Two of their ancestors served with Lord Reay's Fencibles — almost completely Sutherland men. So many were MacLeods that, to avoid confusion, the expedient was resorted to of giving them aliases. And so Dolina, Barbara's great-grandmother and cousin of Norman, had as husband Roderick (Crawford) MacLeod. This method of distinguishing one clan member from another was perhaps less imaginative than that followed in Nova Scotia and in Waipu in later years, where every physical or personal characteristic was avidly seized on, and the nickname passed from one generation to the next. As far as I can discover, the Crawford and Brown aliases did not survive the crossing of the Atlantic. They were, one would feel, the brainwave of some army intelligence officer, an Englishman or Lowlander perhaps, but probably not a Highlander!

When George Collins went to Elphin in 1909, living conditions were much easier than in Norman's time a century before. Virtually all their food, however, was still locally produced.

When our roads became snowblocked, we were seldom taken unawares. Each home had its own store of provisions against such emergencies — a barrel of the finest flour, a meal-chest packed with the oatmeal of Caithness or Ross-shire; a firkin or two of salt herring from Ullapool; a barrel of salted mutton from our own flocks, for this was good sheep country; a stock of potatoes from our own fields. And there might be, there just might be, in one of the outhouses, a barrel of salted venison; but how it got there, well, who could tell? So when the less isolated townships, with their shops and delivery vans frantically sought ways of replenishing their stores and succouring their beleaguered customers, we thankfully drew on our reserves and waited for the weather to change.

The Clearances were further in the past, though still remembered, and it was easier to seek and find work elsewhere. The landscape, which in Norman's time was bleak and harsh, now seemed to have gained a softer side. It was possible for an observer to write like this:

You climb out of Strath Oykell and cross a wide vast of greenish-brown bent, greenish-gold perhaps in the oblique light of evening. Suddenly, something is there that was not there before — something that makes you gasp — the incredible blue cone of Suilven. Then on the right, Ben

Looking south from Clachtoll towards Suilven, Cul Mor, Cul Beag and Stack Polly. The McLeod memorial stands on the green land projecting into the bay.

43

More Assynt heaves into view... You zigzag upward until you are high on a hillside above three of four sprawling lochs. It is what geography calls an alp, an upland pasture isolated by barren hills. You could wade knee-deep in the flowers — creamy meadow-sweet, purple vetch and yellow vetch, red-purple knapweed and blue-purple scabious. The houses are situated beside the road or perched on little hillocks above it.

Elphin had not always been so peaceful. It was originally, George Collins explained to Barbara, the site of the summer grazing for the community centred at Stronchrubie, a few miles to the north-west. Forced to leave there, they moved permanently to Elphin. When Sutherland's men tried to evict them, so the story goes, all the women formed up at the ford over a little stream. They were sufficiently intimidating for the posse to withdraw and not return.

This would have been a familiar landscape to Norman. He would have responded to its strength, its beauty and its harshness. Other things would also have affected him strongly as a boy: the restlessness that came with the Clearances, even though his village was not involved; and the swelling tide of debate with the established church on one side and a revitalised Calvinism on the other. Calvinism came late to the north-west and for that reason made an even greater impact than it did in the south. But this did not automatically mean that life became stern or cruel, and that family life was rigorously governed.

There is an interesting story about the teenage McLeod which says quite a lot about the kind of youngster he was. It is told by Dr John MacLeod, principal of the Free Church College, Edinburgh, in a book called *Bypaths of Highland Church History*. When Norman asked a Macdonald boy to do something for him on a Saturday, the boy refused, saying that he had to learn his Gaelic psalm portion for school on Monday. "Do what I ask," said Norman, "and I'll teach you the psalm myself."

When the time came for the lesson Norman taught him some nonsense verses which began, properly enough, with the first line of the psalm he was to learn. These verses the boy repeated as his school task and, as may be well believed, writes Dr MacLeod, got a sound thrashing for his irreverence. Part of Norman's psalm version was still remembered many years later. It went, in translation,

Ask of me and I'll give to thee
Loch Crocach for thine own
And on the loch the speedy boat
Bringing the fuel home.

Quite an innocuous verse, one might think today, but sufficient then for young Norman to be labelled an irreverent youth. Maturity would make him something very different. In the judgment of the Calvinists, then and later, irreverence was a term that could be easily applied and removed only with difficulty. Among those who carried the Calvinist faith, there were varying degrees of sin, decided on a personal basis. Norman himself, being a man who had built his own faith, differed strongly from many of his contemporaries. As John MacLeod wrote: "Another feature of Norman's examinations was that to reach his standard one must make the profession of a full assurance of salvation. He looked upon the tenderness of weaker believers which was characteristic of the Highland evangelicals as a bit of mawkish sentiment that was beneath contempt."

Much of his energy was directed against established ministers. They associated with the openly sottish drunkards as brethren and fathers, at the Lord's Supper... "Were not," Norman thundered, "John McKenzie, minister of Eddrachillis, William McKenzie, that of Assynt, and Alexander Stronach, of Lochbroom, most notorious inebriates and shameful characters throughout all their ministerial life?" These words were written when Norman was in his seventies and had mellowed considerably. But his style and fervour had not altered.

When Dr John Kennedy, church historian, said Norman "claimed to have been converted in a way unusual if not miraculous", he released another torrent of angry denial: "May Heaven pity both the desperate blindness and presumption of your poor but precious soul on this score." Kennedy's use of the word "miraculous" was particularly irritating to Norman. For him, all valid miracles were contained in the divinely inspired Scriptures. Thereafter, God did not need them. Likewise, the time for divine revelations or intervention in the world of humans had passed. Other ministers thought differently; and this was indeed one of the chief reasons why Norman separated from the Church in its formal shape.

Calvinism could strike in varying ways and with varying degrees of force. My great-grandfather, Ewen McInnes, was one of Norman's close followers and sturdy admirers. It was he who, some say, removed Norman's pulpit from his Waipu church after his master died, saying that no-one else was fit to preach where he had stood. His Sunday observance went so far as to forbid the picking of fruit on that day. His children overcame this prohibition by eating the apples or peaches off the branches. Not long ago I talked to a Presbyterian minister in whose charge there were many descendants of Norman McLeod's followers. We talked about one of the men.

"He was a grand man as husband, father and member of the community. He was very sure of what was right and what was wrong. There was no room for anything in between. No room for doubts, either. He acted as he was sure God would have wished him to do."

Although staunch in his faith, I doubt whether this man would have been very much at home in the company of Norman, who had changed so much from the "irreverent" youth who liked a joke to one who castigated his "friends in the Church for their open and offensive lightness and laughter", who poured scorn and abuse on "Parson William" McKenzie of Assynt, the "hot and hateful drunkard", a man of "rancorous pride and passions".

As a young man, however, Norman was more involved in speaking or preaching than in denouncing the "hornless sheep" in print. As he grew to manhood he was one of a number of young men who were critical of the loose discipline in the church, the abuse of patronage in the appointment of ministers and other current evils. His attitude to the church and its place in his world developed slowly. He was twenty-eight when he began to study with the ministry in mind at Aberdeen University, later attending the University of Edinburgh as a theological student.

But his eagerness to be confronting the world made him abandon his formal studies there after a session or two. He was thirty-four, married with one son and, having renounced the Church of Scotland, could never be ordained in his native land. He was deep in conflict already. In 1813, when his son John Grant was born, he had begun to teach at Ullapool but fell out radically with Thomas Ross, the young minister at Lochbroom. In no way would he have his first child baptised by Dr Ross. He and his wife set out for Lochcarron, taking their young one with them "over moor and mountain". Lachlan Mackenzie, minister at Lochcarron, was related to Norman's mother and might have been thought ready to baptise the baby. But Ross was at Lochcarron before them and would not give the necessary consent to Mackenzie. Norman and his wife had to go home with the child unbaptised.

Norman abandoned teaching and went to Caithness, centre of the East Coast herring fishing. Rugged though he was, it was a life that would have tested his physical strength to the limit, but he still found the time and zeal to hold meetings for his fellow Highlanders in an alien environment. There were friends and followers in Assynt who still kept in touch with him. They were all seized to varying degrees with the fever to migrate.

A steady stream of crofters, the dispossessed and those impoverished by higher rents, went away to Canada where, according to stories that came back, there was unlimited land for the taking. Even less hopeful tales did not dampen the enthusiasm of the migrants. Nova Scotia was a "foreign" place in the full sense of the word. There was the story of a plague of mice on Prince Edward Island in 1813, and 1815 was known as the Year of the Mice in Nova Scotia itself. Codfish had been caught, it was said, with mice in their bellies. The mice, presumably, had been swimming to a place where there was more to eat. This paled, however, in comparison with the year 1816, when Roderick Ross's parents crossed to Pictou. The sun did not shine, blizzards swept in from the north in endless succession, animals froze in the fields and corn froze on the stalk. But Norman McLeod had decided it was time to go. Mary, his wife, was pregnant — their son Bunyan was born in Assynt in 1817 — and it would have been folly for her in her delicate condition to undertake the voyage. She would join him in the following year.

The fever to migrate continued to mount. One of Norman's close associates in his student days was Duncan Matheson, minister of Gairloch. Almost all Duncan's near relatives were among those who would go with Norman to Nova Scotia.

Could Norman's capacity to make ardent followers out of ordinary men and women have been based solely on the harsh, unbending style that in the eyes of some observers was his main attribute? Would the men and women of Assynt have looked deeper, possibly finding within that dour frame a man who was passionately concerned with their welfare; a man who could feed them when famine came; who could, in his own way, support them in their search for truth?

Prohibited from preaching, or from holding a teaching post because of the power of the minister, Norman, if he had stayed in Scotland, would almost certainly have become a violent and angry rebel against the order that he had no hope of altering in his lifetime. Salvation, one might say, came with the move to Nova Scotia. His preaching there drew listeners in their hundreds. Ultimately, as teacher, magistrate, farmer, even as ship-owner as well as ordained minister, he had an impact on many lives that must have been as satisfying to him as his Scottish experience had been frustrating.

Norman, when he sailed away, left behind a Highland population vastly different in many ways from that of fifty years before. Some of the differences he would have approved of; others not so. He would have had to agree with the Moderates in the church in their dislike of the overcharged enthusiasm, the "religious ravings" of many Free Church adherents. He had, however, come to believe that baptism should be limited, along with the taking of communion, to "worthy and righteous persons". In outwardly obvious ways, too, the character of the Highlander who came under the influence of these enthusiastic churchmen was reshaped. Stewart of Garth, an army man with a keen power of observation, was one of those who lamented that the gregarious and sociable Scot was being transformed into a humourless, dour, dogmatic and even melancholic individual. The Scot's taste for music, dancing and all kinds of social amusements had been chilled. Traditional tales from the past and native poetry were neglected, the pipes and the fiddle were rejected and often burned in mass demonstrations. "Deprived of his traditional forms of revelry," writes Laurie Stanley in *The*

Well-Watered Garden, "the Scot now spent his time gravely contemplating the questions of atonement, eternal damnation and saving grace." Stanley adds, with a certain dry humour, "With these attributes the Highlander was ready for his pilgrimage to Heaven or his migration to another land."

A photograph taken late in his life shows Norman McLeod wearing a headscarf round his long, greying hair, making him look rather like an elderly "hippie" of the 1960s. This, together with a flowing blue robe, was the distinguishing mark of The Men, a loosely bonded organisation which aimed at bringing the church back to its original pure simplicity; in particular, at removing the power of the landlords to appoint ministers without consulting the members of the church. The Men originated in Assynt, where many would say the need was greatest. Most of them came from the crofts and fishing villages; self-educated in many cases, their inquiring minds fed from study of the Scriptures and from pondering on the meaning of life and God's purpose.

There were two sides to their campaign. One was to denounce the immorality, the stupidity, the lack of true zeal and earnestness found in many pulpits; the second was to bring men and women back to the basic doctrines found in the Bible. One of the most remarkable of The Men was Colin Sutherland, of Helmsdale. Unable to read, he could correct anyone missing a word in a Bible reading.

Just what had happened to the Christian Church in isolated parts of Scotland over the centuries? Nothing could answer this question more graphically than an extract from George Collins' *Men of the Burning Heart*, describing what befell Alexander MacLeod when his ministry in the parish of Uig began in 1824:

> Mr MacLeod was warned before he set foot in the parish of Uig that nobody there knew anything of Christianity except one herd-boy, and he was reputed to be off his head! If Mr MacLeod thought that his informant had exaggerated, he was given ample reason to change his mind. Uig was indeed in a sorry plight. The religion of the people he found to be a compound of Romanism, Deism and sheer paganism. They told the minister that they believed there were seven sacraments. They regarded the death of Christ as an unnecessary waste. They paid their homage regularly to the sun and the moon. They bought and sold whisky and tobacco at the church door after the Sabbath services. And when Mr MacLeod called upon an elder to lead in prayer at the first prayer-meeting he held in the parish, he could scarcely believe his ears when the poor man besought the Lord to let a ship be wrecked on their rocky shores so that they might benefit from its cargo! Yet there were upward of 800 communicant members in the congregation.

Alexander MacLeod was to move on from Uig and become one of the most revered figures in the Free Church when it broke away in 1843. Three years passed before his Uig congregation was ready to take part in the Lord's Supper. There were twenty communicants who spent the whole night in religious exercises. "While these things were carried on," MacLeod wrote, "the ungodly themselves were in tears, and iniquity for a time dwindled into nothing, covered her brazen face and was greatly ashamed."

I learned about Alexander MacLeod, and his connection with The Men and with Norman MacLeod, in another letter from Barbara Weiskrantz. It seemed to provide a fitting salute — and farewell — to the land that had nursed Norman to maturity. Barbara enclosed some enlightening extracts from *Annals of the Disruption*, by Dr Thomas Brown, and from George Collins' *Men of the Burning Heart*.

The minister of Kildonan, in Sutherland, was urged by The Men in his parish to dispense communion more frequently than once every two years, which was then the custom. A great crowd of worshippers assembled, enough to fill the church twice over. The elders told the minister they must meet outside as there was not room for all. He replied: "If not, there are doors to keep them out." The Rev. Dr M'Lauchlan tells what happened then: "A famous man, John Grant, with another like himself, withdrew with a host of followers to a neighbouring hillside, and kept a meeting of their own while the services were conducted in the church. The spirit that was generated that day continued and spread over large sections of the country, and led to the formation of a party strongly opposed to the Church and its ministers."

There is no doubt that Norman McLeod was one of the leaders in this party. As already mentioned, he named one of his sons after John Grant. He called other young men to his banner, in the war of words with "Parson William" the Assynt minister. Among them was Alexander MacLeod. But as time went on Alexander had his misgivings. Norman's denunciations, he felt, were too sweeping — they included the "godly minority" in the ministry as well as the unsavoury majority.

"Before he was licensed by the Presbytery," writes George Collins, "Alexander was required by the Presbytery to renounce the separatist tenets of Norman. That was enough for Norman! Alexander was cast on the scrap heap with the rest! If he deigned to refer to him at all it was with disdain. A man so lacking in militancy was not worthy of respect! *A chaora mhaol* (the hornless sheep) he used to call him."

An interesting story about Norman the student comes from Dr John MacLeod. Norman had debated through a long night with an "old Ross-shire worthy", *Uisden Buidh*. The old man's verdict: "He was apprehensive that Norman might do mischief in his day. There was a forwardness and a masterfulness about him that he could not hide or hold in check. The old man augured ill from such a disposition wedded to undeniable gifts. He had in him the making of an ecclesiastical Ishmael, whose hand should be against every man, as every man's hand should be against him."

An irreverent reader might suspect that Norman, during the long night, had worsted his opponent in the debate. Be that as it may. The significant thing is that such debates had become an essential part of life in the Highlands by the beginning of the nineteenth century. Clan warfare was ended; cattle-raiding had become difficult in the well-policed lands; a vast gap yawned which, providentially, was filled by religion — no longer formal and entrenched in privilege, but evangelical and breaking old frontiers. When Norman McLeod was to build a church in Nova Scotia that would hold twelve hundred worshippers, he was carrying on a practice that he had seen developing in Scotland before he left.

He had spoken at gatherings in Assynt where men and women in their hundreds, the devout and the curious, the believers and the unsure, met for a day or longer. Biblical texts were discussed, at length, by men whose experience was from life and not from theory. A meeting, followed by prayers, could last more than seven hours. Then the audience, which might number over a thousand and had assembled from many miles around, would slowly disperse, some returning to their homes, others to quiet retreats on the hillside where they would continue to seek and feel the presence of God.

In all these events The Men played a leading role. In many places, depending on the attitude of the minister, there was complete harmony in the parish, and in some parishes the session was almost exclusively composed of them. But this was not always so. What could one expect, for example, in a parish where "the minister was so careless that he passed his lifetime with only three sermons, which he read and read until his whole parishioners found their amusement in rehearsing them?" Or at a meeting where someone like Alexander Gair gave the opening address, and "fairly astonished us by the sparkling brilliancy of his oratory, by his wonderful acquaintance with Scripture — by the ingenious, original, but often mystical interpretations he assigned to many passages, by his scathing invectives against many classes of evil-doers, and by his awful denunciations of 'graceless ministers'." Or again, at a vastly different kind of meeting, where old Andrew Ross, called on to pray, addressed God under the name of "Everlasting Love" — "and as often as the word escaped his lips the whole physical frame became agitated, his voice became choked, and his eyes rained down tears; they were not the tears of remorse, but those of overpowering love". Or to be one of a thousand men, women and children, who have flocked to a meeting at Snizort, in Skye, "travelling over hill and moor, along roads and by-ways, by boats now lying at anchor in the bay, from all parts of Skye and the neighbouring isles".

Led by The Men, the humble people at times like these subconsciously felt their power, as well as the love of God streaming down to them. And they were transformed. There were plenty in the Establishment ready to criticise: "The new religion," says Maureen Molloy in *Those Who Speak from the Heart*, "was so blatantly political that tenants found to be giving shelter to The Men forfeited their leases". But that was not the full picture. The power of their faith swept the countryside, leaving none untouched except some of the factors and landlords and Moderate churchmen. The tide that had started to run in Assynt kept flowing right through to the establishment of the Free Church. Many of The Men went their own way, buoyed up by the support of their fellows. Others with the support of liberal-minded ministers and elders were able to work within the body of the church. And a few, Norman McLeod among them, refused to compromise or alter their stance, and took their departure to seek a freer air across the ocean.

Barbara and Larry Weiskrantz had been holidaying on Barra in the Outer Hebrides and, on their way home to Oxford, paid a visit to Assynt. By this time, Barbara told me in her letter, she had become very involved in the story of Norman McLeod. They had already visited St Ann's. Now, in Assynt, she had hoped to elicit information about Norman from Alec Menzies, still living in Elphin, last survivor of the generation closest to McLeod. Alec, at ninety-two, was in fine form, up a ladder painting the back wall of his croft, but he could tell her nothing new. However, at Lochinver she met Norman MacAskill, OBE, a man of many talents — "a fisherman by trade", Barbara wrote, "but in true Highland fashion much more besides: a maker and a player of stringed instruments, musical conductor, one-time Sheriff, member of the Crofters' Commission and general custodian of Assynt culture and tradition". Nearly one hundred and eighty years after he had left Sutherland, Norman McLeod was still well remembered, and Norman MacAskill was able to tell Barbara where McLeod was born and lived as a young man at Clachtoll Bay, near Stoer. She took photos of the ruined croft that had been his first home, the only sign of habitation on the bluff looking down on the sea. There were old sheep pens still recognisable, too, contrasting with the modest and well-organised camp site near by. And an inlet in the bay nearest to the croft would almost certainly have been where the family fishing boat was anchored.

Norman MacAskill, Barbara said, was the man behind a move to erect a memorial cairn to Norman McLeod on the bluff at Clachtoll. No better place could have been fashioned for that purpose. Harsh and bleak for most of the year, with the fantastic peak of Suilven brooding over the landscape, Assynt is a place to harbour ghosts, wizards and prophets.

"Touring around Stoer Peninsula is a strange experience," Barbara wrote, "a little like stepping back in time, for there's been precious little development there of any kind and it must look today very much as it did in Norman McLeod's day. A sombre place, numerous outcrops of granite interspersed with tufts of coarse grasses and heathers. But beautiful, too, in its brooding inwardness."

Another letter came very soon after Barbara's, this one from Edinburgh, from our cousin Anna Dunlop. It contained very cheerful news, giving an almost fairy-tale climax to Barbara's account of her visit to the lonely land north of Lochinver.

Anna enclosed a clipping from the *Scotsman*, an article by Tom Morton which began: "History was made yesterday when the 21,000-acre North Lochinver Estate in Sutherland was sold to 100 of its tenant crofters... " ("I thought you would be interested," Anna wrote, "in this reversal of the old crofting emigrations!")

The Assynt Crofters' Trust had been formed in an effort to bring an estate under its tenants' control for the first time in Scottish history. It had been a tough, lengthy and unrelenting battle against long odds. The previous owners, Scandinavian Property Services, like many others on the Continent and south of the border, had been tempted to buy holdings vastly bigger than anything they would be allowed to take up in their native lands. But, as the *Scotsman* said, estate ownership is no longer, if ever it was, a honey pot for the monied investor. The Swedish company went "bust", as others had done before them. But in Assynt there were men and women of skill and determination who ventured to buy the estate. Help came from individuals and organisations all over the world. They were able to convince the liquidator and the banks that their proposal was realistic, as was their price of about £300,000, which meant that they gained possession not only of the croft land but also of mineral, sporting and fishing rights, including sea-salmon netting and loch fishing.

That night, the crofters celebrated in the village school at Stoer a victory that could encourage other crofting communities to venture along the same road. Land ownership could be revolutionised. There is much still to be proved, but the spirit is certainly there. The *Scotsman* has a magnificent photograph of Alan Macrae, chairman of the Assynt Crofters' Trust, celebrating the victory. He stands on a narrow, eroded crag, his sheepdog at his feet. His arms reach skyward, one of them firmly holding a whisky bottle. An appropriate backdrop, taking in almost all the horizon, is Suilven, the mountain that overlooks the estate. Later that evening Alan entered the hall while the crofters' party was in full swing. There was a standing ovation. Solemnity, too, as in a voice choked with emotion he told the crowd:

"It seems we have won the land and this is certainly a moment to savour. But my immediate thoughts are to wish that some of our forebears were here to share it. This is a historic blow which we have struck for people on the land right throughout the Highlands and Islands."

The tough battles have not yet all been won. A hard economic struggle lies ahead but, as the crofters face up to the future, they will surely sense an invisible host, crofters and fishermen, and their wives and families, long gone but still giving strength and inspiration to them in their efforts.

Chapter Four

Pictou and the Hunger
for Knowledge

S O, AT LAST, NORMAN MCLEOD farewelled his wife and many of those who had listened to him over the years, and set foot on the shifting deck of the barque *Frances Ann* at Ullapool. Wherever Norman might be, stories gathered around him, and the Atlantic crossing to Nova Scotia was no exception. Murdoch McDonald was not on board the *Frances Ann*. As a small boy, he would accompany his parents to Nova Scotia in 1818 on the *Perseverance*, and they joined grandparents already living at Cariboo, a dozen miles up the coast from Pictou. Murdoch's family were on intimate terms with the McLeods, and what Murdoch wrote in 1885 for Judge Paterson, back in Nova Scotia, should be considered close to the truth:

> The ship proceeded favourably on her course till mid-ocean when, met by heavy storms of westerly winds, she was badly damaged, so that they had to stop the leaks with blankets and whatsoever they could find. Ultimately the captain called a council of crew and passengers and proposed to put back. Everyone on board agreed to the proposal, Mr McLeod alone protesting. He told them that, if they put back, some way or other he would be saved, but no other one aboard the ship would ever see land. He requested them to hold on as they were and, unless they would have fair wind in less than twenty-four hours, he would agree to put back. Before daylight next morning the storm calmed down. Shortly afterwards a smooth breeze of easterly wind came on, they squared the yards and had not to move a sheet until they arrived at Pictou Harbour.

An elaboration of this story explained that Norman, being a good mathematician and navigator from his days with the fishing fleet, had kept his own log of the voyage; and was able to convince the captain that the ship was closer to Nova Scotia than to any ports in Europe.

As Ian Lang would say, the truth is never the worse for a little honest decorating. And that is the story that came down through the years in families that took part in the migration. Of one thing there is no doubt: Norman McLeod reached Pictou on the *Frances Ann*, and his wife and family, including the newborn baby Bunyan, joined him there the following year.

Pictou was spilling over with land-hungry Highlanders, largely impoverished but with their minds fixed on the block of land that would give them and their families security and a measure of comfort they had never known before. Pictou was a frontier town still, after thirty years of exist-ence, raw and unadorned; its chief reason for survival being that it was so much closer to Scotland and therefore cheaper and less difficult to reach than the Carolinas, the other centre for victims of the Clearances. But many of the new arrivals were shocked to find their "paradise" was a wilderness of grim forest and impenetrable swamp, often deep in the interior instead of on the sea coast as they had been promised.

Pictou itself lives in a watercolour painted by J.E. Woodford in 1817. There is a flagstaff; stumps stand crudely out of the rubble from fire and slash; a big windmill on the point, for grinding grain; a scatter of houses with plenty of space around them. And great stretches of water reaching across to Loch Broom and West River, itself already settled. In many ways it could have been a picture of Auckland, the northern settlement in New Zealand, in the 1840s. But beneath the turmoil and restlessness, the disap-pointment and uncertainty, Pictou had a measure of stability and forward-looking citizens working to lay the foundations of an integrated rural society. Many of the first settlers knew no English and were barely able to read or write, but there were others, before Norman, for whom education, espe-cially a liberal education, was an essential part of life.

"Without knowledge," said the Rev. James MacGregor, who had ar-rived at Pictou in 1786, "people can be neither good Christians nor good citizens."

The Rev. Thomas McCulloch, one of the most remarkable men to grace any pioneering settlement, carried MacGregor's ideas even further. He founded a grammar school in the tiny town and then in 1816 established the Pictou Academy, designed to take students to the same levels as Scot-tish universities.

"His twenty students, dressed in the flowing red gowns of Glasgow or Aberdeen, were recruited from log homes within twelve miles of the Acad-emy," writes Donald MacKay in *Scotland Farewell*.

They met in a "modest, two-storey wooden frame building with tower and steeple". And there they were offered a four-year course that included Latin, Greek, Logic, Moral Philosophy, Mathematics and Natural Philoso-phy, most of which McCulloch taught himself. He built a library, a mu-seum for scientific study, with a valuable collection of wild-life specimens and minerals. He established a Divinity class to educate local ministers and train others. He wrote editorials for the local newspaper. He preached twice a day in the new church.

Writing to a friend in Scotland he said: "With respect to family affairs, I may add that I now have eight children and we have food and raiment. I undergo considerable fatigue but upon the whole enjoy a degree of worldly comfort, and also of respectability, I could not have aspired to in Britain."

How successful was McCulloch in his work? Results speak for themselves. Donald MacKay quotes the case of a Pictou shoemaker's son who went to Glasgow University to study for the Master of Arts degree, along with three Academy classmates. All four were awarded MAs without need of further study. In Pictou, most of the immigrant parents were hungry for land; many of the children were hungry for knowledge which would lift them out of the ruck. The people who lived in one fifteen-mile stretch, says MacKay, gave thirty-five clergymen to the Presbyterian Church, "along with a provincial Governor, a Chief Justice and a Premier of the province".

The hunger for knowledge was just as strong in the Highlands as in remote Nova Scotia. The education system there, and the devotion of the teachers, was so great that it was not unusual for fourteen-year-olds, taught in the tiny schools of some remote glen, to be admitted to university on even terms with their elders. But the universities were all outside the Highlands. There is, indeed, a certain irony in the fact that only in the year 1993 were there signs of a federal "Highland University" being put together, from colleges in Inverness, Skye, Stornoway on Lewis, and so on, under the umbrella of the already degree-granting Robert Gordon's College, now Aberdeen's second university. I am grateful to Anna Dunlop for this information. She adds: "The Skye College is at Ostaig, where all the staff are bilingual and the teaching language is Gaelic."

Norman McLeod did not like Pictou, in spite of, or perhaps because of, the Rev. James MacGregor and the Rev. Thomas McCulloch. For Norman, a liberal attitude spelt lack of discipline, and without discipline in religion and education the people would have no protection against the forces of evil. McCulloch's first address as principal of the academy was on "The Nature and Uses of a Liberal Education", and he considered the college "would have a powerful influence by disseminating general knowledge, correcting the vices of youth and instilling in their minds the principle of virtue". This was all much too soft for Norman, especially when the academy was non-sectarian.

It confirmed his feelings about Pictou itself. Here was a bustling little town, a place of rest and recreation for seamen between voyages, with taverns and doubtless other places with gambling and immoral activity available. Equally important to him, it had no place where he could barricade himself and his followers against the many and varied temptations of the outer world. He established himself at West River, along the coast from Pictou, and there, as far as possible from the liberalising or demoralising behaviour of the townsfolk, exhorted those who came under his spell.

There is an interesting and enlightening little book which helps the reader to understand the man: *The Letters of Rev. Norman McLeod, 1835–1851,* written to John Gordon, a disciple of the minister for many years, and still in Pictou. The introduction says: "In these letters the sharp angles and rigid principles of the Rev. Norman McLeod are revealed in a unique way. They show him to have been scornful of other ministers, impatient of all authority save his own, but extremely insistent upon the correctness of his own interpretations and the necessity of conforming to his views. They also show that he went to great pains to kindle and restrain his followers."

Norman would have been no more at ease staying in the Pictou area than if he had remained in Scotland. There must be some other part of this great continent still unspoilt by man, where he could fashion a life according to God's standards; or perhaps even another community looking for a leader such as he. Before too long he would have to seek out one or the other. Meanwhile, he would fight with all his strength against the insidious temptations that Pictou offered his weaker brethren.

Of these temptations, the Pictou Academy was one of the most potent. Already its pupils included the sons of some of his converts. From an initial roll of twenty, the academy, charging a fee of twenty pounds, had increased in strength and in reputation, drawing scholars from a wider radius. All this made it harder for Norman to maintain a position of authority. He would have to move, to find a place where he would be minister, schoolteacher, lawgiver and lawmaker. Other families found Pictou not to their liking. Some of them were older settlers, among them Donald McLeod "Squire" and his family, and Norman McDonald, who have already been mentioned.

Where should he go? Norman had friends in many parts of the United States, some of them former associates in the activities of The Men, now making their way in transplanted Highland communities scattered through the eastern states. It could have been from one of these that, in 1818, a call came to him to be the minister at a Highland settlement, probably in Ohio. It was an attractive invitation, and first steps in another minor migration led first of all to the building of a small vessel, named by the cynics the *Ark*, in which some of the men could make an exploratory voyage.

Details of this first venture are shrouded in a true Nova Scotian fog. Some accounts suggest that the *Ark* would make the very ambitious journey down the east coast of the continent, round the cape into the Gulf of Mexico to the mouth of the Mississippi. From there the party would find transport up the river to the Ohio destination. It is more likely that the *Ark* would have made for Boston, from where there seems to have been, at that time, a migratory trail towards the west. What would today seem the simplest route, to the Great Lakes by way of the St Lawrence River or Halifax, had many difficulties in the early nineteenth century.

Murdoch McDonald, whose father was navigator of the *Ark* on the little schooner's first voyage, gives a simple and credible account. Most of the men involved in the move would have been experienced seamen. The list that Murdoch McDonald gives of the officers is one of the first indications we have of who were Norman McLeod's chief lieutenants in Pictou. It was he — and no committee — that appointed Donald McLeod "Squire" sailing master; Hugh Matheson chief officer; and John McLeod "Arichat" and Murdoch's brother Alex among the crew. These names keep turning up at a various stages of the migration.

According to Murdoch McDonald, who would have learned details from his father, the voyage of the *Ark* was singularly uneventful. Murdoch wrote:

> The wind favouring, they made for Cape North. Then, sailing close by the land and examining the coast, one fine afternoon they arrived near St Ann's Harbour and commenced to fish. They found codfish very abundant and after getting a good catch made for the harbour to pass the night.
>
> When looking round the next morning they were delighted with the prospect, weighed anchor and sailed for the head of the harbour — about six miles. They landed and, after a short consultation, decided to go no further. Each man selected his own locality and with heart and will to clear a plot of ground to be ready for spring work and also put up the walls of a shanty. When such works were finished, they returned to Pictou to spend the winter.
>
> After their arrival in Pictou, they sold the *Ark* to one of the shareholders, A. Munro, and each partner in the *Ark* prepared a small boat to carry his family to Cape Breton.
>
> The Parson's boat was the largest trading boat. The first landing they made was on Prince Edward Island. I often heard the old minister speaking of the great kindness received from the Catholic Bishop of that Island, who when he heard who he was, sent for him to his own house and treated him as kindly as if he was his own brother.

While Norman, after pausing on Prince Edward Island, took his boat round Cape North and down the coast to St Ann's Bay, the other six boats followed what could be a more sheltered route: through the Strait of Canso, now crossed by a causeway and, hauled over the narrow isthmus at St Peters, down the Bras d'Or lakes through the centre of the island to the open sea and round to St Ann's. All the boats came safely into harbour in May, 1820. Their owners were: Norman McLeod, Donald McLeod "Squire", Hugh Matheson, Ronald Ross, Alex Munro, Roderick McKenzie and Norman McDonald. .

As often happens, the best stories are repeated chiefly for their colour and the creative imagination that brought them to life. One of the liveliest appears in *Idyll of the Shipbuilders*, in a section written by the Rev. John Murray. It tells how, with her two hundred passengers on board, "the sails were spread to the breeze" and the *Ark* sailed out of Pictou Harbour bound for the Gulf of Mexico. But she was destined never to get there. All went well until she had passed through the Strait of Canso, and reached the Atlantic Ocean. Here she encountered a terrific gale from the southwest that drove her before it along the south coast of Cape Breton and past the island of Scatari. Then the gale shifted to the east-north-east, and drove her towards the Bird Islands, off the mouth of the Big Bras d'Or.

> In order to avoid being wrecked, the captain steered the ship under the shelter of Cape Dauphin and into St Ann's Harbour, where he dropped anchor in comparatively smooth water. They were saved — all saved, but barely saved.
>
> After the gale had blown itself out and the sun began to shine again, the passengers, who had been under battened hatches during the storm, were allowed to come on deck. After their terrible experience they were all sick of the sea, physically and mentally. They determined to abandon their purpose of going to Ohio, and resolved to make homes for themselves on the shores of this capacious and beautiful harbour.
>
> They all got busy cutting down the primeval forest, piling and burning the trees and 'slash' in order to get at the soil and plant potatoes, oats, etc, so that they might raise food for themselves and their children. It was easy to make a livelihood in St Ann's at that time. The virgin soil, enriched by the ashes of the burnt forest, was fertile. The waters of the harbour, as well as the rivers, were teeming with all kinds of fish. Wood for fuel and building purposes was to be had for the labour of cutting and preparing. Everyone helped his neighbour, and before the winter came on, every family had a warm log house in which to pass its long dreary hours.

A fascinating story, indeed, to tell before the fire on bleak winter nights, embellished still further, no doubt, by the skill of the storytellers who graced every Highlands community. If more drama was needed, they could always go back to the voyage of the *Frances Ann*, to the mid-Atlantic confrontation between the captain and Norman McLeod. One lively version: "The captain was unwilling to take the advice of a passenger and not turn back to Ireland. He blustered, threatened to put Norman in irons, but finally was persuaded. 'Well,' said the captain, 'under stress I will proceed, but you'll find yourself in gaol as soon as we reach America.' 'Of that I will take my chance,' replied Norman. The passengers, many of them fishermen and experienced seamen, manned the pumps, kept the ship afloat, and they arrived safely at Pictou. On arriving the captain was gallant enough to say: 'Well, McLeod, I will say that you are a better seaman then I am.' 'Not at all,' replied Norman. 'It was the Lord's doing.'"

John Murray's story, which embodies the memories of events that took place nearly one hundred years before he set them down, is a classic tale of the search for Utopia: the arduous journey, dangers faced and perils overcome, the arrival at the place that seems like paradise, a place unspoilt by other humans but waiting just for them, a place where, working in harmony and love, they can find food in abundance, shelter and warmth against winter's chills.

In hard fact, this was not quite how it had been, although, for a start at least, everyone worked together under the autocratic but caring eye of their leader. Coming from Pictou they would have known what to expect. A benign summer would be followed by a harsh winter, with meagre supplies of food, ice closing the bay and snow drifts piling high. But their worst imaginings did not measure up to what they found. There were government allocations of seed potatoes, corn and oatmeal, but this did not last long. Laurie Stanley writes: "The Rev. Norman McLeod's following of seventy-seven or more refugees, described by the Surveyor-General of Cape Breton as 'a set of miserable poor', sent piteous requests for relief to the Lieutenant-Governor of Nova Scotia, James Kempt, during their first winter in St Ann's. The government obliged, sending thirty barrels of meal and flour and some blankets and bedding."

However, Stanley acknowledges later in her book, *The Well-Watered Garden*, that "This community, under the tight direction of McLeod, enjoyed a measure of prosperity and permanency, unlike most of the early frail and nondescript Scottish settlements"; and perhaps it was the sort of special pleading thought necessary when asking for government help that made the Surveyor-General call the first St Ann's settlers "a set of miserable poor". There were difficult times for every Cape Bretoner to face, then and later, but the settlement at St Ann's, from its very foundation, was an integrated community. Its people had a wide range of skills. Some were educated and proficient in English as well as in Gaelic. Other could speak only Gaelic, but in a community where responsibilities were shared, that was no disadvantage. Most important of all, they had their church and their minister, who was also their leader in every aspect of their life. Within a remarkably few years, indeed, observers were praising St Ann's for its stability, its comparative prosperity and the feeling of harmony that prevailed.

Reading what contemporaries write about Cape Breton Island in the early years of the nineteenth century can be a startling experience for one brought up on a comfortable story of plain living, high thinking and just rewards. The picture we see is of a great influx of Highlanders and Hebrideans, uncared for, uneducated, so poor that they had to borrow from the shipowners to pay their fares.

"Their doom," said one report, "is one of the extreme privation — spiritually, morally and physically." And again: "Multitudes, even of adults, were unbaptised, and thousands to whom the sacred rite had been administered, sunk into the most deplorable insensibility and grossest ignorance.

There are few here, generally speaking, who can read at all. The Bible, in several sequestered spots, is totally unknown, and the Sabbath entirely forgotten."

Darkest Cape Breton, like Darkest Africa, became the target for missionaries — from the Evangelical wing of the Church of Scotland and from the Presbyterian Church of Nova Scotia. These two bodies became rivals for the souls of the benighted Cape Bretoners. From Scotland came men, indomitable workers who endured great privation on stipends insufficient to nourish them; the Scottish parishes had tight purse strings when it came to supporting those who were out of sight. Many of them were at home in Gaelic, which made social and religious intercourse easier. For the missionaries from Pictou there were, surprisingly, bigger language problems, for men like the Rev. James McGregor and the Rev. Thomas McCulloch, already met in this chapter, could not find the time to do the work as thoroughly as they would have wished. But they had time to carry on a war of words, their target being ministers of the Established Church of Scotland, and also schismatics dabbling in their secessionist pool. Especially Norman McLeod. You could ignore him, but he wouldn't go away. Instead, with complete impartiality, he spoke and acted against the Pictou group as well as against those sent from Scotland to cultivate what they hoped was a virgin field.

James MacGregor had once written: "There is a fourfold zeal in Pictou. Zeal for the Established Church of Scotland; zeal for the Presbyterian Church of Nova Scotia; zeal for lukewarmness; and zeal for Norman McLeod. And who is this Norman?" he asked. "A self-made preacher, who declares there is not a minister of Christ in all the Church of Scotland." Now the same fourfold zeal was to be found in Cape Breton. But there had been one major change. In Pictou, all four were in a state of flux, warring without positive result. In Cape Breton, the war continued, except in the tight little community of St Ann's, which was under the firm control of Norman. And, like the good general and the fervent crusader he was, he defended his principality by raiding neighbouring communities — Middle River, Baddeck, Boularderie — until the equally positive leadership of the Rev. James Fraser, who had worked as a teacher in the fishing villages of Assynt, caused him to retreat.

McLeod's dislike of the Established Church of Scotland had if anything grown stronger. Some of it had been focused on one Donald Fraser, who had arrived at East River, near Pictou, from Scotland, as the Established Church minister and had found his congregation shrinking in the face of Norman's fiery preaching. Fraser became one of the leaders in his church's missionary efforts in Cape Breton. He wrote highly charged reports on the condition of the islanders; reports which Dr McCulloch said wilfully misrepresented the situation. Fraser, for his part, was also able to use words as weapons. He falsely alleged that James MacGregor — a man of culture and dignity — had described the ministers who had come on behalf of the Church of Scotland as "Thieves and robbers, whoremongers and adulterers". Hearing this, his listeners tended to turn away from the Pictou church and give a warmer reception to the missionaries from the home country. Graduates from the Pictou Academy were no longer wanted. Then, in 1820, Donald Fraser in turn became a target, this time for Norman McLeod himself who, in a perverse kind of way, found himself acting as an ally of the embattled Pictou Presbyterians. Fraser brought a case in the Halifax Supreme Court of Pleas against Norman who, he said, had publicly charged him with bigamy, in this way bringing his "good name fame credit and reputation" into disrepute, to the extent of £500. The court ruled that he was entitled to a little over half that sum. But, writes Laurie Stanley, McLeod paid no more heed to the civil law than to ecclesiastical measures of discipline. He refused to retract his charge and defaulted in payment. His personal property was seized.

Libel and defamation were serious charges. Maureen Molloy writes in *Those Who Speak to the Heart* that, after defaulting, he was imprisoned, but I have seen nothing to support that.

Everywhere in Cape Breton, except in little St Ann's, the missionary arguments continued. Why, it was asked, should missionaries not be sent to Cape Breton when the need was as great there as among the savages of Van Diemen's Land or the Cape of Good Hope? Meanwhile, with religious controversy giving an interesting background to their daily routine, the new settlers "dug in" and began to make homes in the wilderness. One sign of their activity comes from Norman himself. The *Ark* arrived in early summer. By December of 1820 Norman was in his first home on land that had been cleared during the year, and was petitioning the Nova Scotian government for over 300 acres between the North and South Gut, on the harbour. This was to be the heart of the settlement, the site of the church that would be the first public building erected, the home of the minister. But spiritual nourishment would avail little if the bare physical wants were not met. And so, led by Norman, they worked desperately all that summer, clearing enough of the land that had been granted to them by the government to take crops of potatoes and oats. These were, it has been said, often planted in the ash from the trees they had felled and destroyed by fire. But it is likely that much digging, with primitive tools, was done too.

The settlers would have known what they could expect when winter set in, having already endured the snow and ice of Pictou. But, as we ourselves found more than a century and a half later, the benign sun, blue skies and warm breezes of St Ann's during summer make it difficult to believe it could all disappear so quickly. We were standing where the ground slopes down to Black Cove, comfortable in our light summer clothes, when one of our St Ann's friends said: "In a few months there'll be a track through six-foot snowdrifts down there!" And, not far from the longest day, we decided to have a swim in the sea. I did not know that I could react so quickly! A first plunge into the water and, as quick as a flash, a reflex backward dive and the feeling that a thousand red-hot needles had pierced the skin. "Was it quite cool?" an interested companion, again from St Ann's, asked me innocently. "A month ago there was still ice off the bay."

The climate provides an answer to why St Ann's should have been uninhabited when the *Ark* arrived. The French had established an armed trading post there early in the seventeenth century; Fort Dauphin also had strategic value, but a hundred years later the French virtually abandoned it in favour of Louisburg. The bay might remain open to shipping until the end of December, but the narrow inlets and sheltered waters would remain ice-bound right through the spring. And for an area that relied on the sea-roads for communication, that was a major problem.

For the new settlers, winter was a hungry season, but spring was even hungrier. However, they were accustomed to that kind of situation in the Highlands and the Hebrides, long before crossing the Atlantic. It was something to endure, even though it cost the lives of the young and the frail. So, as the spring of 1821 came round, their eyes were on the future. The *Ark*, now under the control of Alex Munro, sailed from Pictou with new families, food, seed for crops and pasture. They realised that, for the settlement to succeed, a bigger work force was essential; and in spite of the harsh winter there were sufficient volunteers from the Pictou area, drawn by the desire to share family and religious links.

More and more people were flooding in from the Highlands and the Hebrides, leaving behind them a land where social conditions had never been worse. One migrant to the American colonies, Hector Crevecoeur, had written a little earlier: "What attachment can a poor European emigrant have for a country where he had nothing? The knowledge of the language, the love of a few kindred as poor as himself were the only cords that tied him; his country is now that which gives him his land, bread, protection and consequence." For the Highlander, family links would not be easily broken but, as the migrants were joined by more and more "refugees" from their old clan areas, nostalgia and sentimental recall played a diminishing part in their lives. It is only in more recent years, when the glow of romance has replaced the grimness of reality, that there has been a change.

St Ann's was bursting with energy in that second summer. Plans were made for a school, where Norman taught fourteen pupils. Four years later he was officially licensed as schoolmaster; by then, too, he had been appointed a magistrate in Victoria County. There was only one important gap in his control of the settlement. Although he had told the Nova Scotian government that he was licensed as a preacher of the Established Church of Scotland, which he wasn't, he could not take marriage services until he was ordained. Marriage by a civil authority, he considered, could not protect the celebrants against the temptations, the careless attitudes, of modern life. Only a minister, with the full power of the Lord reinforcing his words, could do that. In 1827 he was ordained by the Genesee Presbytery in New York State. Although many of his enemies refused to acknowledge his new status, he was now fully equipped for his work. In the same year his school, having gained government approval, began to grow in size and range of subjects. By 1835 it had 110 students, as young as three and up to twenty-five years old.

A quotation from Allen Tate in the 1930s could be applied, with a slight modification, to Norman McLeod's aims for his people. Tate said: "Only a return to the provinces, to the small, self-contained centres of life, will lay the all-destroying abstraction of America to rest." The power of the State was not so all-encompassing in Norman's day as a century later, and he still believed he could build a "centre of life" that would be as self-contained as he wished. But it soon became apparent that, sturdy as the barricade might be, the world would inevitably be knocking on the gates of St Ann's and could not be denied entrance.

St Ann's had never been the isolated little settlement that most of its inhabitants imagined. In 1820, the north shore of Boularderie Island was already occupied by other Scottish migrants with no close links with St Ann's. The fertile valley-lands of Middle River, inland from Baddeck, had received their first Scottish migrants in 1806, and Baddeck itself was signalling its future as a port to serve the Bras d'Or lakes area, and also as a centre for boat-building, an industry ideally suited to the skills of the men and the resources of the land. As communications improved, all these places became familiar to the St Ann's people. The first civil marriage in St Ann's was celebrated by a half-pay naval officer, James Duffus, of Baddeck, before 1826.

But the traffic was not all one way. Norman, consolidating his position on the shores of St Ann's Bay, reached out to the other neighbouring communities. Among those he won to his banner were members of the McKay family, notably John McKay ("Ian Ruadh"). In 1834, Alexander Farquharson was introduced to the combined charge of Middle River and Big Baddeck, with the settlers being committed to a bond of £150, paid each year, half in cash and half in produce. John McKay and his followers who, according to Laurie Stanley, were styled "an intransigent group of radicals", refused to sign the bond. There are references to "an unpleasant business" and "a furious contest with McKay". The rebels included about half the church trustees. They referred in a petition to the "miserable and marked inefficiency" of their Minister, and eventually took what was the logical step — withdrawal from the church services.

John McKay was a man of considerable personality. It calls for no subtle thinking to divine what was in his mind when he stood against Farquharson, calling for a minister "more beneficial" to the edification of their souls. Norman McLeod was well aware of the situation, making reference to Farquharson's sleep-inducing sermons. A new minister, if he was to satisfy the McKay faction, would have to be McLeod himself or someone of equal stature.

John McKay was one of Norman's strongest supporters. He must have made life difficult for Alexander Farquharson, who was described by members of his congregation as "quiet, humble, amiable, gentle, affectionate and sympathetic". He was still minister at Middle River when the McKays, who were considerable landowners in the district, moved on to New Zealand with Norman McLeod.

While Norman was consolidating his position at home in St Ann's, he did not limit himself to seeking new followers in the neighbouring settlements. He continued to write to his friends who had stayed in Pictou. The letters written to John Gordon show how urgently, how passionately, he worked to protect his friends against the evils rampant in the world, including Pictou. In St Ann's they were safe, but elsewhere there were many hazards. Norman did his best to categorise them. Laurie Stanley sets them out in a formidable list: "The plagues of the day, such as 'Mere profession, dead devotion and an outward rusty shell of religion, without tenderness of conscience,' wild jests, profanity, horse trading, riotous and drunken behaviour and immoderate dressing all came under his censure."

It is not difficult to see how his Pictou friends, bereft of his physical support, would find his letters a strong prop to their faith if it ever flagged. Typically, Norman wrote:

> If you had any proper sense of your danger from yourselves, you would also fear to live among formalists and wranglers, both in political and religious concerns; and in that case, the merciful Saviour would compassionately, either preserve you from fatal contagion where you reside, or give you an outgate to a place of better spiritual nourishment, in teaching and example. I see plainly that your families after you, are in dreadful danger of being hardened, in the furious and fashionable fashion of your neighbours, in unchristian giddiness and gaudry, vanity and folly, pride and passions. "Evil communications corrupt good manners." With all your ease and affluence you would find your situation alarmingly critical,

if you had proper feelings of your spiritual and eternal responsibilities and concerns. I am seriously afraid that it will be too late when you are truly convinced on this awful ground.

Encouraged by Norman's letter, but equally so by reports that St Ann's was flourishing to a greater degree than had first seemed possible, new settlers continued to arrive. Inevitably, the tight bonds that had held the people together began to loosen. Many of the new arrivals came from Scotland, particularly from the Outer Hebrides; and they were an independent breed, not likely to fall quickly under Norman's influence.

John MacAskill, a lively seventy-seven-year-old when I talked with him several years ago, brought a picture from the past vividly before my eyes.

"The MacAskills came from Harris about 1831," he said. "My great-great-grandfather came to Pictou from Assynt in about 1792. He was Murdoch MacLeod. You must understand that, if Norman condemned anyone in the community, he was a pariah, an outcast. Such a man, towing a raft of logs with a rowboat, was having a hard time off Munro's Point. Mrs MacLeod wasn't going to sit with her six sons and let a man go to destruction because he was an outcast. So she told them to go and help. The minister was told, and in church on the Sunday berated her, even bringing up things that had happened in Scotland. She was a renegade, just like her dead relatives in Assynt. Her husband listened no longer. 'If you're going to take a spade and open graves in Scotland,' he said, 'remember that I know your people as well as you know mine, and I can dig as deep and turn up just as much dirt as you can.' Turning to his wife he said: 'Come on, we're not listening to that fool any more.' And out they went."

John MacAskill's anecdote might have owed much to the talents of the storyteller, but it certainly shows how Norman's autocratic style could bring strong reactions. There are many tales which have lasted, even in garbled form, because they contained more than an element of truth.

This, for example, is one version of a long-living McLeod story. A boy was charged with theft before Norman as magistrate. Found guilty, he was sentenced to having his ear, or a piece of it, clipped. The story had many sequels. One story told how, long after McLeod's death, a party of Nova Scotians were digging in a Mangawhai swamp, not far from Waipu, for kauri gum, a valuable income earner in those days. Some of the party had their origins at St Ann's, others on Boularderie Island, where the Rev. James Fraser was McLeod's implacable enemy. At their first mealtime, mugs were brought out minus their handles. "These must be St Ann's cups," said a Boularderie man, "they've got no lugs!" The remark touched a sensitive spot in the St Ann's men, still loyal to their minister, and a lusty fight followed.

The full story, obviously not known to the people in general, was told in a letter from Judge Marshall to the provincial secretary in June 1834. It is one of the many interesting revelations in Laurie Stanley's *The Well-Watered Garden*. A St Ann's boy voluntarily confessed to the theft of money. At a public meeting attended by the school trustees, McLeod and "other principal inhabitants", it was agreed to punish the boy without delay, rather than have him spend the winter months in a Sydney jail awaiting trial. A lesser punishment, they agreed, would be to "take a small part off one of his ears". "A rough form of community justice" is how Laurie Stanley describes it. Two local men performed the deed, with the "sanction and approbation" of the minister.

While most of the rebels against Norman's fatherly but autocratic control came to St Ann's after the first settlement, some, hopefully without creating divisions, planned to make their own way from the very start. Perhaps the most notable of these was John Munro, brother of Alex who had captained one of the boats that brought the first settlers from Pictou. Both brothers, who came from McLeod country in Assynt, had been well educated — Alex at Edinburgh University — and before going to St Ann's, John had taught school. His mind was set on wider horizons, however and, while Alex became a teacher at St Ann's, John, with his brother's support, looked to the sea and trading for a livelihood. His story is told in a later chapter.

I seem to have moved away from a study of what activated Norman McLeod, and of what his contemporaries thought of him. He did not approve of a man whose purpose in life was to make money, or to enjoy comfort and worldly pleasures while neglecting his spiritual welfare. But for every man of this kind there were dozens of others who followed Norman as long as they lived, steadfast in their faith. And this they would not have done if they had not seen another side to his character.

One of the most interesting comments came from Murdoch McDonald:

His having been my minister for sixteen years, my school teacher for several years and my being always in and out of his house and often at his table like one of his children, and passing many a night in his house and company, I had a better chance than anyone living to understand his ways.

His nature and temper were very mysterious, often almost clashing with each other. One side was mild and lovely as could possibly be while the other was autocratic and domineering. It is impossible to describe his character without a thorough knowledge of his ways. His enemies or his bigoted friends can not or will not do it."

"Tough but tender" is a description that could be applied to Norman as

I see him, darkly though that may be. He was a man of strong feelings — in no way mealy-mouthed. He was fierce in his putting down of evil, equally strong in his love, but that was a private thing.

He lived at a time, and in a world, where there could be more confrontation over religion than over anything else. His people, humble for the most part, took it all in their stride, kept their faith as a fire to warm them, and went on with the business of living and cherishing their families.

Chapter Five

Discipline and a Measure of Hardship

MEANWHILE, IT WAS BY NO MEANS plain sailing in the settlements of St Ann's, Baddeck and Middle River. Ice in the Bras d'Or lakes and St Ann's Bay would bedevil trade. Short growing seasons would mean hardship and sometimes near-starvation. One woman who arrived at Baddeck with her family in 1826 — she was 107 when interviewed — recalled preparing the order for winter supplies to be collected, on foot, from the town of Sydney, forty miles away. The order was for corn meal and potatoes. At that time there were only two other families at Baddeck. Food had to be husbanded during the winter and early spring for, when it ran out, there was no more until the ice melted and the outer world could be reached.

The well-disciplined little community of St Ann's fared better than most in the cruel years that the Cape Bretoners had to endure when storms out of season killed their crops, when a devastating blight rotted their potatoes, when early snowfalls and ice blocked their harbours, lakes and trails. There were reports of families attempting to keep alive on one meal a day of curds and milk. Government relief, when it was available, could be a quarter of a barrel of flour and meal for each family. St Ann's had one advantage over some other parts of the island, where late arrivals from Scotland were attempting to establish themselves on "backlands", as they were called, the better land having been already occupied. Land quality varied at St Ann's, but balance came from a wide variety of occupations — farmers, fishermen, blacksmiths, shopkeepers, boatbuilders, merchants and seafarers. This broader economic base meant that, with normal care, there was less risk of crippling shortages. Until ice closed the bay, the sea was a lifeline.

There are a few first-hand reports of what could happen in the bad years. A correspondent of the Halifax *Herald* wrote in March, 1834, the grimmest time of the year:

> Unparalleled distress now exists amongst the new settlers on the backlands near Baddeck and Middle River, and in other places in that quarter. We have been informed that it is positively affirmed that in one settlement about forty families consisting of one hundred and seventy persons, of whom one hundred and thirty are children, are the most reduced to one meal per day and this consisting wholly of potatoes of miserable quality. It is stated that, after partaking of their scanty and wretched meal, the parents have to contrive to put their children to sleep in hopes thereby to diminish or postpone their craving for more food.

But it remains for Norman McLeod, in a letter to his friends in Pictou, to picture most vividly the wretched state that had befallen the people of St Ann's. He tells of "the scarcity of provision, which has for some time been bordering on famine throughout the island". When he writes, the savage winter of 1848 has passed but, he says:

> There has never been anything like this in Cape Breton. There are several among us who could, without distraction, sustain their own families, if the burden of others around them had not fallen so grievously on their charity; but the general destitution has made it impossible, even for the most saving, to shut their ears and eyes from the alarming claims and craving of those around them, running continually from door to door, with the ghastly features of death staring in their very faces.

That was not the general rule. Most winters were more lenient, and after them came spring, summer and fall, when the physical world was alive and the settlers, too, were able to get busy with living. Not that the winter days were wasted. The McGregor brothers, who in the season would be building boats, could now turn their hand to other crafts: making spinning wheels, for example. There was leather to be worked for many domestic purposes, boots to be made, wool to be spun and blankets, clothing, especially socks, to be woven or knitted. As long as there was a little food for their bellies, the winter would pass.

Resistance to disease was low, except for those lucky enough to build up immunity. What we may often not take into account, so-called childish sicknesses, were killers among the young. Tuberculosis was a scourge that carried off not only children but adults, too. One after another the young men and women in a family could take a fever, waste away and die. In the old cemeteries one sees the names of many children; but in contrast, those who weathered the storm could reach a great age.

The migrants came from a part of Scotland where there were virtually no trees, where houses were made of stone or earth. But they were quick to learn the virtues of timber, its many uses; they must have been saddened later at the thought of the trees that were axed and burned, sometimes needlessly, to provide farmland. There had been magnificent forest trees: white spruce, red spruce, juniper — excellent for fence posts as it did not rot — pine, oak and ash, a hardwood with many uses. As an old farmer told me this, the names of the trees rolled off his tongue like a melancholy poem. The first cabins, and shelters for the stock, were built of logs, but changes came quickly. There are still houses standing that have been lived in for well over a hundred years, with weatherboard walls and characteristic high-pitched roofs. They are houses that combine dignity, usefulness and an often elegant simplicity. But for the visitor from New Zealand it is the barns that catch the eye. Great rounded beams, in an intricate pattern, support a vaulted roof that would not look out of place in a cathedral. The men who built these structures were in the same brotherhood as the boatbuilders. And each skill developed quickly in the first years in the area that embraced St Ann's, Baddeck and — for houses in particular — Middle River. The first boats were not ambitious, though designed to face the storms of the St Lawrence Gulf and the iron-bound Atlantic coast. With clients like John Munro and the McKenzie brothers, the builders soon had a succession of cutters and schooners, up to around eighty tons, going down the ways. Within a decade the growth of population and industry in Britain signalled a market for timber, minerals and other produce that Nova Scotia could help to satisfy. Bigger ships were needed, and where better to build them than in Nova Scotia, with its excellent timber and skilled shipwrights?

Now, instead of the small vessels used on the coast or on the journey across to Newfoundland and Labrador, full-rigged ships at times but chiefly barques — square sails on the fore and mainmasts, fore-and-afters on the mizzen mast — brought fame to the colony. More than a hundred years later, Bill Craig, from New Zealand, stood on a spot overlooking North Gut, St Ann's, where his grandfather, one of the McMillan brothers, had erected his forge to do the ironwork for the ships built there. One of these was the *Margaret*, first of the ships to carry the migrants on their epic voyage to the lands of the south.

The ships built at St Ann's traded to all parts of the world, and with them went the young Cape Breton seafarers. The McKenzie brothers were among them. An interesting story, told to me by Doris Ewen, in Waipu, gives an indication of where they could go.

"I was told," said Doris, "that when the Prince [Duncan McKenzie] was captaining a boat in India, something unusual happened there. The Prince said his next son would be called Dallae — the Gaelic for Delhi." And so, in good time, Dallae Alexander McKenzie came into the world. The name has continued in the McKenzie family.

If ships were necessary to keep the island economy afloat, with a population that was increasing rapidly, it could be said that barns were almost as important in their own way. Sheep and cattle had to be fed and sheltered over the long winter. The growing season for green crops — vegetables for the family and stock feed such as turnips — was two or three months. Hay had to be grown, harvested and stored — in the barn, along with potatoes, leaving room for the cattle and sheep as well. A cattle beast was too valuable to eat. The money earned from its sale bought goods that were essential but could not be produced on the island. An ox might sell for over 230 shillings, while a man would be paid 3s 6d a day for unloading cargo from a ship. Money was not in common circulation; and it says much for the piety of the St Ann's folk that, in 1839, over £50 was raised to support the work of the Nova Scotia Bible Society. Much of the money came from donations of butter and, as Laurie Stanley says, the local nickname, "Society butter", became popular among the people of the community.

The Bible was never out of sight, and rarely out of use in a family that followed Norman McLeod. There were prayers morning and evening, daily Bible readings, impromptu discussion and instruction meetings led by some of Norman's trusted lieutenants. The Bible was, for many, the cornerstone of their culture.

I have in front of me a large, leather-bound Gaelic Bible, the edges of its pages stained dark brown with the years and the usage it has experienced since it was published in 1843 for the Edinburgh Bible Society. As is usual with family Bibles, the fly-leaf bears a variety of signatures. Just inside the front cover is the note, in very faint ink: "Bought of Chales (sic) Campbell, Baddeck, N.S." Facing it are several inscriptions. The first, in a flowing script, names "Mr Hugh Campbell, North River, Saint Ann's, April 7, 1857". Hugh was the anglicised form of Ewen, by which name he was more generally known.

While the children followed the Bible lessons in their native Gaelic, they were also wrestling with an understanding of English, hoping to master that complex language. I have been studying one of their textbooks that has survived: *Rudiments of English Composition*, by Alexander Reid, L.L.D. Alexander was headmaster of the Edinburgh Institution. The 1856 edition of his formidable book was the eleventh printing since first publication.

I try to imagine those St Ann's boys and girls saying a Gaelic goodbye to their parents in the early morning, walking on trails through the forest and fields that were so familiar to them, then through the school doors into a strange new world. Through the year they would be led into the mysteries of English spelling, punctuation, structure of sentences and the thing called "style", indefinable except for a few like Dr Reid. The examples set out for study would have enlarged the minds of the pupils; many of the examples were from the classic Greek and Roman world, others from natural history, from cotton plants to camels, others again from more modern European history and figures like Columbus and King Edward III.

Books such as Dr Reid's could play a part in community development that might not have been expected, spreading beyond the classroom. Parents, as well as the children, discovered a world far different from that they had known in the Highlands or knew now in Nova Scotia. History and philosophy, they found, had many faces. Opinions were able to be voiced in that other world without attracting condemnation. The deeply repressive Calvinist edicts, based often on Old Testament pronouncements, could be used with them to forbid such things as vanity in dress, merrymaking, the use of alcohol, pastimes such as card-playing, even revival meetings with their hectic atmosphere and emotional conversions from a state of sin. But, as the historian T.C. Smout said, the Highlanders had not been very pious in the eighteenth century and, although missionaries and zealots did their best to convert them from the 1780s on, not everything had been erased from the past.

During many generations, it had been the practice of Highlanders to gather once a year for a communal celebration of Holy Communion. It was no ordinary gathering, for many of those present a social occasion as much as a religious one. The famous preacher Roderick MacLeod remembered one such gathering from his boyhood at Dunvegan: "...as soon as the services, which were conducted in the open field, were ended, three pipers struck up music, and three dancing parties were formed on the green."

Men, women and children would come, sometimes in their thousands, to the meeting-place. Even for the majority who did not take communion it was a special time. The harvest was safely done; at the turning-point of the year, with winter looming, they had time to reflect. Instead of being individuals or families leading solitary, monotonous lives, they would instinctively reinforce their position as part of a homogeneous community. It was something that went back to the earliest days of the people, long before Christianity had reached them. A time of thanks, of propitiation, with a history as old as that of the Harvest Festival still celebrated in our churches.

More than that, there was a deep desire to "belong", whether to a clan or, when the clans died, to a community, and this was gained by coming together. The mantle of the Lord was over them. That being so, they could be themselves.

As a social occasion, it had many trappings not always as decorous as the pipes and music that Roderick MacLeod remembered. The communion season became a carnival, a time when young people could get together without too many restraints, when their elders, if that was their wish, could cement a deal with their cattle, when they could meet old friends for a glass or two at the whisky tent and seek bargains from the pedlars who camped nearby.

It was activities of this kind, combined with the complacency and lack of concern for their people, shown by the "Moderate" clergy, that made a revolutionary change inevitable in the Highlands, at a time when migration was in full flow. At Boularderie, before very many years of settlement had passed, there were great gatherings for the communion festival, with people coming in their hundreds from as far as forty miles away. Describing the scene, James Frazer wrote about "a neat tent-box, and a venerable-looking man standing in front of it, holding an octavo Bible and reading to the people as they assemble, and crowds of decent, serious-like people, repairing to the spot, and quietly taking their seats on the grass... I should not forget ten years and upwards, very attentive — having their Bibles, and seriously turning up, and marking any passages mentioned."

This could change quickly under the emotional impact of a powerful speaker and a responsive audience, as at Mira in 1853:

> Serious looks, grave deportment, and weeping eyes, but also more unmistakable indications of deep distress. Thousands were melted. Some of both sexes trembled under the word... Not a few were awakened to a sense of sin, and of their lost, ruined conditions as sinners; others had their bands loosed, and many of God's People declared it was a season of much refreshing of souls.

It was a vastly different scene in both the Highlands and Cape Breton, with the Evangelicals calling the tune, compared with the complacent and relaxed style of the Moderates fifty years before, but not everything from the past could be swept aside. There could be subtle changes. Phrases from the Bible had been commonly used by the unlettered as a charm to avert evil or misfortune. Now, the people had become familiar with the Scriptures and could quote from them in a less superstitious way. But superstition lived on in many ways, especially when it could be supported by scriptural injunctions. A person could still be an ardent Presbyterian and believe in witchcraft long after the move from the land of Macbeth. Indeed, among Presbyterians of the stricter sort, disbelief in witchcraft was regarded as atheism, and flying in the face of God's word.

Although card-playing was to become a popular pastime among descendants of the migrants, for a long time, to many believers, cards were the Devil's Bible. And there was to be no talking in a light sort of way, no singing of heathen hymns, or whistling on Sunday. Whistling was invented by the Devil when he found he couldn't sing psalms.

The communion celebration of the kind that took place at Mira would have been rejected by Norman McLeod. Not for him, or for his followers, did religion require the trappings of a revival meeting with its high emotion, frenzy and fervour. If there was to be any thundering, Norman himself would do it; his disciplined, steely voice would cut through the silence, pouring scorn on the unworthy preachers in the neighbouring settlements. Whether they needed it or not, his listeners would be reminded of their duties to God, of what they could or could not do. In the closely knit community of St Ann's, it would have been difficult not to be involved with the minister. And, in any case, the Sunday church service was one of the few times when the district could assemble in one place. Assemble they certainly did, not only from St Ann's widespread farms but from as far afield as Baddeck, leaving home the previous day to get to the church at Black Cove.

Norman did not conduct a communion celebration, as was normal with the Evangelicals. Communion, in his mind, demanded such absolute freedom from sin that, humbly and with full knowledge of their own weaknesses, his congregation could not honestly receive it. He had also moved away from administering baptism, for the same reasons. But he still drew the people to hear him expound the Scriptures. The first church became too small. While thousands attended the communion festivals at Boularderie and elsewhere on the island, it became necessary to build another church at St Ann's, a church that could seat twelve hundred people, with the congregation sometimes flowing over on to the stairs and passages.

Without their own religious beliefs to ponder over, without those of others to mock or deride, following the example of their minister, life might have seemed a little tame. But any monotony could be mitigated in various ways. It has been noted by observers that the Highlander, whether at home or translated to another land, can be very friendly with his neighbours and at the same time be intensely curious about their doings. Letters written to friends or family members show that the early settlers possessed this disarming quality which, undoubtedly, added a mental stimulus to their quiet lives. And curiosity was no negative thing. In times of trouble or distress, when a family needed comfort or support, the neighbours would be the first to offer help.

The solemnity of religion could not destroy the Cape Bretoner's love of a story, whether true or false. Some might be of the improving kind, but many stayed current simply because they were good stories. "The Boston joke" is a good example. Boston may have started as a puritan settlement, but by the time St Ann's came into being, it had developed its own quirky sense of humour which is today as strong as ever. Seeking work or adventure, many young Nova Scotians found both these things in Boston. Coming home on holiday, they brought with them a high-spirited style that at first seemed alien to their home-staying associates. But they soon got used to it as more and more people came and went. Incidentally, in those days there were no problems over crossing frontiers. You just went. Two typical Boston jokes will be sufficient. They are typical because they can be told today with very little change from a century or more ago. First joke: A girl at Boston airport, pointing to the post box beside the ticket office says, "If I post my letter here will it go to New York?" "Yes." "Oh darn it, I want it to go to Cape Breton." Second joke: "Is the mail in from Iona?" Post official, "How would I know?" "They know at Iona if the mail's in from Boston."

Professor Jim Saint-Clair gave me this story. When Alexander Graham

Bell first came to Cape Breton, he was impressed by the Little Narrows area and asked about buying land. His interrogator looked at him suspiciously. Was he a Baptist? No. Even more ominously: Was he a Roman Catholic? No. As a matter of fact, Bell remarked, he was an atheist. "Humph!" came the reply. "In that case you better go to Baddeck!" And to Baddeck the celebrated inventor went.

Good stories can easily develop into folklore. When I innocently asked what was the origin of "Bear" as a nickname for a branch of the MacLeod family, Hector was first with an answer. "Winter was ending on the Middle River," said Hector, "and with the snow gone Big MacLeod went out to his farm. He took with him his long iron crowbar for digging out boulders and rolling the logs, for you see he was minded to do a bit of ploughing. And he took with him too his young heifer, and every now and again he would pick her handfuls of wild turnips and anything else that might tempt her appetite.

"The fine spring day went on, and the sun became hot, and at noon he led his heifer away to the shelter of the woods, where she could rest and, perhaps, sleep. He himself had his bite of lunch and then began to work again. Now you must know that, during the winter, the great brown bears seek out for themselves a place to rest, nor do they stir again until the warmth of the returning sun awakens them. And then they go foraging fiercely, for their hunger is great. But as MacLeod worked, the bears were far from his mind. He heaped up the big red boulders, and gathered together the timber that would hinder his plough, and he listened to the bell jingling on his heifer's neck.

"Then suddenly he thought: She should be resting. What can be disturbing her? Is it perhaps flies, or other insects? So he took up his long iron bar and went to see. Now it seems that, if a bear encounters another animal that is big and strong, it will kill with one great sweep of its paw. But if the animal is young and tender, the bear will not maul it, but will carefully seek for the nerve at the back of its neck and paralyse it. And that is what MacLeod found when he reached the shade of the trees. His little heifer looking up sadly and hopelessly into the face of the biggest bear he had ever seen.

"MacLeod let out a roar, and the bear jumped to its hind legs and stood up, fully nine feet high. He backed quickly against a tree and looked at MacLeod who, his heart full of anger, looked back. MacLeod grasped the crowbar firmly and began to circle slowly around the tree, and the bear backed around it too. Round and round they went, but with each circuit of the tree MacLeod gradually came nearer, until he measured the distance and knew he was close enough. Before the bear could guess what was happening, he swung the great iron bar hard against the side of its head.

"The one blow was enough," Hector said emphatically, "and the bear did not move again until they cut it up for steaks and a skin that kept the children warm during many a winter's night."

There must surely have been many stories dealing with fishing, back in Scotland as well as in Cape Breton; but perhaps it was too grim a business for there to be much humour attached to it. One anecdote that I was told rings true. A landsman had been persuaded to go out fishing with a friend. The sea, whether the Minch or the waters that batter the Cape Breton coast, got up, and the landsman grew uncomfortable. Finally he had to protest. "Tell me," he said. "Can't you keep in the valleys, instead of climbing up on those hills all the time?"

In other ways, too, fishing was a hazardous and uncertain business, right into this century. I remember Mary Campbell telling me how her crofter father would go out from Glendale on Skye towards North Uist or Harris. If a bad sea came up during the day, he would be unable to risk rounding the point to Loch Pooltiel, where he moored his boat, and, in the stormy dusk, he would feel his way into Loch Dunvegan and walk the seven miles home. Things like that the fisherman would prefer to forget.

Parents, on winter nights, would tell their families tales that they had brought with them from Scotland, tales of heroes who did improbable deeds that were remembered down the centuries. In Nova Scotia they would see fragments of carefully fashioned stone walls, mounds that hid the foundations of buildings more ambitious than anything they erected; and they would learn that it was much the same in the Highlands and the Hebrides: the shells of abandoned houses and castles about which local memories had nothing to say; and even older, circular stone buildings, now reduced to rubble, in which the first people had lived.

Judging by their letters and various reports written after the settlement, the people of St Ann's were too busy to think about the history of the place. The regenerating forest had quickly removed most traces of former occupation. It is only recently that signs have been found of the first French trading fort named St Ann's, established in 1629. On Boularderie Island there had been developments that would have startled Norman McLeod and his followers. One hundred years before the *Ark* arrived, the Chevalier de Boularderie, a nobleman of great energy and agricultural "know-how", had worked up an estate of more than 100,000 acres, furnished with all the equipment that would be used in his home country. The chevalier lived there in his manor house for thirty years, writes James B. Lamb in *The Hidden Heritage*. Today, he says, the patterns of the old French fields can be clearly seen, and the mounded foundations of the great manor house itself.

These and other relics of the past add interest to Cape Breton today, but to people carving out their livelihood this shadowy past seemed remote and irrelevant. Their feeling was for people, not places, and particularly for people with links that made it possible to appreciate and understand them. People like themselves, in fact, but who in one way or another had moved out of the routine that controlled their own lives. Those talked about in Cape Breton are not the famous or the remarkably talented, although there will be a proper pride in their achievements. The modern folk hero could be someone like Giant MacAskill, who, far from being freakish, won the affection of those who knew him because he was an ordinary man who was very strong. He travelled far and wide, performed some remarkable feats, but remained essentially a man of St Ann's. I talked to John MacAskill about him.

"Giant MacAskill — he was born Angus — was my grandfather's brother," said John. "He grew to seven feet nine inches, and weighed somewhere between 195 and 240 pounds. Three of his brothers that I remember were all over six feet, but not anything like him. Grandad Norman was six feet one and a half, and weighed 195 pounds. Duncan was six feet two and a half, John, the youngest, six feet three. The children of the three sisters, Christy, Mary and Catherine, were of average size."

A couple of years at school saw Angus start to grow, and by the time he was fourteen he was well over six feet and amazingly strong. His father was busy raising the ceiling of the family home and building a bed, eight feet long to hold him, and a chair to match.

Before very long, tales began to circulate through the district about the young prodigy. There was the great log that his father and two of his brothers, working together, could not lift on to the saw horse. Scolded because he had not been there to help, Angus quietly went out and lifted it into position by himself. Some of the early stories are delightfully circumstantial. The American skipper, for example, confident in his three hundred pounds weight, who challenged Angus to a wrestling match and was tossed over a woodpile ten feet high and twelve feet wide. James Lamb, who gives an account of the young man's career in his book, describes him as well proportioned, good-looking, with pleasant manners and a fine musical voice. The bad times of the late 1840s had hit St Ann's, and, when a Yankee schooner skipper and entrepreneur, Captain Dunseith, offered to put him on the stage, Angus decided to accept.

It is said that he toured Europe and that Queen Victoria presented him with a Highland costume. Another report linked him with the famous P.T. Barnum; sadly, a photo showing Tom Thumb sitting on the giant's outstretched hand is considered a fake. He returned to St Ann's after some French sailors in New Orleans dared him to lift an anchor lying on the shore. He lifted it easily enough, though it later proved to weigh nearly a ton and a-half. But the anchor fluke caught his shoulder, causing an injury that he never shook off. A friendly man, possibly too kind-hearted to be completely successful in business, he ran a store at Englishtown, a grist mill that had once belonged to John Munro, and also a fishing boat. He died at thirty-eight in the year 1863. His grave is visited still by tourists who marvel at the story of a remarkable man.

Men to catch the public imagination there were in plenty, in late years as well as in Angus MacAskill's time. *Middle River: Past and Present History of a Cape Breton Community* is a delightful story, full of close detail; full, too, of human interest. One of the most unusual characters is "Camera Eye Dan". As a young man, Daniel MacLennan left Middle River to seek adventure in the far west. In 1909 he joined the Seattle police, and soon established himself as a diligent detective with a remarkable talent: once he had seen a face or a photograph, he never forgot it. His fame spread all over the United States, and he was respected by the underworld also. They labelled him a "square shooter", the highest possible praise in their code. Here is one of several stories about him, told in *Middle River*:

Tom Kelly had shot and killed a policeman in Los Angeles during a hold-up. He had been captured and broke jail. His picture was sent to Seattle, showing him wearing a moustache and Dan saw it briefly. Eight years passed. Kelly was forgotten. Then one day, standing on a street corner, MacLennan saw a face pass by which he remembered. The "Camera Eye" did not fail. "Hello Kelly," said Dan.

"Hello Dan," said Kelly. He was smooth shaven. Eight years had changed his looks. But the unfailing blue eyes of Dan MacLennan had picked their man.

Dan MacLennan died at forty-nine and left no family. But his sister Dolly Nicholson at Middle River kept a scrapbook detailing his exploits, and his name is still green in his native Victoria County.

There is another man whose story, if he were not so modest, could well be told in detail, and not just because while I was writing this he was in his ninety-seventh year. John A. Nicholson visited Waipu with his daughter Barbara, but that was in no way the sum of his journeys from quiet Middle River. As a lad of twenty John had gone off to see the world, and found himself in the U.S. Navy when the United States entered the First World War. He was in ships operating out of Plymouth, England, and after the Armistice was minesweeping near the Shetland Islands. To John, a healthy, growing young man, food was of great importance. "We had good officers, and always fed well," he said.

"Did you have a regular cook?" I asked.

John chuckled. "I was the cook!" To my puzzled look he explained: "Before I joined the navy I was always hungry; I worked in a lunchroom in Chicago so I could get enough to eat. When I enlisted they asked me what my last job was. I said in a lunchroom. So they made me the cook.

"But it was a great life, even when we were stuck at sea during stormy days. In the summer of 1918 there was a fierce storm in the Irish Sea and we had to shelter on the Isle of Man. There was no rationing, and they treated us royally. I wanted to go back." John's grandmother was born on Harris and his grandfather on the isle of Raasay, but he did not visit either place.

John stayed in the navy — until he went back to Middle River to see his parents. "There was plenty to do," he said with a grin, "and the days went by… But that's all a long time ago. My captain lives in Chicago. He's two months younger than I am. He comes to visit me." John's long life ended in 1993.

John's father had 160 acres, most of it under timber. He had a shop and made windows and doors. I wondered how the young sailor home from the sea took to the land. "Did you farm?" I asked.

"I'll have to say I did!" There was a succinct Cape Breton humour in his reply. "There were two horses, two milking cows, six, seven or eight sheep. At the last, the sheep were down to four. They mixed with others, so I told them to go."

He planted an apple orchard, but the rabbits got them. However, wild apples came up and the rabbits didn't touch them. They were good eating, either raw or cooked. "We'd cut them up and freeze them." In 1923 he bought a house and a watermill, cutting timber for lumber. Fifteen years later, a freshet took the stream away. John got a portable mill, moving from one lumbering operation to another for several years.

A happy man, John found great pleasure in his family. "Seven of my children are around me here — five sons, all retired, and two daughters. And another son in Sydney." Nor did he forget his extended New Zealand family. Angus Nicholson, who married Mary McInnes and went to New Zealand on the *Gertrude*, was his grandmother's brother. When John wrote to me not long before his death, he confessed that he was confined to his rocking chair due to the snow and ice of winter. "How I wish I were back in New Zealand these cold and stormy days! One day last week it was minus thirty degrees Celcius. But now," he concluded with unquenchable optimism, "they could expect some fine, sunny days."

If life is a river, these are some of the figures thrown up on the surface to catch the eye. But down below there is the strong, steady current that keeps pressing on — unseen, perhaps, but nonetheless effective. To drop the analogy: while some went away, did something out of the ordinary, many more stayed at home, interested in whatever news came back to them, but most interested in tilling the land, turning trees into useful timber, raising stock and children that would be a credit to them. And at times they may have dwelt on the sentiments expressed in a North River epitaph: "Is there not an appointed time for man on earth? Are not his days also like the days of a hireling?"

But for most of the time they were too busy for melancholy reflections. Mrs Alexander Smith told me how her people came from Harris and Lewis in the 1830s. She herself spoke the Gaelic all her life — she learned it as naturally as English. "How did they manage in the early years?" Evelyn Smith wondered. "They wouldn't have been able to leave Scotland in the winter, which meant that, by the time they had set themselves up in Nova Scotia, there was no chance of growing food to keep their larders full during the following winter. They had to depend on the sea and the forest," Mrs Smith said. "The early ones were quick learners. Of course, there were no great difficulties with the sea, they were familiar enough with it in their home islands, but the land was a different matter."

There was indeed much to learn, although help had come from the Micmac Indians in the Pictou area when the first settlers arrived: such things as the virtues of maple syrup, the fruits of the forest that could keep them healthy during winter, methods of building and roofing their first huts. There were still a few Indians at St Ann's in the early years, survivors of a once proud and powerful race that had held its own with the French a century before — until defeated largely by introduced disease. Eventually the Indians were gathered together on reservations, but for many years migrants moving inland from Baddeck would squat with impunity on Indian land.

They were family memories that Evelyn tapped, not just personal memories. She had been born not far from where she lived all her life, and tales from the past came down to her as if they had been part of her own experience. Every year repeated, to a great degree, the pattern established before. "We grew potatoes, hay and oats, and raised a few sheep. Also fished for herring and cod. There is a journal kept by one of the family in 1916 when they had a lobster business and general store. Lobsters were quite a bit cheaper than they are now! The lobster season lasted from 15 May to 15 July. On 1 August, look for work in Sydney! At first we had no horse or wagon, but the neighbours were good and I didn't feel isolated. But life tended to improve in some ways. The first year we fished from a rowboat, the next from a motorboat. Lobster boats are now much bigger — concentrated on a harbour at Little River, not working from along the coast."

Alex MacLeod was nearly ninety when I talked to him and Norrie, his wife. The present MacLeod farm has seen six generations of MacLeods. Alex's grandfather, another Alexander, came from Big Baddeck to buy the property. Life was full and varied, and their memories hold lively little pictures; such as Norman McLeod's big church, far from a solemn place when the children were playing in it, running up the stairs on one side, across the balcony and down the stairs again on the other side. Nor was there anything solitary about the ways of farming in those days. At a building frolic, when a barn was being built, there might be twenty or twenty-five men helping. Looking at the MacLeod barn with this knowledge in mind, one can understand how those mighty beams were lifted and fastened in place. In a busy summer, Alex recalled, there was also time to help the widows and old maids with their haymaking.

"It was oxen first, then horses, then tractors," said Alex. "The horses were fast, but the oxen kept going. And when the oxen were there, the feeling of the frolic was strongest. The horses wouldn't have minded when the tractors took over. On a hot day they would turn quite white with sweat, and you'd have to let them go."

Our conversation was enlivened with many fascinating comments, as Alex warmed to his theme. "Bears? If a bear can get a good fat lamb he'll do it up — gather up all the bones and skin and wrap them up and hide them in a hole, they're that cunning.

"Herring? First there are spring herring. Catch them, open them up, rip their guts out, turn them inside out, salt them and hang them in the sun. That's what they call 'hard herring'. The July herring is very different: big and fat. You couldn't dry them.

"The best fish? There were plenty to choose from: codfish, mackerel, hake, salmon, haddock, turbot. Turbot you got in deep water. They were grand eating."

There were animals on the MacLeod farm too. They had eight or nine milking cows, about twenty-five sheep, some of them Blackface. The lambs would be ready for market at three or four months. They would dress out at around fifty pounds. There were usually one or two litters of pigs around. A little pig would fetch three dollars.

Alex, so closely anchored to the past, would nevertheless move with the times. He loved the rhythm of the scythe, the singing sound as it cut through the long grass, the orderly way in which the grass fell from the blade. And so, each year when haymaking time came round, Alex would be out cutting his crop with his trusty scythe. Until one day a friend said to him: "Alex, why don't you try one of these horse-drawn mowers? They do the work well."

Alex did so, and was converted. But when nearly ninety he still enjoyed scything the five-acre meadow by the house, once every year.

Most of the families could recall stories about their ancestors or contemporaries. None more so than the clan Macaulay. Murdoch Macaulay took his two sisters down to sail for New Zealand. Then he called to someone to take the horses home. He was going too! His mother, the story says, was heartbroken. Murdoch, safely settled in New Zealand, married his cousin Isabella MacLean.

The Macaulays transplanted well into New Zealand soil, and those who stayed in Nova Scotia flourished also. A few years ago, when Bonnie Thornhill was preparing to visit New Zealand with her husband Roland, at that time Minister of Tourism and Culture in Nova Scotia, she began to investigate her family tree. She found that her great-great-grandfather, Big Angus Macaulay, was the son of Murdoch who had come to Nova Scotia from Uig, on Skye, with his parents in 1812. And Big Angus, born at North Gut St Ann's in 1825, was the elder brother of Murdoch who had so suddenly decided to accompany his sisters, Christina and Catherine, to New Zealand on the *Ellen Lewis.*

So, when Bonnie and Roland joined the colourful crowd on the Caledonian sports ground at Waipu on New Year's Day, 1989, it was far more than a routine visit by a Canadian politician and his wife. Roland himself made this quite clear when he spoke with warmth and conviction about the ties that linked his province with the settlements that still proudly remembered their Nova Scotian identity at Waipu, Whangarei Heads, Mahurangi and elsewhere in North Auckland. I was left in no doubt about the strength of those ties when, in July of the same year, my wife, son and I attended a reception at the Gaelic College at St Ann's. There were many familiar names; there were faces that would have looked as much at home at a *ceilidh* at Waipu as they did here. And there was a warmth, a quiet ease of contact that I found very moving.

In the last few years, possibly because air travel brings countries much closer together, there has been a growing appreciation of the fact that the migration, from Scotland to Nova Scotia and then to New Zealand, was much more than a series of dates in a minor chronicle of history. It was something vital that happened, something that did not die. More and more people move every year between Nova Scotia and New Zealand. Like the celebrated Dr Johnson on his tour of the Hebrides, they are more interested in people than in scenery; the living people who, in some strange way, continue an unbroken story through to the present day in their memories and personal encounters. Places are important, too. The New Zealander cannot fail to be moved by the tranquil beauty of a summer sea penetrating deep between forested headlands in St Ann's Bay, the bold strength of the coast viewed from the magnificent Cabot Trail, the houses nestling so unobtrusively beside the Bras d'Or lakes. And in reverse, the Nova Scotian returns home from a visit to Waipu remembering the deep, clean green of farm and forest, the shining blue of the bay that stretches across to the dark, ragged profiles of Manaia and the Whangarei Heads. The recent "twinning" of Waipu with St Ann's and Baddeck brings them even closer together, emphasising that, in essence, they are still one people — as varied in temperament and character as they ever were!

Contacts could come about in many ways. Malcolm Rutherford MacCharles, born in Cape Breton but practising as a doctor in Winnipeg, wrote to Betty Powell at Waipu in 1984. Thirty years before, he was a passenger on a plane from Vancouver which he had boarded at Winnipeg to fly to Ottawa. A friend already on the plane greeted him with these words: "How strange that we should meet like this! I've ridden all the way from Vancouver with a cousin of yours."

"I've no cousins in Vancouver," said MacCharles.

His friend replied: "She's from New Zealand, going to Nova Scotia for a celebration of the hundredth anniversary of some of her people leaving Cape Breton for New Zealand."

Dr MacCharles sat with her and they had much to talk about, for the details of the migration were hazy in his mind. On her way home after the celebrations she stayed with the MacCharles family in Winnipeg for five days. "Her name," Dr MacCharles wrote, "was Mary Sutherland. She was a nurse, and had been in Egypt with the Anzacs in World War I. We had a marvellous time with her and I think she enjoyed it too."

Right from the start there was intense and very natural curiosity over what the migrants would find when they reached the other end of the world. But while they wondered, those still in Canada had more material things to occupy their minds. A letter from Kenneth McKenzie to his father Donald allows us to see how one family fared, and also shows the dilemma that many must have faced. Kenneth had left Cape Breton and taken up land at Kincardine on the shores of Lake Huron, now one of the most attractive farming areas in Ontario. He wrote to his father on 30 August, 1856:

> You informed me in your letter that you were intending to emigrate to New Zealand and also what might be my own views as to my removing there also. I shall try to shape you an answer. I am now in a fair way of making a tolerable living after a deal of hardship and under the circumstances I would likely value its worth, the dangers and hardships attending such a long voyage should be fairly weighed before a person situated with a good prospect for the future (as I am situated) should sell it in a short time and not likely make out of his property its real value 'to embark on a wild goose chase'. However as I could not dispose of my property to advantage to join you before you sail to those distant regions I shall content myself for the present where I am, and on your arrival in the promised land you will write me a correct account of your prospects and according to your advice and the hopes of better prospects I shall likely follow.

You wished also to be informed about my brother John's intentions towards emigrating to New Zealand, a task which I am not able to ascertain. You often stated yourself the impossibility of finding out John's intentions (I am in the same fix). It matters not wherever John may be situated he cannot or will not be an agreeable neighbour. Whenever anything crosses his mind which will not be satisfactory then he will be for leaving the place.

The rest of Kenneth's letter is interesting for two reasons: it shows the strength of the ties with those still in Cape Breton had not been weakened by the sturdy but minor migration to Ontario of which Kenneth had been a part, and it also shows how ably they had adapted to yet another style of farming.

As regarding your friends and acquaintances I shall give you a short sketch. My uncle Hugh and family are in health and doing as well as you could expect a man with such limited circumstances as he was placed in could do, he is in as good condition as anybody could expect. We had a very dry summer here, yet the most of the crops turned out well especially the wheat. I have about 200 bushels, but the oats has suffered on account of the drouth, the rest of my crops are tollerable good. Farquhar McLennan left here yesterday for Boston, Mass, to join his brother-in-law at Wereham, about 60 miles from Boston to take passage direct for New Zealand by the first opportunity.

Kenneth remained on his Ontario farm. His father Donald duly sailed to New Zealand on the *Spray* with some of his children. He would certainly not have wished to return to Scotland after reading a letter from his brother William at Clachtoll. "Poverty has got such a firm hold on the people in general as to affect their morals," said William sadly, "and disable them from any attempt to emigrate to any of these flourishing British colonies." Not so Donald at Clashmore. "He has been foolish enough to expose occasionally in the public prints doings in Suthlerlandshire, and thereby exposed himself to the displeasure and ill-will of the Rulers who have the Clergy, both Free and Bond, at their option. He would willingly leave the country if able."

Many other families were split, permanently or for only a short time, by the migration. Among them were the MacMillans, described by one scribe as great breeders of sons, and, therefore, likely to have members hiving off to other parts of the American continent even before Australia and New Zealand came into favour.

There were problems in communication. Norman McMillan says in a letter dated 10 October, 1864:

The reason we did not write a letter long ago was that we had no account of your brother John since four years and the address of the place where he was is as follows: Timbuctoo, Yuba County, California. Donald seen two men that worked with him for six months... Donald was home last winter and his wife along with him. She was a small black chicken of the Irish breed and if you remember Mary Collins she resemble her very much. He got marrit before he heard of his mother's death and he came home last fall without a cent in his pocket. Since three and four years he used to write home to his mother, telling her he was to get marrit with a Yanky girl. She thought he was only funning and used to write to him if he would get marrit that he might stay there. He didn't dare to come home as long as his mother lived, because he had a notion of getting marrit, he came in expectation of getting some of his father's property, but then he didn't dare to ask anything of his father, only he was wanting Malcolm to give him a share of his place he bought. Before he went in the spring, Me and Malcolm offered to buy a good farm for him, but when he seen that his father gived him nothing, he was so angry and wouldn't take the offer. If you write to Donald you won't say a word that I told you that his wife was an Irish woman. Don't tell that you heard by any at all, he will have a grudge to us. He is making a good living. He keeps a boarding house.

Malcolm continued to farm at Buchanan's Mountain, Middle River, and also to write to his brother William in New Zealand with local and family news. His report on farming in Cape Breton would have been enlightening to his New Zealand brother:

We still keep heavy teams of oxen and two horses. We have a double waggon which cost 21 pounds. Bought in Nova Scotia. We are clear of debts and has enough to eat and drink. The wheat begins to grow pretty well in C.B. — one bushel growed 13 bushels for us last term. We dug a hundred barrels of potatoes last fall. We winter from 25 to 30 heads of cattle and about 35 sheep on the two farms. If only I could converse with you face to face, I could tell you plenty interesting stories. Write as soon as this comes to you hand, delay not for a year.

Malcolm himself decided to go adventuring, as so many of his family had done since leaving the island of Muck, in the Hebrides, half a century before. In December, 1874, he wrote to William from Eureka, Nevada:

I came to Nevada last May. I worked for one man five months for 65 dollars and board a month. Since the first November I work in a furnace for $4 a day. The reason I came out here was I always had a notion of having a route through those western countries. I believe this is a very good country for a poor man, plenty of work and good wages and plenty land and good price for all kinds of produce. I saw potatoes as high as 10 cents a pound, butter 60 cents, beef 15 cents, mutton 20 cents, pork from 25 to 30 cents a lb, flour 16 dollars a barrel, tobacco $1 a lb, tea 1 dollar. Labourers' wages is from $3 to $5 a day. It is very expensive to come here from Cape Breton — it took me twenty-five days to come from Baddeck. I left Baddeck by the stage to New Glasgow, took the cars from there to Halifax and from Halifax by the boat to Portland, from Portland by the cars to Montreal then to the city Detroit. From there to Chicago and from there to Omaha and Nebraska and through the Rocky Mountains; then came to Wyoming Territory in Utah the Mormon country. There are men in Utah that has twenty wives, the most of the Mormons has from 6 to 10 wives. I saw that very queer.

I saw labourers losing 200 dollars here one night by gambling. They don't value money here as it is plenty. This is a very dry country. I saw very few showers of rain all summer. We have no snow yet — warm days and cool nights. They don't feed any stock here in winter, only working horses and mules. I saw farmers here having 2700 sheep and two men herding them. A farmer handy where I live branded 1500 calves last spring and has all other kinds of livestock... I will look for a long letter and all the country news in a short time.

It did not take long for the McMillans, and others of the migrants, to build a dry American humour on an open-eyed Highland foundation. Or perhaps it was there all the time. For example: "Ann got her leg broke and with the interest of getting her leg broke, she has got a young one." "Dam hard and dry" is the uncharitable description applied to a woman who has stayed single. It was indeed a male-oriented society, judging by comments such as this: "We was especially proud of your multiplying in boys. And I suppose at the time of receiving this letter you will be waiting and ready to write us home the name of the next boy if not two." Boys, no doubt for their muscle power, would be as useful in New Zealand as they were in Cape Breton, for he adds: "I suppose the boy called Norman will rip and tare a good-sized root of the New Zealand second growth."

One of the problems that the modern reader faces in interpreting the letters is that they are truly family epistles, with successive sentences written by different people. "You will understand," says (I think) Norman McMillan's son, "that all of us is about writing this letter." And yet, more than a century later, they give a vivid and entertaining picture of how a family, with close personal ties of kinship, coped with the great dispersal. They maintained contacts for several generations, but then other interests took over. The letters of the old patriarch Norman take on a new poignancy. "I am seeing myself very lonesome — how my family is scattered," he told William in 1859. "They are as sheep without no shepherd, but the Lord says He is the shepherd. But I have to say they are very mindful of us." In the same letter he writes: "We are sending you a small box — cloth for you to make a pair of pants and five pairs of stockings and some thread for your Mrs."

Eleven years later, unable to work for five years and in bed most of the time through rheumatism, he made another plea: "Dear Son you will not forget me — while I am living I hope please let me know the names of your children. God bless you all."

There was, in many hearts as well as that of old Norman McMillan, a melancholy that settled deep in the 1860s. More than seven hundred men, women and children, many of them at an age when they could give much to the community, had gone to New Zealand from the comparatively small Baddeck-St Ann's district. In addition, Canada, as it was called to distinguish it from Nova Scotia, and the United States were constantly draining away many of the ambitious and the talented. Not all yielded to the lure of foreign places or academic ambition. Neil MacLeod's father was determined that his sons should all qualify at university, and Neil duly attended. When his years of study were rewarded with a degree, he threw the parchment down before his father and said: "Here's what you wanted — now I'm going farming." And that is what he did.

"I was working in Ontario for seven years," John MacAskill told me. "It was all right just to work in, but not for living!"

Those who remained on the family land held tenaciously to what they had been taught to help them survive. The communities might have shrunk, but they were still largely self-sustaining, with their own blacksmiths, glaziers and so on to support the builders, who were nearly always farmers too. "They knew the best timbers for different purposes," said John, "and there were plenty to choose from. Spruce and fir were the basis. Pine for doors and window sashes; juniper for boat timbers. They were building boats for lobstermen about fifty years ago. They had many tricks to call on when needed. How did you stop wood from shrinking? It would be planed, finished and put out in cold frosty weather and left for a while. Then it would never shrink."

John Munro had gone to New Zealand but the stores continued to supply goods that could not be grown locally. In the 1930s, the little steamer *Aspy* was the lifeline, coming round on regular calls. "In October the *Aspy* brought the winter supplies for the community," Isobel MacAulay Jones recalled. "Bulk staples such as sugar, molasses, flour, baking powder. Potatoes were already stored, the fish sundried, milk also. Fish tended to take precedence at certain times. I remember someone complaining when they went out to the clothesline and found fish hanging there to dry!"

Alan MacLeod told me a tale that hints at a more illegitimate period than that they knew. When working at Neil's Harbour he was told of an American family, two sisters and two brothers, who lived there in a fine house a long time before. There was plenty of gold. Where did it come from? It turned out that, when ships came into Meat Cove at Neil's Harbour, this grim quartet would go on board, slit throats and steal the gold.

They were pirates! Eventually their activities were discovered; they were handed over to the Americans and executed. The story might be a little short on hard facts, but any community needs something that will break the monotony of day-to-day living, and tales like this had a valuable place in local folklore.

With the quietly turning years, changes came so gently that they would not be noticed at the time. There would be more and more letters written to sons and daughters who had gone away. Houses and barns, no longer used, would slide slowly to ruin. In the 1930s the farms were all in pasture, with potatoes grown on the higher land that suited them so well. As Alan MacLeod recalled, even in the 1930s you could look across the whole of the MacLeod and the Macaulay farms — all in pasture. "The work they had done! What strong backs they had! The land all ploughed for pasture and potatoes, all the stones picked up and placed along the boundaries. The heartbreak of seeing it all go back to forest after all that work! When the dog died, the white-tailed deer would be down eating mother's flowers around the house."

We went along a road that led up into the hills. It was a bright and beautiful day. There was a sparkle on the green young forest that was bursting skyward all around us. We stood there in silence until Alan said: "All this was once in farms…"

The past is kept alive in many ways. The Nova Scotia Highland Village at Iona recreates graphically what life was like from 1820 onward. There is pleasure as well as an insight into old ways to be gained at St Ann's Gaelic College. Both these centres can help the visitor to discover more about the men and women who founded families that have now spread far and wide. But chiefly, just by looking with an observant eye and a sympathetic mind does the visitor reach down into the heart of the island.

And what sort of impression does the first-time visitor gain from the St Ann's-Baddeck area? I have quoted already from Barbara Weiskrantz, descendant of a first cousin of Norman McLeod who, after discovering the relationship, was not happy until she had followed the McLeod trail to Pictou and St Ann's. Here is something of what she saw:

We happened to be in Pictou during what was called "Pictou Week". This is a week set aside annually to celebrate the coming of the Scottish pioneers and it was thus that we had our first, but by no means last, exposure to Scottish music which Nova Scotians nurture with enormous enthusiasm. We were given tickets at our hotel to attend a ceilidh that evening in the small town. A bagpiper and side drummer heralded the concert-goers as they arrived, standing on the rocks at the mouth of the harbour, romantically silhouetted against the evening sky. Inside we were treated to a wonderful assortment of singing, fiddling, piping and —

The Gaelic Mod draws holidaymakers in their hundreds, many from distant lands, and piping and dancing competitions make a lively scene. There is growing emphasis on traditional music and language.

new to us — step-dancing. This is an art form which, so we were told, had once been common in Scotland, but not now. It's still very popular in Nova Scotia and has been considerably developed. It's wonderfully rhythmic, requires much skill, artistry and energy and we just loved it. The whole evening was an eye-opener because we had not realised what a vibrant contemporary Scottish-Canadian culture there is. Having been previously inclined to regard Canadians' nurture of their Scottish heritage as quaint, I now realise that theirs is an entirely viable, living and developing tradition, rooted in Scottish culture, possibly even more lively than that in the old country. It is happy, outward and forward looking and positive.

I approached St Ann's with strong feelings of anticipation. At the head of the bay there is a modest motel and here we stopped for coffee beside the still waters of the bay. We suddenly heard the sound of fiddles tuning up and, mystified as to where the noise could be coming from in this deserted spot, we walked round to the front of the motel. There, casually leaning against their cars, were three fiddlers just enjoying playing together in the most delightful way. We learned from one of their wives that they were from Ontario and were there to attend an event at the Gaelic College a few miles up the road. We bought a cassette tape of the group to which these men belonged and it's a delight to listen to it now and experience again the pure *joie de vivre* with which they performed, amateurs all, the leader being a minister of the United Reformed Church.

Not knowing exactly where to find the monument commemorating Norman McLeod and his band of followers, we drove straight to the

Gaelic College of Celtic Arts and Crafts, renowned as the only such college in Canada, where we hoped to find a lead. The college was a big surprise. It stands by the highway with no other habitation in sight. It comprises several modern buildings spread around an attractive campus and, as we drew up to the entrance gate, there was the monument. It consists of two millstones, set one upon the other on a wider stone base. A plaque set into the upper stone reads as follows:

Reverend Norman McLeod
1780–1866
As clergyman, schoolmaster and magistrate he
moulded the character of this community for a
generation. Born at Stoer Point, Assynt, Scotland
he emigrated to Pictou in 1817, led his band of Scots
to St Ann's in 1820 and remained here until 1851
when he again led his followers first to Australia
and finally to New Zealand.

The same legend is then repeated in Gaelic.

We lingered long in the college. It was the nearest we could get to that early community and it was always a lovely, welcoming place to visit in its own right. In the gift shop someone told us about Black Cove and suggested we might like to walk through the college grounds to the spot, now marked by a monument, where Norman first landed and where his

The Gaelic College of Celtic Arts and Crafts stands on the land at St Ann's where Norman McLeod lived and preached for over thirty years. His memorial is in the foreground.

Eveline McLeod, one of the first students at the Gaelic College when it was founded by the Rev. A.W.R. MacKenzie, is a key figure at the college.

second church was built. We learned that an extensive summer school operates at the college, during which classes are held in bagpiping, drumming, Highland dancing, Cape Breton step-dancing, violin, piano, Gaelic language studies, kilt-making and weaving. The Great Hall of the Clans museum depicts the history of the Highland Scots.

The next day being Sunday, I attended morning service at the Ephraim Scott Memorial Presbyterian Church. I was very taken with the quiet, reflective hymn-singing of the fifty-odd congregation. Afterwards several people came up to welcome me. One lady in particular, Mrs Eveline MacLeod, introduced herself saying that a descendant of Norman had married into her family and she herself was a member of the Waipu Twinning Society.

We made one other call before leaving St Ann's. Beside the highway a sign reads: MacLeod Pioneer Cemetery. A rough dirt track leads off, maybe three hundred feet, to an opening in the woods and there, on a small bluff overlooking the tranquil bay, are the graves of more Highland immigrants, many from Sutherland. In the middle is the imposing memorial to two of Norman's children who died during their time in Cape Breton. The legend was barely decipherable...

Mary McLeod was pregnant when Norman sailed to Pictou. John Bunyan McLeod was born that same year, and died on the brink of manhood, aged twenty-one. His epitaph reads: "Gentle and lovely in life. Humble and hopeful in death." J. Edward McLeod had died in 1829 at the age of two. His epitaph has a poignant simplicity that seems to say something about his father and mother. The words are: "Short spring. Endless autumn."

And the "gentle Mary" and her strong but tender consort would lose more sons, in the unsparing Australian colony, before they found their final resting place in New Zealand.

Chapter Six

The Minister's Fold: Within and Without

"W HENEVER YOU THINK PROPER to start for New Zealand, see that you be a good boy and take care of yourself on the passage. Keep plenty clothing on your back and plenty of brandy in your belly, and there shall be no danger to you."

This was the sisterly advice from Miss Martha McRae, a passenger on the *Margaret,* to her younger brother Farquhar, still in Cape Breton. I suspect that her views may not have been completely shared by all on board the *Margaret:* many would have been as enthusiastic for abstinence as the minister himself. Until Norman banned its use among his followers, rum had been the sovereign protector against the cold and wet of a Nova Scotian winter. Brandy may have come into a different category, being taken for medicinal purposes rather than as an aid to conviviality. Obviously, Martha McRae had no inhibitions against its use. She was following a long tradition; there are those who would have said that, without whisky or brandy as a standby, it would have been difficult to survive the dampness and chill of a Highland winter.

There was a sturdy family strength in Martha, who appears in the *Margaret's* passenger list as the head of a group of seven, including cousins as well as sisters. She was, obviously, within the minister's fold, but I feel that she would have raised her eyebrows if anyone had suggested to her that she followed Norman with a "doglike devotion", a term that James McNeish, writing about the migration, applied to Norman's zealous congregation.

A scenario showing the St Ann's community as a homogenous group, all of one mind and purpose, would be very far from reality. Right from the early days in Pictou, through more than thirty years at St Ann's and the surrounding district, there were men with minds of their own — and women even more so — who followed their own consciences and beliefs; agreeing, one might say, to differ when the minister set his own individual course. Life went on tranquilly enough until a few years before the sailing of the *Margaret* when, for a variety of reasons, the placid surface was disturbed. The minister himself had changed with the seasons. Norman McDonald, a leader from the time he left Assynt until shortly before the first party left for

Australia, and perhaps the minister's closest friend over all those years, parted from him because of his increasing arrogance in civil and religious matters.

Norman McDonald was only one of a group of men who, as natural leaders, found that their relationship with Norman McLeod was changing for the worse. It would not have been easy for McDonald, who had been navigator on the *Ark* when she sailed to St Ann's.

Donald McLeod, the Squire, had been a close friend of Norman from boyhood, and was connected with him by marriage. At St Ann's he was a notable citizen: magistrate, school trustee, a staunch member of the congregation. But the Squire suffered the harshest fate that could be visited on his modest and self-effacing nature. Suddenly, he was brought on trial before that same congregation by the minister, who announced that Donald McLeod would henceforth be refused any "private religious fellowship". He was expelled from the circle of his friends for what might now seem a trivial reason. His son had been courting one of the minister's daughters when the minister had other ideas for her future. He had, it seemed, secretly passed a letter to the girl from his son without informing the minister.

It is possible, of course, that there were other reasons for his action that Norman McLeod chose not to mention. Some teachers on Cape Breton Island, and many parents, were firm believers in the saying, "Spare the rod and spoil the child." Indeed, one parent, bringing his son to school for enrolment, told Hugh McKenzie, the teacher, that the boy should be flogged

The Cabot Trail, running through St Ann's and other charming villages on the rugged Cape Breton coast, is followed by many summer travellers.

every day whether he deserved it or not. The teacher refused! There was an occasion, however, when schoolmaster Norman McLeod was about to birch a girl when the Squire's young son, Isaac, intervened. With his help the girl escaped home, but Isaac never went back to the school, going instead to Boularderie. N.R. McKenzie says, with some complacency, that Isaac did not suffer from his rebellion, becoming a teacher, successful businessman and a colonel in the Canadian militia. The Squire, like Norman McDonald, stayed in Nova Scotia when the *Margaret* sailed.

Among leaders in the Cape Breton community were John Fraser and John McKay. John Fraser had a longer connection with Nova Scotia than most. He traced his descent from one who had been at the capture of Quebec with General Wolfe, and took his discharge from the Fraser Highlanders in Nova Scotia. An able man who put his local knowledge to good use, prospered and, by the time the *Margaret* sailed, had a family of five to accompany him and his wife.

John McKay had arrived at Middle River from Lochalsh in 1820. Scholar as well as farmer, he quickly became one of Norman's strongest supporters. While the McGregor brothers built the *Margaret* — Neil and Roderick McGregor were famous shipbuilders — the bills to cover their work were for the most part paid by John McKay and John Fraser.

Nor could Norman find grounds for criticism of two remarkable brothers, Captain Duncan and Captain Murdoch McKenzie, known respectively as the Prince and the Captain. Duncan and Murdoch were never close followers of Norman, but they respected Norman and he respected them. In those times, if you were a sailor on the Nova Scotian coast you were automatically a deep-water man. But the McKenzies were as much at home on the land as on the sea, as shipowners and storekeepers at Baddeck; good businessmen, good seamen, endowed with a formidable dignity and presence. Duncan, it is said, gained his nickname "Prince" because of his resemblance to Prince Albert, consort of Queen Victoria. The role they played became increasingly important as the years went by. They owned the *Highland Lass* which followed the *Margaret* to Australia and, having sold her, bought the *Thistle* which took the first party of Nova Scotians from Australia to Auckland. Then, after some deliberation, Duncan, with a few comrades, reconnoitred the coast north of Auckland in an open boat and made the decision to settle at Waipu.

There was another St Ann's notable, like Norman McLeod himself a son of Assynt, whose falling-out with the minister was on a scale that eclipsed even that of the Squire. John Munro came to Nova Scotia with his brother Alexander on the *Perseverance*. They had been well-educated and taught school, both near Pictou and later at St Ann's. But in a few years, with that enviable versatility so many of the migrants possessed, John built the first of several ships launched at St Ann's, some for fishing and trading to Newfoundland and Labrador, others to carry timber to Britain and to bring back goods for sale in his store. He was a strong-willed man, as independent as he was subtle, and the minister kept a sharp eye on him. He would have heard reports that John was smuggling spirits into St Ann's from St Pierre, the French island off the Canadian coast, and he decided to act. In 1849, the year of the great potato blight, food and work were desperately short. A Gilbertian situation developed, with Norman writing urgent letters to the government, calling on them to bring in provisions for the hungry, while at the same time he was virtually destroying Munro's business by forbidding his followers to deal with him, to sell him the timber that would enable them to buy food for themselves.

John Munro was resilient. Some reports would suggest that McLeod's actions forced him into bankruptcy, but it is difficult to reconcile this with his later career. Not long after the *Margaret* had taken Norman away, the Munro ships, stores and two grist mills were thriving again, as were his opportunistic trading ventures. In 1854, there were two events with far-reaching results. Munro, who had embarked on a political career, was defeated in an election for Victoria County government; he also salvaged and repaired the brig *Gertrude* which had been wrecked at the entrance to St Ann's. The first migrants had by now reached New Zealand, and favourable reports were coming back of the conditions there. He decided, at very short notice, to take the *Gertrude* out to New Zealand, and invited those to join him who were wishing to follow the earlier migrants.

The decision was an interesting one. Norman had not only accused him of using his three vessels for smuggling cargoes of brandy, wine and gin, but he brought up other alleged dishonest practices. The most serious of these involved the handling of money for "Society butter" which the people gave to support the work of the Nova Scotian Bible Society. John did not take this lying down. The local newspaper published a contribution from him in the best tradition of polemic writing. It contained a warning to the minister carefully designed to catch a raw nerve. It reads in part, with a veiled reference to Garibaldi's expulsion of the Pope from Rome: "But these are years of changes, and no doubt, will be remarkable in history for revolutions and the upsetting of old dynasties. The other Pope has got a start, and who knows but the chair here may soon begin to totter too."

Meanwhile, the *Gertrude* was being made ready for the long voyage and John continued to ship butter to Halifax and cattle to St Johns. More importantly, from the goodwill point of view, he was paying local housewives threepence a pound for carding wool. There was welcome casual employment for the men, too, discharging cargo from a Munro ship. The general wage was three shillings and sixpence a day. An important part of Munro's income came from buying herring from the local fishermen; this also generated useful income for the locals.

The decision to sail to New Zealand did not mean that he had signed a truce with the minister. Far from it. But he was big enough and shrewd enough to see that New Zealand should be able to provide a base for his own operations and still allow the minister to go his own way. His pen, sharpened in keen debate with Norman, could still serve its master well. A few years later, recalling the time when he left Nova Scotia, he wrote a lively letter to his old friend the Prince. Times were already bad, and the situation seemed impossible when the departing families all put their properties on the market at the same time, depressing the sale price even further. John wrote: "I had to step in and buy all their lands from my passengers for their passage money. When the little short-toothed creatures saw they were thus foiled they very gladly came to me and gave four times as much for the same land as they offered first." Then, as now, land sharks were a common species.

This was only one part of a quite remarkable operation which proved what John Munro could do when his organising ability was given full rein. In just two months the *Gertrude* was re-rigged, provisioned and fitted to carry one hundred and eighty passengers, 12,000 miles around the world.

But that was not the end. He knew, before leaving for New Zealand, that, although land was reserved for Nova Scotian use, the way in which it could be taken up was an unresolved problem. John proved that he fully deserved the nickname "Diplomatist" given him by the appreciative colonists. Two things happened. First, he saw Governor Grey, gone from New Zealand to Cape Town, and was able to tell the New Zealand Government officials that, if they did not sort out a solution quickly, the Nova Scotians would be welcome in South Africa. Secondly, the politically wise George Grey, it is said, advised Munro to get elected to the provincial council, where his voice would be heard.

Eventually everything worked out reasonably well, although it was not until 1861 that a select committee, with John Munro as chairman, confirmed that passengers on the *Breadalbane*, fifth of the six ships to sail, were entitled to grants of land. For passengers on the *Spray*, which had arrived not long after the *Gertrude*, there were not so many difficulties. A number of them were joining relatives already on their land and others, accompanying Captain Angus and Captain Duncan Matheson, moved down the coast to what is now Mathesons Bay, near Leigh.

Even after the migrants had been settled on the land — not all of it as close to the centre as they might have wished — John Munro remained a colourful figure. His nephew Donald chose to live in Waipu, within nodding distance of the minister, but John made his home discreetly apart, near the Whangarei Heads. However, he must have had some contact with Norman in New Zealand, or at least been aware of what he was doing. Maureen Molloy reports that the Auckland Waste Lands Act, which had some importance for the Nova Scotian settlers, was drafted in 1858 by Williamson, the Auckland Superintendent, and Donald McLean, Commissioner for Native Lands, "with the advice of Norman McLeod".

In *The Gael Fares Forth,* N.R. McKenzie tells an amusing and characteristic story about Munro.

> Marriages were usually contracted in the orthodox manner, but now and again there was a deviation from the normal procedure. A notable example of the latter was the marriage of James Irwin Wilson and Miss Johanna Munro, daughter of John Munro.
>
> Wilson was a fine type of man and was chief surveyor for the Auckland Province — but he was an Irishman and Munro abhorred Irishmen. He would not consent to his daughter's union with a man of the detested race. But when an Ulster man and a Highland lass agree upon a course of action, it is not easy to thwart them. They enlisted the sympathy of a number of friends. The lady was smuggled from her home at Whangarei Heads to Auckland and the couple were married at Mr Dilworth's residence.
>
> Munro arrived in Auckland shortly afterwards and it was rumoured among the Nova Scotian friends that he had bought a revolver to shoot Wilson. This caused some alarm until George McLeod, in a humorous Gaelic remark, assured the people that Munro would do as much damage with a big blue potato as with a revolver.
>
> When the first child (Mrs Storey) was born, Munro forgave the Wilsons. They came to live on a farm adjoining his own and he became very much attached to his son-in-law.
>
> When Henry S. Wilson married Munro's youngest daughter, no objection was made. On the contrary, Munro expressed regret that he did not have a daughter who might become the wife of the third brother, Dan C. Wilson.

There is a certain irony in the fact that John Munro Jr., grandson of the man who in years long past would smuggle brandy and other spirits into St Ann's, should become "coast waiter" at Marsden Point, where vessels, including those trading to New Caledonia and other South Pacific islands, called to have their cargo checked for uncustomed goods. Young John found it at times a frustrating task. When he went out in his rowing boat to carry out an inspection, there was one vessel that would keep edging away — quite innocently! — with grinning faces looking down on him. He would keep rowing, and the boat would keep moving.

It could be said that the contest between Munro the Diplomatist and Norman McLeod ended in a draw with, I should feel, a mutual respect lurking behind the fiery words. Two remarkable men, each a natural leader, the minister more obviously so, but it would be impossible to ignore the qualities of John Munro who, at short notice, could organise a voyage half way round the world and, when that was done, help significantly to resolve the land problems for those on the next three ships, the *Spray*, the *Breadalbane* and the *Ellen Lewis.*

The other strong men of Cape Breton must not be forgotten. John Fraser and John McKay, having helped to finance the building of the *Margaret,* set their considerable talents to the task of making the new settlement a practical reality. The McKenzie brothers, the Prince and the Captain, along with the many others who followed the sea, kept the lines of communication open to the outer world. They were still seamen first, with the wide ocean their domain. But the sea could be a cruel mistress. Some years later the Prince's son, Captain Kenneth McKenzie, a man loved by all who knew him, was lost with his ship in the Tasman Sea. The Prince, when he heard the news, fainted and did not speak for three days.

But the Prince had another son Norman, known as Tom Prince, who took enthusiastically to the land and made a success of it. He planted an orchard, ordering various trees from Yates, the Auckland firm. The account listed peach and apple trees, two burbank plums, two satsuma plums and one gratis. Later, with pride and also a sense of humour, Tom Prince might say to a visitor: "Would you like to try a burbank plum, or perhaps a gratis?" The orchard thrived. Many years later the earliest plums of the season would reach a house in the Waipu centre; a kerosene tin full of ripe Christmas plums from Tom Prince's orchard. More than eighty years later, Beulah Campbell still remembered them.

Chapter Seven

New Ocean, New Land

"**D**OWN TO MY KNEES IN MUD amongst holes and ditches along the newly-formed streets, jostled about by rough looking men with long beards, loitering about with careless gait or drinking to excess, and whom I concluded to be diggers, I feel disgusted at the town, and consider it the very counterpart of Cork in Ireland, and the very opposite of the golden hopes I held out to myself on landing."

That was Melbourne, foster-parent of one of the world's richest goldrushes, as Alex Nicholson, schoolmaster on HMS *Hercules*, saw it in 1853. Cork had been unkind to him and his fellow-migrants, with fever, smallpox and primitive living conditions all on offer. Melbourne was certainly no better, with law enforcement almost non-existent, the bodies of strangled men littering the gutters on most nights, and bushrangers lying in wait to rob or kill the successful gold-diggers on their way back from the diggings.

It was something of a coincidence that Norman McLeod, with a number of his followers from the *Margaret*, should also have been in Melbourne at that time. He would have echoed even more explicitly and vigorously Alex Nicholson's opinion of the town. Norman had frowned at what he had seen in Pictou, in Nova Scotia, when he had arrived there from Scotland nearly forty years before: its violence, its drunken sailors, its loose living and, in his opinion, lack of true religion; a youthful town, the undisciplined resting place for misfits, adventurers, and those back from long spells at sea. Norman had summarily rejected Pictou. Melbourne was so much worse, and even less qualified to be a home for him and his people.

But where to go? They lived for a while in tents on the Yarra River, a crowded area riddled with disease that was to destroy Norman and Mary's three youngest sons. They scouted the country in the hope that some suitable place might yet be found. Some of the younger men tried their luck on the goldfields, a few with moderate success — enough to help buy a farm at Waipu later.

For a few of the migrants Australia may have had some attraction, but not for the bulk of them when the whole purpose of their journey was to establish themselves as a close community free from the pressures of the outer world. In a letter to George Grey, the New Zealand governor in 1853, Duncan Prince spelt out their wishes. They required, he said, sufficient land not only for themselves but for others who would follow. And Duncan went on: "We speak the Gaelic language, and there are many of our old people who speak nothing else, so that it becomes a matter of the greatest importance that our people who speak that language only should, as far as possible, be located in the same place; and more especially we unite with our Pastor, Mr McLeod, in desiring that this should be so on account of devotional purposes."

Much the same argument was used by Donald McLeod, the minister's son, in a letter to Andrew Sinclair, the Colonial Secretary. This letter was written in February, 1854. The Nova Scotians began to take up land at Waipu seven months later. This bald statement might make the whole operation sound simple, which it certainly was not. Although the first land came to hand quickly enough, it took seemingly unending negotiation over several years before there was sufficient room for the arrivals from the later ships. It was only after Waipu had been chosen, and the setting aside of land approved, that the people of the *Margaret* and the *Highland Lass* crossed over to Auckland from Australia. The winter was behind them; it was time to put up shelter for themselves and start growing crops on their own piece of land.

They had seen many inviting places as they sailed north out of Auckland Harbour on the last day of August, 1854. The Great Barrier Island, deep in forest and with many sheltered bays, was on the eastern rim of the sea; on the mainland itself there were coves tucked in behind jutting capes, white sandy beaches and deep inlets where a boat could safely lie. All the way north they had watched the coastline intently. Now they were sailing across a broad, open bay, keeping close enough to the shore to see that the land was flat, mostly covered in fern and scrub, running back to a range of blue hills. A little disappointing, perhaps, at first glance, but the Prince and others had explored all likely places from Auckland north, and this was the one they had chosen. And now the Prince was himself bringing them north on the *Don*, his little seventeen-ton schooner; he called out to them to make ready to disembark.

There were sixteen of them in all: Duncan Ban Mackay, William Beag McKenzie, Hector McKenzie with their families. Norman McLeod was also on board watching — and doubtless handing out some good advice — as the new settlers went ashore. Hector McKenzie was in charge of the first group. They transferred to a small boat easily enough and rowed away towards the land. The boat grounded in shallow water.

"Alex, you're the youngest," said Hector. And so Alex Mackay, son of Duncan Ban, rolled up his trousers, took the painter in hand and went over the side. With his help the boat edged gently through the light waves to the dry beach; and Alex had staked his claim to a small measure of fame as the first of the Nova Scotian party to reach Waipu. It was the first day of September, 1854.

The *Don* sailed on to Whangarei Heads, not many miles away. There it took on its cargo for Auckland: a modest amount of wheat, 16 dozen eggs, six tons of firewood. As they sailed back across Bream Bay the minister and the *Don's* captain would both be thinking of the three families and the new life they were beginning. Perhaps Norman would also have in mind that, at seventy-three, he could leave the initial pioneering to others, while he continued to take services at St Andrews, the first Presbyterian Church in Auckland, and also keep the future wellbeing of the settlement in the mind of the Government. At all events, by September 4 Norman was back in Auckland, refreshed after his voyage along the coast and happy that, at last, the people of the *Margaret* and the *Highland Lass* would be moving to the promised land.

As they busied themselves on shore, the new settlers would inevitably have been making comparisons with their old Cape Breton homeland: St Ann's sheltered by enfolding hills; Boularderie and Baddeck divided by the narrow waters of the Bras d'Or Lake. Here, in contrast, the sky was open and, even in springtime, brassy with the sun; and the waters of Bream Bay, exposed to every wind, with nothing to break the sea's force but a few rocky islands on the horizon; and to the north, mountains as rugged and inhospitable as the Cuillins in Skye. But between the mountains and the sea there was this block of land, 60,000 acres in all, which would allow a community to fulfil its fondest dreams: to continue sharing the leadership its members had known in Nova Scotia, to worship together, to ensure that the old people could enjoy the security spelt out by the Prince in his letter to the Governor.

Such a place had not been easy to find in a colony where there had been many extraordinary claims for land by speculators; and where, even if there had been a generous goodwill toward the Maori, owners of this particular area were not easy to find. Under the stress of tribal war in the 1820s, the Waipu district had been deserted. Norman McLeod and his fellow negotiators showed considerable skill and an even more important quality, persistence, over long months that at last brought them success.

Now, however, with the first settlers safely established, the empty land began to fill up. By the time the *Ellen Lewis* had arrived in 1861, there were over eight hundred Nova Scotians taking up life in an exciting new country. Not all of them kept their feet on the land. In Nova Scotia they had been seamen first, in many cases, and landsmen second. That same situation would continue, with the South Pacific and the Tasman Sea — blue waters and sudden storms — contrasting with the winter ice and the creeping mists they had known before. A huge challenge lay ahead, a challenge that had to be accepted, for several reasons. First and foremost, without their own small craft the settlements would be isolated from their markets. The *Don*, with its intimate little cargo from Whangarei Heads, indicated how important this was. Secondly, these were deepwater men, quick to see the opportunities on a larger scale, with Australia and the islands of the Pacific, and even further afield. One of the first to make his presence felt in the Auckland shipping world was Hugh Anderson. In 1850 a barque on which Hugh, a young son of Aberdeen was mate, came into St Ann's to load timber, and was caught in the winter ice. He met Margaret, Norman McLeod's youngest daughter, and they fell in love. The ship on which Margaret and her family would sail to Australia would be leaving the following year, and the young lovers would be parted — unless something drastic could be done.

Hugh disappeared from his ship, without trace. A few days after the barque sailed in the spring he reappeared, having been hidden in an empty cabin by his friends. Flora Macpherson writes in *Watchman Against the World*: "He boldly approached Margaret's father and offered his help with the work of rigging the ship, and as navigator for the voyage. He also declared himself a suitor for Margaret's hand. His work was immediately accepted; his proposal was ignored. But Hugh Anderson could be patient. He sailed as an officer of the ship and, two years later, in New Zealand, married Margaret McLeod."

Captain Hugh Anderson saw his future in the busy port of Auckland rather than in Waipu. He commanded several ships trading overseas and ran his own ship chandler's business for many years. Two sons went in different directions. One, bearing the loyal name of Norman McLeod Anderson, served in the Boer War, became a rancher in the Transvaal and, though well over age, rejoined the army in the First World War. A second son, Edward, gently spoken, decisive, tall and of distinguished appearance through to his eighties, extended his father's interests notably. He owned Henderson and Macfarlane, one of the country's largest marine trading concerns; and his financial reputation brought him a post as director of the Reserve Bank of New Zealand.

Hugh Anderson's courtship of Margaret reminds us that in St Ann's — and elsewhere in the Highland settlements — the Victorian doctrine of female submissiveness to the man did not rule. A father might very properly suggest to a daughter that her choice of a partner was unwise; the mother could well say the same. And it is possible that Norman had stricter rules for others than he did for his own family, who some would say he spoiled. But there were other marriages similar to that of Margaret and Hugh which started off under a cloud and eventually flourished in the sunshine. Unlike the meek little bride-to-be in Victorian legend, the lassie from St Ann's was ready, in many cases, to take the measure of a suitor and decide whether he was the one with whom she wished to spend the rest of her life.

While Hugh Anderson was busy establishing himself in Auckland, other Nova Scotian seamen were already trading up and down the coast and across the sea to Australia. The list would grow and reach impressive proportions. The Prince and the Captain — Captains Duncan and Murdoch McKenzie — have already been mentioned. The McGregor brothers, builders of the *Margaret* and the *Highland Lass*, carried on in New Zealand where they had left off in Nova Scotia; building for the Prince the cutter *Flora McDonald*, the first boat to be constructed at Waipu. Then the Prince commissioned the McMillan brothers to build a larger cutter, the *Thistle*, which could carry up to thirty grown cattle. Loading the stock called for fortitude and skill. The *Thistle* would lie off the Cove, just south of Waipu; the cattle would be taken out in a small boat pulled by a rope from the ship, and would be hoisted in board by hand with a block and tackle. The Prince supervised the whole operation for his clients, seeing the cattle brought ashore in Auckland, checking the sale at the markets and bringing the proceeds back with him on the return trip. The *Thistle* was wrecked in 1868, striking rocks off Bream Head on a black, stormy night with the loss of two passengers. All on board had performed bravely as the vessel broke up in the wild breakers. Two brothers suffered broken legs but the rest formed a human chain to bring the injured ashore. The tragedy, like others in which the Prince was involved, hit him hard; but it was a measure of a man's strength not to yield to such harsh blows. He commissioned a schooner, named the *Jessie* for Mrs McKenzie; bought another cutter also named the *Don* for trading to Auckland; sent the *Jessie*, which drew too much water for the Waipu bar, to the Pacific Islands where two of his sons sold her; purchased another schooner, the *Cambria*, and traded with her until he retired, to spend his old age on his Waipu farm.

As a small boy on my father's farm on the banks of the Piako River, south of Auckland, I would watch the Northern Company's steamer, the *Hauiti*, sitting high on the flowing tide as she made her way upstream to Kerepehi. "Watch for her when she comes back," my mother would say, "and take this cream out for the captain when she stops at the wharf." There would be a cheerful wave from the wheelhouse, the whistle would sound and away the good ship *Hauiti* would slide on her way to Auckland.

The man at the wheel was John McKenzie, one of several descendants of the Prince to become sea captains. They were my mother's cousins. The Prince helped a son, Norman, and his nephew, Duncan Hector, to buy a small schooner, the *Sunbeam*, in which they traded to Auckland, taking cattle to the market. When the cattle began to be driven by road, the cousins decided there was not enough for two. They tossed up as to who should retire. Duncan Hector kept the boat and Norman went farming. It was a sign of the times that, after a few years, Duncan Hector should sell the *Sunbeam* and go bush-contracting.

I have already mentioned how Kenneth, the Prince's third son, was lost with his crew when the schooner *Rona* was wrecked off the west coast, near the Kaipara Harbour. Captain Alex, the youngest son, gave up the sea to be a farmer; but one of his sons, Ronald, holding a master's certificate, entered the Chinese Maritime Customs Service in the 1930s, working with a fleet of motorboats to prevent smuggling on the Canton delta. Four generations of the family, from Scotland to Nova Scotia and then to New Zealand, had produced sea captains.

Murdoch the Captain, the Prince's brother, having taken over command of the *Highland Lass* in Cape Town, and afterwards sailing the *Gazelle* across the Tasman with the first migrants, did not stay ashore very long. He entered the South Sea island trade with the schooner *Wentworth*, and owned and commanded a variety of vessels. On these he sailed to many parts of the world — Africa, China, North America and Australia among them. He died on the barquentine *Winona*, sailing near Bluff, New Zealand's furthest-south port; and the old seadog's body was brought back to Auckland for burial. His son John, famous for his seamanship, was deputy harbourmaster of Auckland in the 1880s. He resigned to go to Mexico, where he died.

Discussing a community which, it was claimed, produced more sea captains per head of population than any other in New Zealand, it would be impossible to give full details in one chapter. One of the most remarkable was Captain Donald Hugh McKenzie, who was registered as part-owner of fifty ships between 1864 and 1886. He also had a ship-chandlery and agency in Auckland. "D.H." was not related to the other McKenzies discussed here, but there must have been a close affinity between that clan and the sea. Yet another McKenzie was a crew member of the *Spray*. He figures prominently in a later chapter.

However, most of the other clans were also well represented. Kenneth McGregor, of Whangarei Heads, had fifteen ships registered in his name between 1859 and 1897; McLeods at the Heads owned several ships, some of them employed in Pacific Islands trading; Colin McDonald became commodore of the celebrated Currie Line; Robert Campbell had three sons who became master mariners — Angus, Dan Neil and Robert; and, among tragedies that happened all too often, Murdoch Sutherland and Hugh Ross both took ships to the South Pacific and were lost without trace.

At one time there were fifteen ships in Auckland Harbour with their captains from the Nova Scotian settlements. There would have been many a story told on that day. But better roads were made and eventually the railway reached Maungaturoto. The Northern Steamship Company, which had been founded by Sandy McGregor, was obliged to amalgamate with the McGregor Company. The cutters and little schooners disappeared, the fleet of steamers lasted for a few years more, and then joined the old scows as relics of the past. Today, the highways to the north are pounded by giant eight-wheel trucks carrying goods up and down the island, the container ships, one might say, of the land.

They might not go to sea like their husbands or sons, but the wives and mothers were just as closely tied to the sea. What a lifetime of experience Ann McKenzie had! Born Ann McRae in the year 1778, she married Captain John McKenzie and spent her early married life on Prince Edward Island. Back then to Applecross with her sons Duncan and Murdoch. Away again to Nova Scotia and, thirty years later now a widow, to Australia on the *Highland Lass*. Finally to Waipu, where she died at the age of ninety-three in 1871. She covered the whole period of migration and resettlement, but hers would have been a vastly different story from that of the men who took part. Ann McKenzie would have had the tougher role. Births, bereavements, the small, familiar details of running a home; and, behind it all, the anxiety, subdued but never to be ignored, of husband and sons sailing on uncertain seas.

On a less sombre note: not all those of Nova Scotian descent were familiar with the sea. They offered fertile ground for the sailor's humour. One such man, Neil, was the subject of many tales that my friend, Kenneth Ainslie, heard from his mother. It seems this man had not moved out of the area where he was born, and had not seen a vessel of any size or presumably a steamer. He eventually was offered a trip to Auckland in a ketch.

"Next day," said Kenneth, "it was decided to take him down to the waterfront and show him the big ships. So down the old wooden Queens Wharf they strolled. At the end, the *Maheno* was berthed, getting up steam before sailing for Sydney. The smoke was rolling out of the funnels and, after Neil had had a good gaze at her, he was asked what he thought of her.

"After some considered moments, he spat out a chew and replied: 'No wonder baccy's so dear when those big buggers smoke'!"

Life for the seafarers had a more or less ordered progression. Sail gave way to steam but the basic rules remained much the same — care for the ship and for those on board, a watch on weather and currents, endless checking on position with reading of instruments. On land, however, change from conditions in Nova Scotia came quickly. The handling of stock, the cultivation of the soil under a warmer sun, called for new skills or the refinement of old ways.

Many of the farmers adapted well. Back in Nova Scotia, it had been an initial practice to grow crops, particularly potatoes, in the ashes from burnt trees, and this they continued to do. Where it had been normal, in the Highlands and Nova Scotia, to keep one or two milking cows, selling the calves or using them as replacements, a herd of milking cows, yielding milk virtually all the year round, could now bring in a steady income. It meant hard work and long hours, particularly before milking machines were developed and factories were set up for making butter and cheese. And, to maintain production with intensive farming required the use of heavy quantities of fertiliser.

A letter written in 1857 by Martha McRae to her brother Farquhar in Nova Scotia shows how quickly the settlers adapted to different conditions. An acute and objective observer, Martha brings "the Waipu", as it was called, vividly to life, especially in economic terms. Ships' carpenters would not do well, she told her brother. A fall in the price of produce in the Australian colonies had left everything dull and money scarce.

> Carpenters' wages are about 12s a day. Joiners and masons are the best tradesmen for this country under the present circumstances, as they always get plenty to do, for this being a new country there are always new buildings going on, but farming is the best trade of all here; a person having 100 acres of land paid, which he can purchase from the Government at 10s an acre, and to have £50 cash to commence with, might be well enough off in two or three years. The Waipu is a fine settlement, very kind and fertile soil. Rodk [McKay] has sown about 7 bushels of wheat last year which yielded him about 100 bushels and there were several in the Waipu who had a better increase than that.

A sequel to Martha's letter has been preserved, written to Farquhar McRae in 1889, but this time by Catherine McRae. Martha was dead, but her husband was still in Auckland with her two daughters, the Dingwall girls, who were "doing very well" as dressmakers. Catherine, also in Auckland, kept in close touch with her Waipu kin.

"Most of the old people who came from home are dropping off," she reported. Mrs Donald McGregor, in her nineties, was "looking as rosy as any of her daughters... Mrs Rory Campbell died a year ago. She was over ninety. John McKay and his wife are dead, he was ninety-seven and kept so well till the last and could ride to church. His family are getting old men and women now." She scolded her brother for not writing. "It is a long time since I heard a word from Cape Breton."

Catherine covered a wide range of topics, including the sad state of New Zealand in a severe depression. Donald Gillanders, her nephew, had gone to Melbourne. There was no work in Auckland for engineers and carpenters. She further writes:

New Zealand is in a bad state of trade. Nothing seems to be doing well, so many people failing. The New Zealand Bank failed and there was £30,000 they could not account for. The manager and directors were dismissed. A great many of the large business people fail in the ten to £40,000 and in about a month open in the new, and then so many honest people lose all they have through such failures. There is too much roguery in Auckland.

The country has borrowed so many millions from England and now three millions of that cannot be accounted for. The country is on the verge of bankruptcy itself. Taxes are now very heavy and a person is safer to pay rent than own a house, all to pay interest on borrowed money, badly laid out. They say the Parliament is the ruin of New Zealand.

These words will have a familiar ring to those who lived in the same city of Auckland through the 1980s and early 1990s.

Food is very cheap now — bread 3d a loaf, meat from 2d to 4d a lb. It does not pay farmers, a cow is only about 25s, and when they pay train or boat it doesn't leave much. Cheese from 4d to 10d a lb, butter 6d to 8d and eggs 8d a dozen. The climate is very fine here and the people who go to Australia feel the hot winds very much. There seems to be a change all over the world. What is on earth will soon pass away, but there is a better time for which we must prepare.

And with these comforting words Catherine ends her epistle.

So, for the first years, farmers at Waipu did well enough. A kind of prosperity continued, in fact, until the withdrawal of the troops brought in from Britain to fight the Maori; a corollary to their presence was an increased demand, at good prices, for farm produce. The dairy farmers were on the fertile flats. Those who arrived on the later ships and had to look to the frontier lands, as it were, found themselves in a different world. Different from what they had left, different too from the land below them which stretched blandly towards the ocean. Forest was something they all knew about, but how strange was this great mass that enveloped the hills!

It had to be cleared, eventually, but even before it was felled the bush brought an unexpected bonus. Any animals that strayed off the grassland put on beef just as quickly in the green wilderness as their more civilised brothers nearer home. It took a good stockman to round up the strays, for they were suspicious of humans, but when a farmer managed to extricate a bullock and send it to the market, it might fetch up to £25. Before long many farmers were deliberately sending some of their young stock out, and profiting from it. In a way, the bush might correspond to the summer grazing high above the village that the crofters used back in the Highlands.

There was usually plenty of work waiting to be done on a farm, but extra income to pay for development was always welcome. Gangs formed to build roads linking Waipu Centre with the Cove, the Braigh and other outlying areas. The contract rate at one time was £40 a mile. Needless to say, the roads were fairly primitive, with three tracks in the dust — two for the cart wheels, one in the middle worn down by the horses' hooves. Local work was welcome, but more and more the young men were drawn away in two directions, to the town and to the bush.

Over the ranges from Waipu, on the west coast of the North Island, was the far-spreading Kaipara Harbour. Bush on the shoreline was already being worked for kauri timber when the first Nova Scotians reached their new home. Before long, young men from the settlement were making their way over the hills to join a logging camp. There was rain and mud to contend with, and danger too. A falling tree could split, and launch itself like a giant spear in an unexpected direction. Logs could roll and crush a leg. But rheumatism from the working conditions was probably the worst menace of all.

Life in the bush broadened horizons in many ways. Here were men of many nationalities all working together. Ex-army men, driving the bullock teams, named the big, ponderous creatures Captain, Sergeant and so on. Down where the logs were loaded, usually for Australia, there were tantalising glimpses of a different life. In spite of all the distractions, however, the men kept close ties to home. There was one keen worker who, having come home for the weekend, decided to make a start back to camp after attending church. He was censured by the minister for this breaking of the Sabbath.

It would be impossible to estimate the amount of timber that went away through the Kaipara in those early years. And, if millions of feet were exported, an even greater quantity was destroyed as farms were made out of forest. One labour-saving technique was highly spectacular. On a bush-clad hill face, the trees would be partly cut through until the bushmen reached the crest of the hill. There a key tree, big and wide-spreading, would be felled so that it would crash down on the nearest of the partly-cut trees. Like dominoes collapsing, these would fall, taking with them in turn the trees below them. They would be left to dry, and then burned in a blaze that would be seen miles away, with the smoke darkening the sun.

Much of the land that was cleared in this way proved unsuitable for farming, once the initial fertility had gone. There is a cheering irony in studying the career of Roderick Duncan Campbell, born at a time when the bush-burning was at its peak. A son of Waipu, Duncan was educated there to the sixth standard, then left school to help his father when the family moved to Parua Bay, near Whangarei. While still a youth he set up his own contracting business — bushfelling, pitsawing timber, supplying hardwood puriri for wharves in Auckland.

From this time Duncan gradually began to see the true worth of trees, not only for their timber but for preventing erosion and for conservation in general. When he was appointed the first Conservator of Forests for the Auckland district he was able to introduce his own quite revolutionary ideas. Frank Simpson, in an article in the *Auckland Star*, summed up the career of this descendant of forest-clearers:

> On assuming his new office Mr Campbell found that many high-forested areas in the Far North were being planned for settlement. He was satisfied that the removal of trees from these high-ridged areas would create grave erosion and flooding problems… These forested hill areas are now preserved.
>
> Another important move for which he was directly responsible was to preserve the main kauri areas, permitting only dead and over-mature trees to be taken out. He was always interested in the preservation of regenerated kauri. Through his influence a large area was acquired at Great Barrier Island, and a start was made with acquiring some thousands of acres extending from the Bay of Islands southward.

All this may have redressed the balance to some degree, and allowed modern generations to enjoy some vision of a past that might otherwise have vanished.

Chapter Eight

Log of a Voyage, and Letters
Across the Ocean

W HEN THE BARQUE *Breadalbane* sailed from Big Bras d'Or in December, 1857, among her 160 passengers were two young people, a boy and a girl, whose lives would be closely linked for many years. Seventeen-year-old Hector Fraser was the son of Roderick and Marcella, who went to Boularderie in 1817 from the Western Highlands. Roderick was a miller. Dolina, nine years old, was the daughter of Roderick McLean, usually known as Rory, and Margaret. He was a bootmaker, and something of a character. As Enid Mansell, a descendant, wrote, "He lived until he was 96 or 98. By that time he had gone back to talking in Gaelic, which saved his family much embarrassment as he would tell all visitors that, in Scotland, the Government had taken his castle from him, and that he and a friend had set up a whisky still. They were caught and put in jail for six weeks."

The *Breadalbane* made port in Auckland. The Frasers and the McLeans, along with most of the other passengers, went to Waipu; nine years later Dolina, now eighteen, married Hector at the beautiful St Andrews Presbyterian Church in Auckland. Dolina must have had tremendous strength and vitality. When she was forty-five, she bore her nineteenth child, Ivy, who died at the age of eighty-seven in 1981. Seven of her children reached their eighties, three lived into their nineties and Jessie Grant, known as Mina, was 101 when her full life ended.

Dolina had her share of adventure, some of which she would later recall with amusement. The family had moved to Okaihau, a district still in an unsettled state after the wars with the Maori. Hector had bought a farm which Dolina and the older children looked after while Hector was away on road-contracting work. At such times, an elderly Maori woman would call and ask Dolina for flour, sugar and other food, frightening her so much that she would give the woman whatever she demanded.

"One day, a Sunday, she came while Dolina and the older children were at church," Enid Mansell wrote. "When she found Dolina was out, she settled down on the doorstep and went to sleep. She woke up to find Rory, who was just a young boy, pointing a gun at her. He told her to go home, and she went. The next day she turned up again and pleaded with Dolina to sell Rory to her. He was just the kind of boy she liked."

Dolina died at seventy-nine. There are photographs of her taken in later years. They show a lively woman with a trim figure that was the admiration and envy of many in a younger generation.

The men and women who waited to board the *Breadalbane* on that December day in 1857 were as well prepared for what lay ahead as anyone could be. They had seen the *Margaret*, with Norman McLeod and many followers, set sail for a strange land; and in the next year, with a festive skirling of the pipes to send her on the way, the *Highland Lass* had slipped past Boularderie to the open sea and an uncertain future. They had read letters from friends and relatives who had completed the great adventure. Many were attracted by the idea of migrating, but needed to have their confidence boosted by accurate or optimistic information. They would have been heartened by news following the arrival of the *Gertrude* in December, 1856. The *Gertrude*, with its politically acute owner, John Munro, on board, had brought reinforcements to the advance guard that was seeking to establish a settlement area where the people could live as a close-knit community and, as was frequently emphasised, where they could look after the old folk, many of whom could speak only Gaelic.

The *Breadalbane* passengers knew before they left that there would be a warm welcome awaiting them and, equally important, sufficient land for them to live on. They would also have been advised on what food and clothing to take with them. But how, we may still ask, did they make plans that would help them to survive for six months at sea in close and unhygienic conditions? In Nova Scotia, similar planning was essential in preparation for the long, harsh winters — that discipline would certainly have helped them to adjust to life at sea. But even so they faced daunting obstacles of a kind not easy for us to visualise today.

Fortunately, we can to some degree put ourselves in the place of the passengers by reading a journal kept by Murdoch Fraser during the voyage. The part that survives covers the first sixty days at sea. Murdoch, obviously a very intelligent young man with wide-ranging interests, later taught school in New Zealand before becoming a minister of the Presbyterian Church.

A bland report in the Auckland newspaper *The Southern Cross*, published the day after her arrival, gives a very comforting account of the voyage of the *Breadalbane*. "She has experienced a remarkably pleasant passage, having had nothing but fine weather until she made the New Zealand coast..." I doubt if Murdoch would have agreed. The *Breadalbane*, as was proved on the first day out from Kelly's Cove, could roll with the best of them, and a great number of the passengers were very seasick. In addition, as Murdoch grimly relates, they had to put three of their boxes on deck so as to have a little space in the steerage. Perhaps it was the change in the climate that made Murdoch more genial. After two days, the snow, ankle deep on the

113

deck when they sailed, had begun to melt. Soon, the seasick sufferers were emerging from down below, the men moving about in shirtsleeves and bare feet. Murdoch, but not the women, I imagine, could say that, when a heavy roll of the ship tore loose the lashings of one of the fireplaces, smashing pots and kettles, "everything that was loose rolled about in a very comical manner".

Before long the ship had settled into a routine. Constables and J.P.s were appointed and the first mate measured out the water — half a gallon daily for each person. There were grizzles about the owner, Charles Campbell, later a Nova Scotian politician:

> ...a cold-hearted, gold-loving villain who packed the passengers into his ship close enough to be compared to a slaver. What but a soulless and heartless wretch would be cruel enough to pack thirty-two souls into a space small enough to contain six persons, the half of that room stowed up with part of their luggage, the rest exposed to all kinds of weather and to the mercy of the waves?
>
> Our captain true enough is a very nice man, but his niceness is only a poor substitute. No doubt the vessel is strong and stiff enough, and that the only merited point about her. She was leaky above [through the deck] and below, wet and unsteady and not such a fast sailing vessel as was reported.

Murdoch celebrated New Year's Day, a day of high wind and big seas, "hanging up in the rigging to dry myself out", after having been given a thorough good ducking on the quarter deck. But the wind had one thing in its favour — it continued to blow from an appropriate quarter, sending them well on their way. The journal shows that fair winds took them through the doldrums, feared by sailormen for their long calms and sudden thunderstorms. On the thirty-first day out, "at four o'clock in the morning we were startled out of our sleep by a shrill note blown on a trumpet, an intimation from Neptune that he came aboard and that we were crossing the Equator". It was a fine day with a clear sky which led Murdoch to issue a graphic warning to immigrants in that climate not to expose their heads to the sun or the moon. "The covering for the head should be straw hats, with paper inside the crown. Paper is a good preserver from sunstroke. We had some persons aboard who were very sick from that cause and especially by sleeping with their faces to the moon."

Meanwhile, life on board seemed to proceed smoothly enough. Initially the fireplaces, of which there were two — one to port and the other to starboard — caused some trouble, with the bricks breaking away in heavy weather. They were rebuilt quickly, "our captain being the principal mason employed in the work". One of the crew, Donald McDonald, obviously out of favour with the mate, resigned. Murdoch McDonald signed the ship's articles in his place. It seems that some of the crew were selected from men wishing to migrate, while others were "professional" seamen, ready to go wherever their work took them. On an insufferably hot Sunday, when even windsails inserted down the hatchway could not make conditions bearable down below, Murdoch took refuge high in the foretop with one of the sailors. They talked about the kind of life he led. "I am like a man shut up in prison for a number of years ignorant of the manners of society," the sailor said. "When I have a chance to go among society, I feel the time long till I shall spend my all, and when that is done I must ship again, to earn and to spend." What if old age should catch him penniless and friendless? "Am I not in that position always?" the sailor replied. "Who are my friends, and when is my pocket with money? As for old age, I am sure it will never catch me... I never intend to pray, neither do I intend to go to heaven, but I do believe that I with a great many of my shipmates go together to Davy Jones' Locker." Murdoch showed an admirable objectivity in reporting the sailor's words which I feel sure would have figured in a graphic style in his talks from the pulpit when Murdoch became a minister. The sailor concluded in this way: "A sentimental sailor would not do, for the moment they get religious they must quit the sea and go to preach gospel to the land lubbers, and have no word about their old shipmates, who put their life in jeopardy for their sake. Let our blood be on their heads."

In cramped quarters, with only an occasional passing ship to relieve the monotony, some friction would be expected among the passengers. Murdoch makes little reference to this, except to say: "Aboard of a ship where idleness is the general occupation, a disturbance is very easily raised, and should the disturbance be raised by children, as it most generally is, men must set it right."

As the voyage went on, Murdoch gave more and more space to a subject which could easily have become an obsession — food. The store of potatoes, which might have been an important part of their diet, rotted in the damp heat and had to be thrown overboard, a welcome relief as it robbed the hold of a sickening smell. Murdoch consoled himself by saying that:

> Potatoes should not be used for they are a regular nuisance aboard ship; at the best they contain only twenty-five per cent of nutritive food. A little of them pickled would be very useful. If the immigrant intends to take any vegetables, which no doubt are very useful, let him take a small quantity of various sorts such as cabbage, carrots, turnips, beets etc, etc, all pickled in different strong crocks well covered, and kept in a rough strong box; but if any evil-disposed person be aboard, as in our case, he must watch his effects pretty close, or he will risk the danger of having them destroyed as well as consumed.

Murdoch is equally informative about meat. "There is no use in taking too large a quantity, as if it is not properly packed and salted, it will decay in a short time." Mutton and pork were best, with a little fish for a change. Later, however, fresh fish came on the menu. They saw large schools of flying fish, "darting through the water like so many birds flying from their enemy at the report of his gun"; attempting to escape the dolphins that pursued them, they landed at times on the deck. Murdoch adds a curious comment. "Both dolphin and flying fish are eatable, excepting those on the copper banks, and to find out the eatable ones I give the following receipt. When the fish is boiling put a silver coin along with it into the pot. If the coin retains its original colour it is eatable. But if the coin turns to a copper colour, it is not eatable."

Bread made at home before sailing kept well for a long time. And, to get rid of the bad taste of stale water, first-rate quality lime juice should be added, or good vinegar for a change.

To cure a fever and alleviate another common ship-board complaint, diarrhoea, Murdoch made two recommendations that would certainly have been acceptable to some of the passengers. Cream of tartar was good for fever and, "one part cream of tartar mixed in gin and molasses is very useful to cleanse the blood and regulate the bowels. I knew one case in which it gave great relief in rheumatism." Diarrhoea could be cured in a very simple manner if taken in time:

> Take a tumbler full of strong dark brandy, which pour into a larger dish. Burn some loaf sugar over the brandy by means of a bar of iron made red in the fire, on which place the sugar, and as it drops, it will set fire to the brandy; leave burning one minute or more, add some ground pepper, mix well, drink all up — it will cure in a short time.
>
> Good brandy is of service in case of seasickness, therefore a good supply of it would be useful. Chocolate and coffee are the best drinks to use. Rice being a light diet is very serviceable for healthy persons as well as invalids.

Entries in the journal are not as full over the last thirty days, except for the description of a furious storm that carried the *Breadalbane* before it at fourteen knots, not long before the desired sighting of Tristan da Cunha Island. It would have been interesting to read Murdoch's account of their stay off Capetown and their arrival, after a stormy crossing of the Tasman Sea, off the west coast of the Auckland peninsula. There they encountered a canoe load of Maoris, which caused some apprehension until they were hailed by a white man who proved to be Donald McLean, later Sir Donald, who was engaged in land purchase for settlement. Apparently, on the *Breadalbane's* small chart, the name "Auckland" extended from the town centre on the Waitemata Harbour across a narrow isthmus to the Manukau

Harbour on the west coast, with a treacherous bar and many sandbanks. McLean explained that, to reach their desired port, they would have to sail north round the cape and down the east coast.

I was interested to find that Murdoch Fraser, when he wrote his mature and well-balanced journal, was only twenty years old. He was the first teacher at North River School. In his late thirties, however, he became a student minister at Coromandel — his success in this field had two sequels: the recruiting of a number of other men as home missionaries, and the start of an odyssey that took him all over the young colony. During twenty-four years he pioneered or developed new charges at which he liked to stay for no more than two years, among them remote stations such as Kaikoura, Waipawa and Westport. He was the first minister at Chalmers Church, Dunedin, and finally returned to Waipu from 1905 until his retirement at the age of seventy.

There were two Roderick Frasers on the *Breadalbane*, but the one we are concerned with was the Miller, who set up his home beside a stream now called the Millbrook. A placid enough stream when I saw it, coming down from the hills and coiling across the floor of the valley; but one which, I was told, could carry a good body of water. There is a magnificent por-trait of the Miller, a fine romantic study which makes him, with great beard, flashing eyes and defiant pose, the Highlander as we imagine him to have been. Murdoch was his eldest son, married but with no children; there was John who had six children; there was Isabella who married William McDonald from the *Highland Lass* and bore him nine children; and there was Hector, who introduced this chapter and who fathered nineteen chil-dren. I have seen photographs of the girls in Hector's and Dolina's family as they moved through to young adulthood: smartly dressed, all strikingly attractive. Their faces, and those of their brothers who could be caught by the camera, show a zest for life and an inner happiness. Another photo-graph, taken on one of the rare occasions when they came together in adult years, showed the whole family, complete with mother and father, except for one son who had died young. Sadly, the only surviving copy of the photo had suffered a tear which eliminated four of the family. I hope that an unspoilt copy will be discovered some day.

The Miller was strict on Sunday observance although, like many of the migrants who came from Boularderie Island on the *Breadalbane*, he was not a follower of Norman. Enid Mansell remembers being told that, if your boots hurt on the long walk to church, you were allowed to take them off, but not to carry them in your hand; you had to leave them in the bush on the side of the road. A regular routine was achieved in a farming family with children of many ages. While father was away working in the bush for ready money or engaged in road-making, mother would be looking after the babies and the older children would milk the cows.

As the years passed, farms tended to become too small. The Miller had his mill to bring in an income, but Hector and Dolina needed more space. In 1882 they moved to Okaihau. Jessie Fraser was only three when the move was made, but details of the journey remained in her mind for the next ninety years. Their belongings were taken to the open coast, where a lantern was waved to attract the attention of those on the boat to Opua while it passed at night. But the signal was not seen; no boat came in over the surf to pick them up. They had to wait another week, with their luggage at a relation's house, before the boat took them on the next stage of their journey.

"Times were very hard," said Enid, "but they were a happy family." Dolina certainly found pleasure in the little domestic chores. The children had to be well-dressed for school. Flour bags were bleached until they were snowy white, made into aprons and trimmed with lace, for the girls to wear to school. Jessie remembered, too, how they would sometimes go to a local dance although their parents did not approve. They would hide their supper plate under a log in the paddock during the day, slip out the bedroom window at night, catch their horses and ride off to the dance. There were times when it was three in the morning before they got home. "Jessie did this only a few times," said Enid, "as she felt very wicked."

That, ruthlessly abridged as it is, gives a glimpse of how one family group fared from the time they sailed from Nova Scotia until, a generation or so later, the eyes of most of the descendants were fixed on a new life in New Zealand. For the old folk it might have been different, but even for them the Gaelic-speaking days in the Highlands had lost their clarity, fading into a nostalgic or fanciful dream.

The Frasers were, as far as we can tell, fortunate in the way fate treated them. They enjoyed good health; the children too, were healthy and active; they found occupations and land on which they prospered in a modest but happy way. They had breathed confidence in themselves as they left Boularderie, and this confidence seemed to grow under the challenge of a new environment. A study of correspondence that has survived from the time the six ships sailed shows that there were widely variant attitudes among the people. For some it was a joyous venture; for others, a desperate attempt to find happiness that had eluded them, an attempt to escape living conditions that became harder to bear with every wintry blast or taste of famine.

Dolina Fraser bore her nineteen children with apparent ease, and watched them grow up into a closely knit family. How different for another woman who died in her ninth childbed. In the course of her married life she had seven stillborn babies, one that died when a few weeks old, and only one that survived her mother.

The letters I have seen, written in New Zealand to Nova Scotian kinsfolk, from Canada to cousins and other relatives in New Zealand, usually are designed to bring up to date the roll-call of births, marriages and deaths. For this reason, life being what it is, they are a mixture of joy and sadness. Others, however, give an interesting picture of what the immigrants thought of their new homeland. Incidentally, in one letter the writer uses the word "home" to refer first to Nova Scotia and, in a later paragraph, to Scotland. And by then the sons and daughters would think of home as some part of New Zealand.

John McInnes and his family came to New Zealand on different ships, and some of the brothers and sisters seem to have gone their own way from the start. Ewen, who was a close follower of Norman McLeod, travelled on the *Margaret* with two of his brothers. Perhaps because he stayed in Australia for a couple of years, and married Mary McBain from North Uist there, his children had no close links with those who left Cape Breton a few years later on the *Gertrude*. This section of the family had more than its share of tragedy. Angus Nicholson had married Mary McInnes, a daughter of John, back in Nova Scotia. A letter that he wrote to his sister Margaret, back in Nova Scotia, in 1887, gives a cheerful picture of a farmer's life at Okaihau, a hundred miles north of Waipu, where he had moved ten years before. He now had 470 acres of fertile volcanic land, compared with one hundred acres at Waipu. The family milked dairy cows, with a good market for their butter in the sawmills working the forests on all sides. Potatoes, too, were a considerable cash crop. Angus is proud of his sons, flourishing physically in this new land.

"Alexander is the biggest of the boys," he writes. "He is six feet four high and weighs 223 pounds. John is six feet three and a half inches and weighs about 200 pounds, while James is only five feet eleven inches and weighs 170 pounds."

But tragedy hit some of their cousins, with two drowned in separate accidents and consumption killing others at an early age.

Letters to Cape Breton relatives gave background details of a lifestyle that would have seemed strange to Canadian readers. Within sight of three volcanic cones, "cold probably since the days of Abraham", they could grow three crops of potatoes in one year. There were springs of hot water boiling up not far away, good for rheumatism and skin diseases. In the forest, "lovely tree ferns grow, some to a height of forty or fifty feet, with green fronds spread out like a gigantic sunshade. But the monarch of the forest is the kauri, a species of pine tree, general size a diameter of four to eight feet and a height of barrel without a limb of from sixty to eighty feet; but trees are often met with twenty feet in diameter."

"Dances are very frequent and continue all night," Angus Nicholson wrote. "They dance quadrilles, waltzes and polkas and I don't know what beside. I never attend them myself. I think God meant us for something more rational and useful than injuring our health dancing all night. We have a Mutual Improvement Association here which meets once a month, where we are given lectures, write essays and have debates."

And so, in Okaihau as in most other places, life went on; the elders improving their minds, many of the young ones reverting unconsciously to the way their ancestors had lived a century or more before, slipping out at night to enjoy music, dancing and the company of other high-spirited friends.

It is interesting that, in spite of the fact that a number of the Nova Scotians had served in the war with Napoleon, and earlier still in French Canada, the letters that I have seen say nothing about it. The world they describe was an intimate one. Over a generation or two perhaps it was possible to erase from clan or family memory what it was pointless to dwell on.

The earliest letter I have read was written on 10 April, 1850, by Hugh McKenzie to his friend Donald McLeod in Adelaide, South Australia. Donald, a son of Norman McLeod, had taken a cargo of local produce to Europe in a ship owned by members of the family, and later had gone to Australia where he worked as a journalist. Hugh, like the McLeods, was a native of Assynt in Sutherland where he was born in 1817. He seemed likely to remain a bachelor, a sober member of the Cape Breton community, until Mary Fraser caught his eye. Mary was to accompany her family on the *Margaret*. Hugh did not want to go, at that time anyway, and so, like a Nova Scotian Lochinvar, he carried her off to Boularderie Island where, a fortnight before the *Margaret* sailed, they were married by the Rev. James Fraser and stayed behind. Let it be said that, along with a son and two daughters, they rejoined their families in 1857, travelling on the *Spray*. They had five more children in New Zealand, among them N.R. McKenzie, like his father a notable teacher, and author of *The Gael Fares Forth*.

All this was in the future, however, when Hugh wrote to Donald, replying to a letter he had received a few weeks before. Donald had already been successfully urging a move from Nova Scotia to Australia and, as Hugh now told him, "The vessel intended to convey your friends thither is carried on with great dispatch. She is very strongly built, has an elegant model, and appears to be a first-rate 'clipper'. She will be a barque of nearly 300 tons. Your Reverend father is fully determined on leaving Cape Breton for Australia as early in the next Fall as possible, or at least before the navigation of this coast will be obstructed with ice."

Hugh mentioned one obstacle that could cause delay. Land values had dropped because of an economic depression, and the removal of a good number of settlers all at once would cause a further fall. The previous year's

This cottage in the Braigh was built in 1857 for Hugh McKenzie, great-grandson of Simon Fraser, who commanded the 78th Regiment of Fraser Highlanders at Quebec.

crops had turned out well, but reciprocal free trade with the United States had resulted in heavy competition in the fisheries off the coast. And, even in April, "we have still several feet of snow on the ground, and the weather extremely cold". However, Hugh said confidently, "...those who have made up their minds for Australia do not flinch or waver in their purpose, but manfully and perseveringly prosecute their design, and so will certainly surmount every difficulty which may arise to obstruct their plans, for 'Fortune favours the brave'."

Then there comes a significant passage in his letter: "I feel very grateful to you for your explicit description of New Zealand, for I was totally ignorant of its real characteristic until given by your kindness. You will be pleased to write me immediately on receipt hereof, in case I will not leave this place so early as is anticipated, and tell minutely of the state of the country, physically, politically, morally, so on, if you will have leisure at your disposal to do so."

Hugh relaxes a little as his "insipid rigmarole" draws to an end. "I am still as confirmed a 'bachelor' as yourself. Surely our temperaments in this respect are alike or, to use phrenological terms, our Amativeness and Adhesiveness are very small, but these organs are largely developed in our St Annian young men and women for they weekly get married in scores, notwithstanding the ominous depression of the times."

Not long after Donald in Australia had received that letter, his correspondent would have been married, starting his family of eight sons and daughters. So much for the conceit of bachelors! Mary his wife was the daughter of John Fraser, one of the leaders of the community and the descendant of Simon Fraser, of the 77th Regiment, Fraser Highlanders, who had taken his discharge after Quebec.

Highly articulate, possessing that special quality that helps the student happily along the paths of learning, Hugh was ideally suited to carrying out an important task at a critical time in the people's development. Gaelic would still be spoken commonly in the home and in the church but, without an ability to speak and to think in English, it would have been difficult for the young Cape Bretoners to make their way in the world when they left their homeland behind.

One of those who decided that Ontario was the place for his future was Hugh Matheson, another Assynt man, who left Clachtoll when he was twenty-four in 1818. From Pictou he went with many other followers of Norman McLeod to Cape Breton Island, taking with him his bride Christina McLeod. Their married life was a succession of tragedies, Christina dying in her ninth childbed. His second marriage was very different, although it had its share of hardship. Hugh and Margaret had five children under the age of thirteen when they went to Ontario in 1851 with, in the father's words, "a helpless family and scant means of maintenance. By hard work and good providence we surmounted our difficulties." He fell out with his family, and it was only about ten years before his death — at eighty-nine — that natural sentiment brought about a reconciliation.

"Religious animosity" was at the bottom of the rift. Hugh, even when he wrote to his nephew John at St Ann's in 1872, was a bitter man with a long memory for fancied and other hurts, revealed in this letter:

> In St Ann's in those days our social atmosphere was so much tainted that even the strictest bonds of natural affections were dissolved, and replaced by hatred and persecution as far as the civil law would permit, and very often a step beyond, and all that caused by "Norman heresy" of which (persecution if I may call it so) I got my good share of suffering. I was of necessity alienated from my mother's children without any other crime imputed to me by man, but endeavouring to preserve entirely the dictates of my conscience in defending truth against error. I hope the above is sufficient apology for any neglect of communicating with friends, especially when I have reason to suspect that such friends might be prejudiced against me.

Communication was made more difficult after he went to Ontario because his brother Angus, living at St Ann's, could neither read nor write.

Rather sanctimoniously, Hugh continues his letter to his nephew John:

> I wish you would notice that I say nothing prejudicial to Norman personally, as he is now in a state beyond human comprehension, but a

man's good or evil doctrine or example may long survive himself, and may bear good or evil fruit to others. Ancient Jerusalem was destroyed by God's judgement for the sins of King Manasseh long after Manasseh was believed to be in heaven.

Elsewhere there are other revealing glimpses of the way life went on in Nova Scotia and in Canada. Alexander McLeod at Kincardine, Ontario, wrote to his old friend Murdoch McKenzie back in St Ann's in 1855, before the *Gertrude* sailed:

I am very sorry to hear that Donald McLeod and the Macdonalds are going away [to New Zealand]. When I'll think of the happy times we used to have in the Glen and will never meet again, I'll feel lonesome. Tell your father that my father says that he is very glad that he did not go to New Zealand, and it is a wonderful thing if those that are going do not repent, for he did come but a short distance [to Ontario] and he felt it troublesome enough.

The letter from his old friend in Ontario was not sufficient to keep Murdoch McKenzie in St Ann's. Little more than a year later, Murdoch was on his way to New Zealand on the *Spray*. From Cape Town he wrote to his friend Roderick Fraser in St Ann's, and Roderick replied in September, 1857, giving a vivid picture of the situation in Cape Breton which, in the last few years, had lost many hundreds of its inhabitants to New Zealand and Canada. To some with long memories, the effect must have seemed as debilitating as the Highland Clearances. Although a number of families had already paid half their passage money for the next ship, some had changed their minds because of recent news from New Zealand.

"Fortune-seekers," said Roderick, "are beginning to fear that New Zealand is not an exception to other places in regard of acquiring a fortune without troubles and a chance of disappointment." The main disappointment was "the sad and solemn account of Mrs McLeod's decease, for some who had promised themselves the pleasure of seeing her and enjoying the happiness of her association after their arrival". A well-deserved tribute to one who had suffered sad bereavements including the loss of three sons from typhoid in Australia; who had endured the rigours of raising a family, in different countries and always in difficult conditions; and whose whole life had been lived in the shadow of a strong and sometimes overbearing husband, although he seems to have always been considerate of his gentle and delicate Mary.

Murdoch McKenzie had some very good correspondents. John McLeod writes in a warm and effervescent style. His 1859 letter is full of news about friends, marriages and bereavements, those who have gone away and those who have returned home. He is far from the type of Highlander, rigid and uncommunicative, that some have depicted. Can one detect a romantic undercurrent in this paragraph?

> I was at your uncle Kenneth's [Matheson] a few days previous to my leaving home, they are all well. I saw Peggy [Kenneth's daughter] after coming home from the States, she went there sixteen months ago and got married last January in Manchester, Mass; her husband is a stoveliner and bricklayer by trade and I believe he is doing well. He did not come to St Ann's with her, she said that he was busy at the time. She is the same wild and laughing Peggy, looks nice, only pale and thinner than usual. She enquired earnestly about you, asking if ever you wrote to me or if you have mentioned her name in the letter you wrote from the Cape of Good Hope. She complained hard that you never wrote to her, she is to go back in August.

The *Ellen Lewis* sailed for New Zealand in December 1859, the last of the six ships to carry the migrants from Nova Scotia. John McLeod's name is on the passenger list. But what became of the "wild and laughing Peggy", who had gone to Massachusetts, I have not been able to discover.

The Clan McRae crops up in a letter written to John McKay by his nephew, Alexander McKenzie Junior, in 1864. Alexander's home was South Side, Boularderie; he taught school at Kempt Head where he had £40 and his board. He writes about Rory McRae who, he says, "is the greatest merchant in Baddeck, with the exception of one man from Nova Scotia named Tupper. Rory had been a clerk at Charley Campbell's for a number of years. And the time that Charley became a Tory they fell out and Rory commenced business himself and now is superior to Charley in business, but Charley says it was by his money that he started. He calls Rory's property his own yet."

Alexander is adept at passing on the details, large or small, of life in a Cape Breton that had lost so many of its citizens so recently. "Murdoch my uncle is still living and dawdles about between the house and the barn, and he is as good as ever to take in water for the girls. Mr Munro is as good as ever in regard to the Temperance cause. We are not as great in friendship with Munro's family; but we are not bad friends."

The winter had been fine, such as they had never had before in Alexander's experience. And, as so often happens in such a situation, there had been a lot of sickness. "It is just what we call 'the cold', but in most of the cases this year, it was accompanied by a fever, so bad that some persons were confined to bed for five or six weeks, and some have died." He estimated that one-third of the people had been affected since winter set in. From this distance, it seems possible that Cape Breton had experienced its first influenza epidemic.

There is mention of Captain McKenzie (the Prince) coming to Cape

Breton — he paid a number of trading visits there. A sad little story tells of Angus McKay, who built a house where he lived alone on Philip McRae's place in Middle River. "But the Middle River scoundrels commenced to make fun of him by throwing stones on the house when he would be asleep. They carried on that sort of work until they at last made him take his house to pieces and drag it up to the woods about a mile and there he lives now, all alone."

One more hopeful story from Middle River tells of gold-mining the previous summer about a mile from the Drover's place. "It proved first-rate," writes Alexander. Those who were washing made good wages averaging about £6 a month for every man which was very good, when they had not the right means for washing… Coal-mining is carried on to a great extent in Cape Breton since the beginning of the year 1860 and there is every indication of more improvements being made."

Coal-mining continued to flourish, but the goldrush to Middle River would bring little in the way of riches before it fizzled out.

Chapter Nine

Mary McBain:
A Journey from North Uist

THEY HAD MADE THEIR WAY, slowly, across the island to Lochmaddy, carrying their few possessions and making time for the little ones: Mary McBain herself, her father, red-headed Donald, his young second wife Catherine, and the rest of the family. Lachlan was twenty-four, then came Mary two years younger, and then Marion, Ann, Catherine, Murdoch, Christy, John and baby Alexander. The last four were much younger, being Donald's children by his second wife.

They had left Baleshare, their croft and ten bleak acres, under a lowering sky, harsh December weather with the wind whipping almost unobstructed across the island. North Uist, remote in the Outer Hebrides, had become a hungry place. Donald did not want to leave, for it had been home to the McBains for generations, but he knew he had to go. Starvation and an early death were the only alternative. Now, a gruelling journey would take one of them to a grave in Ireland, the rest to Australia and Mary, after three years, to a happy home in New Zealand.

And now at last they saw the steamer *Celt* coming into Lochmaddy, a sight never to be forgotten — paddles thrashing through great seas, smoke streaming from the funnel and blending with the spray from the breaking surf as the little vessel butted through the waves. Mary looked at the steamer curiously as it was secured at the wharf. It was easy to understand why she was late arriving. The box covering one of the paddles had been smashed by a great wave which, they were told, had also broken the ribs of the helmsman. Down below, out of the reach of the weather, there were already ninety-five emigrants from Harris. Taken from the estates of Lady Dunmore, they had been loaded on to the *Celt* in lighter boats in about three hours, during a heavy storm of wind and rain. Mr Chant, the man in charge of the operation, had plenty on his mind, but his feelings show through in his report to the emigration commissioners:

> The most painful scene I have ever witnessed… Women hung on the necks of friends, and were in some cases removed by force. As the vessel steamed out of the bay they stood on the poop, threw their arms in the air giving full vent to their grief, as they gazed for the last time on the black peaty glen and bleak rocky hills over which they had been accustomed to roam, and to which they were so devotedly attached.

126

They had, to some degree, reconciled themselves to leaving their island, but for the McBains and the other families it was not easy to take the final step. Embarkation time was noon, but by the end of the day about sixty of the 164 migrants had not reported. Messengers were sent out and the reluctant travellers were at Lochmaddy two days late. There was, however, one extra would-be migrant. James Macdonald, from the Perth settlement, did not want to be parted from Margaret McAskill who was going away with her family. He was warned that, if he continued to stow away, he would be prosecuted. He countered by declaring in the presence of witnesses that she was his wife — a legal form of marriage which would make it impossible for her to go without him. In addition, some of his young friends threatened that, unless James could go, they would upset plans by preventing the migration of some of the families that had already been approved. Once again it was Mr Chant who had to make a decision. Laws must not be defied, he reasoned. James was convicted under the Passenger Act and fined one pound, or fourteen days' imprisonment. After five days in custody other emigrants "whipped in" to pay the fine and he was discharged. Rather than have the schedule of migrants disturbed, Mr Chant decided to allow the young man to travel. A minister on the migrant vessel would "solemnise the marriage according to the rites of the Church of Scotland". And so the romance of the twenty-year-old bridegroom and his twenty-one-year-old sweetheart got away to a promising start.

This little story is possibly worth telling because it suggests that, in spite of being treated at times with a certain sanctimonious condescension proper for largely unlettered savages, the natives of North Uist, in this year of 1851, were not as naive and unsophisticated as some people thought they should be.

But meanwhile the McBains, along with most of the other migrants, were waiting in the cramped between-decks of the *Celt* for the late arrivals to appear. The *Celt*'s sea-going certificate allowed the carriage of 224 passengers, but on the application of Sir John McNeil, on behalf of the powerful Highland and Island Emigration Society, the officer in charge was given authority to carry more if he thought it could be done safely. Mr Chant, the responsible officer, set the figure at 350 passengers of all ages, and with these tightly stowed down below, out of the ferocious weather, the *Celt* left for Campbeltown, near the entrance to the Firth of Clyde, early on a Friday morning. There was a gale from the west-south-west, bringing up a heavy beam sea. Mr Chant gives a vivid description of what followed:

> In the course of a short time the people became very sick, especially the women, who were much alarmed at the rolling of the vessel, and they shrieked dreadfully every time the sea struck us. Depression of spirits brought on by exhaustion, seasickness and hysterics rendered strong

127

stimulants necessary. By the application of vinegar to the head, warm water to the feet and a liberal use of hot brandy and water, some soon recovered; but there were others who were unconscious for hours, and required mustard to the soles of the feet. Even this strong remedy was very slow in giving relief. At noon it blew a hurricane and we were obliged to run for Canna harbour, which we made a little before dark. The women suffered greatly during the night, and required constant attention.

There was to be another day of seasickness and misery in close quarters, with no means of finding relief apart from the ministrations of the good Mr Chant, before the *Celt* drew into the sheltered waters of Campbeltown, and the migrants could attempt to sort themselves out.

There are a few eyewitness descriptions of their arrival at Campbeltown; some of them blandly designed to present the best possible picture to the reader. But others seem to bear the mark of truth. "On her voyage from Harris and North Uist, the *Celt* had a stormy passage that would have been perilous in a less efficient vessel. Some of the women were on board for five days and nights with their infants in their arms..." It is not surprising that, wracked by seasickness and fear, many of them were still exhausted when they reached harbour. "The women did not seem to be conscious of where they were or what had brought them there. The men looked dark and stern, like men about to confront danger, and not likely to shrink from the encounter, but relaxed into a smile at the first kind word."

Then there is the terse comment from Mr Mollath, the surgeon: "The greater portion [on arrival at Campbeltown] was exceedingly dirty and very many prostrated by excessive seasickness." Ideal conditions, as he would know, for contagious disease to develop.

The McBains and their fellow travellers would have known that they were to travel in an English warship to Australia, but its size and dimensions would have been far beyond what their wildest imaginings could create. HMS *Hercules*, built as a 74-gun, line-of-battle ship, measured 176 feet on her gun deck and had an extreme breadth of over 47 feet. The *Celt* drew alongside, and the migrants were mustered through hatches to the lower deck. A long, wide open space, this provided the main sleeping and eating area. There were narrow wooden bunks in tiers from floor to ceiling, and partitions to provide some privacy between the sexes. Here the migrants from Harris and North Uist waited while the indomitable *Celt* steamed away to bring a further 375 men, women and children from Skye. Mr Chant writes:

Lord MacDonald was at Armadale, and watched the embarkation of his people with great interest. The emigrants from Sleat had been collected, housed and fed at the Castle for some days before our arrival. When the embarkation had been completed, I went on shore to take leave of his

Lordship. He was much affected at parting with his people. Indeed, his feelings so overcame him that he was obliged to give vent to his grief, and I left him in tears.

Lord MacDonald certainly had enough problems to reduce most men to tears, apart from the wrench it must have given him to see the final departure of so many loyal clansmen. In *The Highland Clearances*, John Prebble tells some of the story:

In 1849 Lord MacDonald, who had a wide property on Skye and North Uist, debts of £200,000 and impatient creditors, decided to evict 110 families, more than 600 people, from a square mile of flat ground in the north of North Uist. After violent confrontations with police brought from the mainland they were compelled to sign a bond of emigration under threat of pulling their houses down. They were crowded into some narrow, swampy spots, their former cultivated land added to the huge farms of the tacksmen. In July, 1850 they were still there; in September, they were moved to Loch Efort in the south of the island and each family was given twenty acres of land. One season of failure finally broke their morale and they petitioned MacDonald to send them to Australia. He eventually agreed that those who were young and healthy could go to Australia.

There are some inconsistencies between Prebble's report and the McBain situation. Donald and his family were not in the Loch Efort area; and the family lists from the Highland and Island Emigration Society state that they lived on Baleshare Island. It also mentions that Donald had ten acres as his holding. Prebble has some startling stories in his book. He says that, "On North Uist, when clansmen refused to leave their beloved island, the minister used his dogs to round them up. Elsewhere, the biggest estates, the largest flocks, belonged to the minister, while his people starved on the bleak hillsides."

One might say that HMS *Hercules* had been a victim of the peace that followed the defeat of Napoleon. Launched in September, 1815, three months after the Battle of Waterloo, she was laid up in reserve for twenty-one years and her first real duty came in 1852 with her refitting as an emigrant transport. The need was there, for gold had been discovered in Victoria, upcountry from Melbourne and, when the news spread to the rich pastoral land of South Australia, the sheep stations were depleted of labour as just about every young shepherd or worker took off for his share of the wealth to be dug from the soil. Something had to be done if the sheep industry was not to grind to a halt.

The solution in Britain was to form the Highland and Island Emigration Society, designed to overcome two pressing problems: the Australian farming crisis and the overpopulation of the Highlands. The society had a formidable committee, under the patronage of Prince Albert and including such men as the Duke of Buccleuch, the Earl of Shaftesbury, Sir Charles Trevelyan, Baron de Rothschild and two leading clan chiefs, MacLeod of MacLeod and Cluny Macpherson. Apart from interviewing landlords, commissioning transport and working out a way in which the whole project could be financed, they hit on a master stroke: the aim would be to send away whole families instead of individuals. In this way, they hoped, the young men would not go rushing off to the goldfields. It was also important to balance the sexes.

There is one report that, because young unattached men would not be acceptable, they were scouring the neighbouring island of Benbecula in search of wives. In this respect, the McBain entry in the society's family register has a special interest. Donald McBain had been twice married, it states, and had four children under the age of twelve. His passage was approved, however, "in consideration of the adult females the family contained". It could be said that the decision paid off. By his two marriages, Donald had seventy grandchildren, many of them in New Zealand.

Once aboard the *Hercules*, their troubles were not over. Christmas Day, if it concerned them at all, would have been a miserable time, and New Year's Day even worse. The *Hercules* sailed from Campbeltown on December 26, into the teeth of a storm that split her sails and left her at the mercy of the elements until she struggled into Rothesay "after five days of intense anxiety and great fatigue", in the words of Captain Baynton. "The ports could be opened only once since we left Campbeltown, and the emigrants have suffered much in consequence, many of the women very ill."

There was an ominous sentence in the captain's report to the society. "You will be sorry to hear we have a case of fever [typhus] and another of smallpox and measles on board."

It was not until sixteen days later that the *Hercules* was able to continue her voyage. By then, the morale and health of the migrants had been improved by the addition of fresh meat to their menu; ropes in the rigging, broken by the ferocity of the storm, had been replaced, and the torn sails repaired. On January 16 she sailed from Rothesay, and on January 20 arrived at Cork, with nearly eight hundred still on board, and with virulent smallpox prevailing. This is how a report to the Land and Emigration Commissioners described it:

> Although it would have been of the greatest importance to remove the passengers on their arrival from an infected to a fresh and healthy atmosphere as well with a view to their restoration, also purify and prepare the ship for so long a voyage, it was found impossible for a whole week to take any measure for doing so as there was no hulk or receiving ship here to which they could be transferred.

130

Mary McBain, who survived a horror journey from North Uist in the early 1850s that took her to Australia and then to Waipu as the wife of Ewen McInnes. A singer and bard, she loved "the old language" and never learned English. Inset: Beulah Williamson, grand-daughter of Mary, died in 1997 at the age of 95. Her lively mind held countless stories from the past.

When it was suggested that the cases of smallpox should be put ashore at Queenstown, the townspeople rose up in protest. Who should go ashore, the sick or the healthy? The argument continued while the numbers of sick and dead continued to rise, with Lord Palmerston at Westminster and the Lord Lieutenant of Ireland, at Dublin Castle, having their say. In the end, those ill with smallpox were taken to the Haulbowline Hospital; the hulk *Duc d'Orleans* arrived and harboured those with fever; the migrants who were still healthy went to the old military barracks. The facts are hard to credit. The *Hercules* had arrived with twenty-seven cases of smallpox among the emigrants and seven among the ship's crew.

The crewmen went to hospital instantly; a full week passed before the sick emigrants, now numbering thirty-two, were allowed to be landed. And for an incredible seven weeks Mary McBain and her family, along with more than seven hundred other Hebrideans, remained cooped up in the stifling atmosphere of the warship before they were disembarked.

In the barracks, their new home, conditions were shocking. "No proper segregation could be maintained," wrote Surgeon Mollath, "and it was only when the disease became well marked that the numerous cases were sent to Haulbowline or the hulk. In consequence of this," he added, "when the emigrants were re-embarked there appeared to be a smell of disease among the greater part of them."

The barracks, built to hold two hundred, were forced to accept over six hundred; although that number gradually dropped as death and illness took its toll. The healthy went into the barracks on March 14. The weeks crawled slowly by. Nearly three months had passed since the migrants had left their island homes and there seemed no likely end, save death, to their present torments. Faith, that imponderable quality, continued to sustain most of them but it was sorely tried. As the Scottish historian, T.C. Smout, wrote in *A Century of the Scottish People*, "As long as the Bible continued to be regarded as the inspired word of God, it was very difficult to avoid the conclusion that He was eternally hellbent, dooming to everlasting torment most created souls."

Then the thing that the McBains had feared came to pass. Lachlan went down with smallpox and was taken to the hospital. Just about this time, a decision was made that, with the sickness continuing to increase, it would be prudent to send the healthy away in the *Hercules*, the sick to follow in other ships as they recovered. It was a time of confusion and despair. The surgeon, the minister and the matron had all been taken ill; the surgeon and the matron died at about the time that Lachlan went to hospital. Left behind in Queenstown, he would need a family member to look after him and to accompany him to Australia when he recovered. Mary was chosen to stay. Then Lachlan died. The *Hercules* sailed for Australia shortly afterwards with 380 of the original 760 migrants on board. Mary was not among them. Mourning her beloved brother, with the rest of her family departing, she had to stay behind in quarantine.

This is how her grand-daughter Beulah, one of the last alive to remember her, described Mary: "She was a happy person, with laughing eyes and no severity anywhere about her. And she never mentioned, to me or in my hearing, the terrible things she and her family suffered after they left North Uist. Nor did she speak about the island itself, where McBains had lived for generations; nor about her favourite brother Lachlan."

Suddenly, as I write, I am overwhelmed by a rush of emotion. Images and words come to life in my head. These are no cut-out figures from a page of history, to be picked up, moved about, studied objectively. I feel Mary alive in me, her great-grandson, as she is in so many other descendants. I see her there, seemingly isolated in the press of people. For all her life she has had the support of family, but now she is alone, her brother dead in a strange land, her father Donald and his wife, her other brothers and sisters gone away. What to do? Mary, we know, drew on a deep well of courage, an inborn faith; not sunk in despair, not with resignation but with an almost serene acceptance of what each day would bring. For that is how she was right to the end of a long life.

Meanwhile, the *Hercules* sailed south, the smell of disease gradually fading. The passengers carried with them personal reports made to the Highland and Island Emigration Society when the emigrants were being chosen. In much the same way, one feels, a herd of cattle might have been checked, virtues and defects set down objectively. Here are some of the comments:

> "A first-rate family, all capable of Labour (Seven children from 28–13), the girls good house servants, the men accustomed to herd sheep and cattle."
> From Harris: "Very destitute family lately dispossessed of his croft."
> From North Uist: "Man seems to have suffered from want of food, wife and children (7 in all) healthy."
> "Very poor family, man reported to be a good labourer."
> "No stock or crop. Very poor family but good one for Australia (9 children from 25–5)."
> "Very destitute family — children nearly naked."
> "All of the daughters have been in service and can dairy."
> "Had neither land, cattle or employment. Very poor and destitute family."
> "Dispossessed of croft in May. Employed at the fishing for a few months."
> "Has maintained herself by knitting in winter and outdoor work in summer."
> "Annually to herring fishing. Carting stone to Raasay earning about 6s 6d a week."
> "Mother maintains herself by spinning. Can earn about 3s 5d a week."

They were assisted in various ways. Colonial funds had been set aside to pay for the passage of efficient labourers; owners of properties from which the migrants departed would pay one-third of the total cost; the migrants themselves would pay what they could, and they also signed promissory notes issued by the society which they were expected to repay from the abundance of their Australian earnings.

Mary eventually sailed in the *Olivia*, one of twelve ships that took the rest of the migrants, in dribs and drabs, to Australia. But some did not sail. The bones of Lachlan and fifty-five others lay in Irish graves.

Did Mary find the rest of her family when she arrived in Adelaide? One of her daughters, reviving a tale that she had heard when she was very small, said Mary had to go seeking blindly for any trace of them. It certainly seems that, when HMS *Hercules* unloaded what was surely one of the strangest cargoes to be carried by an English warship, there was work waiting for everyone and they would have been hustled away to all parts of the state. Her duty done, the *Hercules* departed for Hong Kong, there to act as a floating hospital for the many servicemen fallen victim to fever, syphilis and other diseases in that insalubrious port. The McBains seemed to fall on their feet. There is a portrait of Donald, a big man with flaming red hair, wide-spaced eyes under a lowering brow. He is standing rather awkwardly with one hand on the shoulder of his wife Catherine; he wearing a dark frock coat, she in sober black sitting beside him, submissively it might seem, a brooch at her throat her only ornament. Nowhere is there a mention of Mary in those early days. The first hard facts come with her marriage in Adelaide to Ewen McInnes on February 20, 1855. There were several migrants on the *Hercules* named Ewen McInnes, but this one, son of John McInnes, of Portree, Skye, had reached South Australia by a different route. One of Norman McLeod's most firm supporters, he had sailed from Nova Scotia on the *Margaret*, which arrived at Adelaide in April, 1852. When McLeod and most of the others moved on to Melbourne, Ewen stayed behind. He was still there when the first party of Nova Scotians sailed on the *Gazelle* to Auckland, across the Tasman Sea, in September 1853.

Ewen was a practical man who could also plan ahead. He was determined to have a farm of his own, but he knew that, to develop a raw block of land with any efficiency, it was necessary to possess a certain amount of capital. There was work in South Australia, well-paid work with so much of the labour force having caught gold fever and disappeared. Ewen worked hard, saved his money and then, at the most favourable time, discovered Mary — Gaelic-speaking like himself, industrious, young and charming. He had kept in touch with passengers on the *Margaret*; there were others related to him on board, and the link with New Zealand was strengthened with the arrival there of his father from Nova Scotia on the *Gertrude*, third of the migrant fleet, which reached Auckland in December, 1853. And so there were friends and relatives in plenty to greet Ewen and his bride when they reached the new country. There was also land to clear, to prepare for crops and cattle.

What of Mary in this new, strange setting, memories of her well-loved brother still fresh in her mind, her father and family scattered across the broad, sunburnt South Australian countryside? She was happily introduced into a sociable community with its own Nova Scotian qualities but not too different from what she had known in North Uist. Scotland and Nova Scotia had suffered the effects of the potato blight, the decline in fishing returns. Here in New Zealand they hoped all would be well. Mary lost contact with her Australian kin. Indeed, it was not until a few years ago that this contact was resumed through the activity of Anne Finlayson, a fourth-generation descendant of Mary, who diligently sorted through much confusing detail to discover where the McBains had gone.

Anne lived in Cairns, in the north of Queensland, about as far as one could get from Adelaide. She often spent her lunch-time in the Cairns

Genealogy Office, where a friend, Pam McLennan, was on the staff. Quite by chance they discovered that Pam's husband Wayne had a great-uncle who had married Mary McBain's sister, Catherine. His name was Alexander McQueen, and he had also travelled from North Uist to Adelaide on HMS *Hercules.*

Ewen and Mary thrived in their new environment. Worship at Norman McLeod's church, about five miles from their farm, filled their Sundays, and also gave sociable Mary the chance to talk to the other women about the things dear to the female heart: babies, health, spinning, singing. Before very long there were five children in the McInnes cottage, all nurtured in the old ways, with a proper pride in the language and legends of the Gael. Ewen was a mature man of thirty-four, twelve years older than Mary, when they married. He knew what was right, unhindered by doubts, and was equally confident that his children would follow his example. Mary was gentler by nature, more accommodating to the changed viewpoint of the younger ones. The three girls, Catherine, Anne and Margaret, had plenty to occupy them at home, but the world, even in conservative Waipu, did not pass them by. Later, there were dances — held on bridges on the long summer evenings — and Mary would help the girls to slip away after Ewen had gone to bed. The farm, limited in production during the developing years, would not support the full family. The two sons, Dan and Sam, went away to work as bushmen in the kauri forests. When the great trees were felled and trimmed, the squared logs would be dragged by bullock teams down to the harbour, to be taken either to Australia or to other parts of New Zealand where building timber was in short supply. Later, however, they returned to the North River and farmed there for the rest of their lives.

Ewen McInnes was seventy-six when he died in 1897; Mary survived him for another twenty-one years. For many of those years she lived on her own, with her sons' farms nearby. Her grand-daughter Beulah Williamson remembered visiting her there regularly as a little girl. "She was lovely. So soft. So warm. When I walked with mother up to the North River house to see Granny, her eyes would fill with tears and she would hug me, crooning in Gaelic 'malina, malina', which I think meant 'my darling'. She would keep holding me tight as if I was her baby.

"Granny was eighty-five when she died. She had been with her daughter, Auntie Margaret, for some years. They had a lot of fun together. Granny could speak only broken English. She would start off a sentence in English but before long it would have become Gaelic. They'd roar with laughter, in which Granny would join. When her grandsons, the Finlayson boys, were away at the Great War, they all wrote special letters to her. They loved her too."

Alex Gow Finlayson, who had married Margaret, farmed near Maungaturoto. Their house, as Beulah recalls it, was large, full of people and just as full of fun. They were a lively family. Margaret, like her two sisters Catherine — Beulah's mother — and Anne, was an excellent horsewoman and rode in competitions everywhere.

"The Finlayson girls had gone to school in Auckland, and most winters the family took a house there for a couple of months. They had a wide circle of friends, in country as well as town, and Auntie Margaret and her children loved to entertain and be entertained. She was tall, straight-backed, beautiful and kind. She ran the big house easily and efficiently. The girls had everything they wanted but they were also taught to cook and to manage a home. The farm was big and prosperous and there was plenty of butter and eggs."

One of the daughters, another Mary, lived into her nineties. She was alert, very intelligent and forthright, and played a keen hand of bridge almost to the end. The two Marys, Granny and grand-daughter, got on very well together. In spite of her lack of English, nothing much passed Granny by. Among visitors in the years before the Great War, Beulah recalled with a chuckle, was Eddie Aickin.

"He had his eye on young Mary, but the war came and Eddie went off with the New Zealand troops. Writing home, he did not forget Granny, with whom he had had so many conversations in which she gave her own entertaining version of the English language. The war hadn't destroyed Eddie's sense of humour. She must have thought she was talking to him, in the old way, when they read her his final sentence in one letter: 'You make it them to look after you while I'm away'!"

By the time Eddie and Mary were married, her father had died and her mother was living in Auckland. She gave the bride away herself. "I can see her now," said Beulah, "standing there erect and proud before the minister."

Mary McBain, who became Mary McInnes, lived for over sixty years after her marriage to Ewen. She had had her bad times as well as her happy times, but I'm sure she would have felt it had been a good life. Her old language, which English never replaced, was very important to her. She was singer as well as bard. It would be good to hear some of the songs and stories she loved to tell. On Ewen's tombstone there is an inscription which she composed. It reads:

> Duine cothromach bha beusach air
> an robh eagal De. Fior Gaidheal aig
> an robh mor speis do chaint.

In an English translation: "An able (or steadfast) man, upright in his

The Waipu cemetery, serene and tranquil, with the ocean not far away.

life, in whom was the fear of God. A true Gael who had a great love for his language."

And so, in God's good time, Mary was buried next to Ewen in the cemetery at Waipu, a beautiful place, serene and quiet, looking out to the ocean which had brought them to this land.

It all seems a long way from the ten-acre farm on North Uist, from the horror voyage of the *Hercules*, from the girl who, a stranger in a strange land, met another Gaelic-speaking wanderer and established a new and vital family.

Chapter Ten

Settling In

I DON'T KNOW JUST HOW Cockatoo McLeod got his nickname, but there is one thing certain — it was a very necessary thing to have. He was one of three Donald J. McLeods flourishing in the Waipu area at that time, and without a nickname he would have found life even more confusing than usual. Cockatoo was one of the first generation to be born and brought up in the new country; a sturdy breed facing different challenges from their fathers, but fashioned also to a great degree by the beliefs and lifestyle of the Nova Scotian homeland.

On his farm at Finlaysons Brook, Cockatoo had as a neighbour and close friend D.A. Finlayson, known generally by his initials instead of his Christian name which could also have led to ambiguity. At a later date "D.A." would tell, with some sadness, a story about Cockatoo. "Plans were being made to celebrate the arrival of the first migrants at Waipu," he said. "Cockatoo had a most unholy hatred of the Reverend Norman, and objected strongly to a proposal to place a memorial window in the church. He felt so strongly that he wrote me a four-page letter, amazed that I should be willing to go on the centennial committee and agree to the memorial window. I wrote back that, with the passage of years, it was time that so much bitterness was forgotten. Cockatoo never spoke to me again.

"Strong feelings," D.A. concluded, "tended to stay with the Nova Scotians. Friendships could end — and did so — very often over what might seem trivial disagreements."

This was not something that began with the move to New Zealand. Stubbornness, or strong-mindedness, went back a long way with the Highlander, and it was not confined only to the men.

"My grandfather Roderick Finlayson, eventually a passenger on the *Highland Lass*, didn't want to go," D.A. would recall. "But he was married to Catherine McLean, a strict follower of Norman McLeod. Roderick was planning to go with his other brothers out Vancouver way. Catherine said she was following McLeod whether my grandfather came or not. A strong-minded woman, indeed!"

Religion, of the Cape Breton kind, held sway in the Finlayson home. Young Finlayson remembers visiting his grandparents one Sunday. He was playing around outside, a barefooted six-year-old, when his grandfather saw him.

"He was a big dark man, with a beaver to match. He looked at me and growled: 'You mauna whistle on the Sabbath, laddie!' The words stayed in my mind."

Changes in religious attitudes may have come only slowly. But for the majority of the migrants who exchanged a farm in Cape Breton for land in New Zealand, although the basic agricultural principles stayed much the same, differences in their application brought them into a strange new world. That most of them adapted so quickly says much for their versatility.

It was, in many cases, a matter of adapting or going under. The McKenzies of Limestone Hill had moved, literally, into a different world from what their fathers knew. It was strong country, fertile on its steep faces, with strange shapes of eroded limestone, like exotic sculpture, breaking through the soil or scattering huge boulders down the valley slopes. Where the bush had been cleared the grass grew well; the cattle were good and strong. They were also pretty wild and had never seen anything approaching civilisation. For the McKenzies of Limestone Hill they offered a challenge. Sometimes the men would win, sometimes the cattle.

The railway from Auckland to the northern settlements had just been opened, with the nearest railway station at Oakleigh about ten difficult miles away. A mob of cattle, mostly two-, three- and four-year-old, were persuaded to come down from the hills and, during a long day, were driven down to Oakleigh. The holding yards in those days were made of anything that came to hand, but the cattle seemed tired and went in behind the makeshift fences without too much trouble.

Then the train came in and began to shunt. The big wheels moved slowly, half hidden in great clouds of steam, a sight that made the cattle back up in fear against the back fence of the yards. The railwaymen did not know what to expect. Then a piercing whistle sounded. The cattle, their eyes rolling, turned and burst through the side of the pens as if they were made of wet paper and, with the ground shaking as they went, headed for home and the country they knew.

It was, in a way, a measure of the adaptability of these transplanted Nova Scotians that they could tell this story later — and laugh as they did so.

Age can bring a golden glow to memories of childhood; Mrs Malcolm McLeod's own memories of "settling in" on a new farm at Waipu are full of happiness and delight in simple pleasures. She arrived with her parents, Hugh and Catherine McLeod, on the *Ellen Lewis*, and lived first in a shack belonging to relatives in the village. Their land was six miles out through the bush. Every Monday her father loaded the week's provisions and his tiny daughter on his back and set out for the roughly marked section where he would build his home. Help would come from a neighbour who, in time-honoured fashion, he would later help with his own building.

But first he had to get shelter from rain and sun. A whare, or hut, made from the fronds of a nikau fern, came first. Then he began to clear space for his house, for a simple garden and for the sowing of grass seed to sustain a beast or two. Hugh felled a kauri tree which, with his neighbour's help, was sawn into planks, sufficient for a four-roomed house.

Mrs McLeod would recall with joy those early days when she would play at housekeeping in the lonely clearing and keep her father company. She did not want to leave when Saturday came round and they rejoined her mother in the settlement, making their way along a dark track through thick bush. Hugh McLeod was a versatile man, and his life gave this quality plenty of scope. He had been a teacher in Nova Scotia. In New Zealand he became, of necessity, a builder; his cattle thrived in the bush which supplemented his pasture and the young steers, trained as working bullocks, brought good prices. He tanned leather from which he made boots for his family and neighbours. He also cut out clothing for men and boys. In a matter-of-fact way he and John Munro brought a cargo of flour from Auckland to Waipu in an open boat along a coast that, then as now, offered danger in plenty. He died while comparatively young, leaving a widow and eight children. They stayed on the land that Hugh had developed and, through hard work and the mutual help system that had come to New Zealand with the migrants, built a prosperous farm.

It could be said that, in some ways, the first arrivals had an easier introduction to the new life. The land fringing the coast was mostly flat and largely clad in fern and teatree, much easier to clear than the bush. This could be burned, and crops or grass seed sown in the ashes in the springtime. The principal crops were potatoes and corn. Some wheat was grown, but oats, still the favourite for porridge, had to be brought from Auckland. The easily worked land near the settlement itself meant that, in a surprisingly short time local produce, including cattle, could be sold in Auckland or exchanged for other goods. And so the settlement survived and flourished.

But looming in the background over the land which the migrants on the *Margaret*, the *Highland Lass* and the *Gertrude* took up, was the forest. In Nova Scotia they had been well accustomed to forest, but how different it was from this!

The forests they had known near St Ann's had contained trees of many kinds and varied uses. Some were softwoods, easily worked. Others, such as the mountain ash, were hardwoods. Whatever they were, their virtues became familiar over thirty years, and full use was made of them. But chiefly the migrants remembered, nostalgically, how the forest would, at times, blaze with colour, strong and splendid and somehow friendly, so different from the bush they saw in New Zealand with its muted shades of green. The Cape Breton forest, to their backward-looking eyes, had shape and

Kauri logs, burnt standing timber and cattle — the story of the first pioneering years.

form, a kind of natural discipline. The bush that closed in around Waipu was a riotous mixture of wilderness gone mad: giant kauri trees with flawless cylindrical trunks losing themselves in the vague green of the upper air; tree ferns, black and curving under the weight of their hanging fronds; dead trees crumbling to the ground or supported by a network of vines; smaller shrubs and mosses, masked in green, giving an impression of turbulent, unrestrained energy; saplings, with all the beauty of youth, that would in a century or two themselves be giants; all in a luxuriant, tangled confusion through which it was difficult, at times impossible, to make any progress.

Some bushmen have told me how overwhelmed they had been when the bush first closed around them, the night, and a vast silence, claiming them as they sought the comfort of their blankets. But the men from Nova Scotia, and their sons, quickly came to terms with this new environment. They attacked the bush with axe, saw and fire as if it was an enemy. Once it was destroyed, they would be able to build homes, barns, get on with living. Later, when the fever and the urgency had died, many a farmer would say: "We wasted so much good timber; we did away with so much beauty." And they would look, with some regret, at stands of native bush that had survived. But there were still some who affirmed that, if a choice had to be made between grass and forest, grass must win.

The Birdgrove McLeans, one family among many with similar impulses, would have been too busy slashing and sweating to think for long of beauty destroyed. Their land was south through the Braigh from the Waipu centre.

141

John and Dolina McLean had nine children, and there was at all times plenty of work to keep their hands and minds occupied. Clearing the bush proceeded logically: the men cleared the trees, the children tackled the undergrowth. The kauri was milled but the other trees were left to dry and were burned at the end of summer. A few years later, the stumps of the trees were levered out and burnt.

When seed had been sown and the crops came to maturity, there was more work to do. Wheat was harvested with a sickle; afterwards, the ground had to be cultivated to prevent the regeneration of fern and teatree. There were potatoes to be dug and stored; crops to be gathered. Ground laboriously and monotonously in a hand mill, the corn meal came quickly into use for bread and porridge. The recipe for bread: flour, corn meal, baking powder, butter and salt. The bush, directly or indirectly, supplied most of their meat, wild pig and native pigeons being supplemented by an occasional sheep or cattle beast. Much of the mutton and beef would be salted for future consumption.

By the time John McLean was forty, he was selling eggs in Auckland, along with two hundred sheep. And there was a good market for his tasty Northern Spy apples. Changes came to the farming routine, notably with the opening of a dairy factory at Waipu in 1901. A larger milking herd was developed and fewer sheep carried. There was a good return also from the sale of kauri timber. Not all of it was sold. Between 1903 and 1910, four houses were built for the new Birdgrove generation. When Dolina died at the age of seventy-six, John had the house pulled down. He lived for the rest of his life with a son, dying in 1929 at the age of eighty-nine. He had, in truth, seen the passing of one era and the full development of another.

The McLean men were — and are — an interesting breed. The early ones were bushmen before they became farmers, and they were also pianists of more than average ability. Virtually without exception, they had a special gift with animals, whether horses, cattle or sheepdogs. They also loved racing. The racecourse was the social rendezvous for the family.

When "Flick" McLean was eighteen, about the year 1893, he rode eight winners out of nine at the Waipu races. Next day, he rode down the coast to Mangawhai, then on to Warkworth and Auckland. There, he took the train part of the way to Hawke's Bay, about two hundred miles south, collected a mob of sheep and drove them to Waipu. There was the time, the family delights to recall, when Flick was driving cattle through Waipu itself. A bull entered a grocer's shop where there was a display of china. As the McLean history says, "The bull inspected the china, signed the visitors' book in the only possible way a bull could, and left the shop without breaking a thing."

When he was 76, twelve months before his death, he fell from a horse while riding bareback and broke a bone in his hand. Men and women alike, they loved farm life, the busy dealing in stock, the open country in general. Jessie Tom McKenzie was the wife of Danny Birdgrove McLean, who had a good amount of the McLean quirky humour. There was the time when they were travelling through the steep and tricky Waipu Gorge. Jessie was driving when the car's brakes failed. Danny hopped out and his passing remark to Jessie as she carried on down the hill was, "Stick to it, Jessie!"

Motorcars figure in the folklore of the McLeans almost as frequently as horses. William McLean, farming at Maungaturoto beyond the Brynderwyns, aroused some speculation among his family when he suddenly told them he was going to Helensville, the most noticeable town to the south. It was only after he arrived home that night that they discovered that he had bought a car, and had driven it to within a few miles of his home before it went over a bank. In those carefree days it did not matter that he did not know how to drive; indeed, that he had never sat behind the steering wheel of a car before. After all, if a man bought a horse it was logical to expect that he could ride it. Neither William nor the car was damaged. But he had learned his lesson and spent several days teaching himself how to control this new monster by driving round one of the farm paddocks.

Macaulay "Cauley" McLean was a progressive and naturally optimistic farmer. He was the first in the area to use topdressing, and one of the first to buy a milking machine. Browntop grass seed, later known as Waipu browntop, had a humble beginning, having been brought in bedding from Nova Scotia and thriving when the mattresses were emptied. It was a fine grass, very suitable for low-fertility land and as civilisation took over, for bowling greens and sports fields. Caulay saw its potential, growing it extensively and selling the seed all through the country during the 1920s. In 1926 he bought a handsome Nash motorcar for £620, all from selling the seed.

Today, where not so many years ago cars laboured through mud in winter or choked the travellers in dust, there are tarsealed roads that seem to mock the trials of early years. The main road north from Auckland climbs effortlessly to the crest of the Brynderwyns, where a parking area invites a pause. Down below, if it is the right sort of day, there spreads a view that would have few equals on New Zealand's varied and beautiful coast. There is still native bush to left and right, but elsewhere green pasture, with occasional dark shelter belts, spreads towards the sea. Sheep, cattle and houses are lost in this broad expanse of open country. But the eye quickly leaves the foreground. Far to the left a superb range of mountains with ragged volcanic crests is dark against the cloudless sky and the sparkling, restless waters of Bream Bay. Bream Head reaches out to the ocean. Like the peaks of another great volcanic range a chain of islands breaks the sharp line where sea meets sky: the Hen and Chickens islands, their colour changing in shades of blue as the day goes by; Sail Rock, looking like a full-rigged ship coming up from the south. Still further south, Bream Tail with its bold headland contains the beaches, occasional cliffs and slow-flowing streams that bring colour and variety to Bream Bay.

It is a view that wrenches the heart of a returning exile; as powerful in its appeal to the sons and daughters of Waipu as is the first sighting of the Cuillins to the returning Skye man, or the Cape Bretoner's recognition of the long, shining waters of the Bras D'Or lakes after years away.

We have lingered long enough on the crest of the hill. Now we follow the road leading down to the sea, past alien pine plantations that cloud the hills to the south. The country beside the road is Birdgrove country. Danny McLean had farmed it in the early days. His son Murdoch, fired by his love for good cattle, expanded the two hundred acres that had been sufficient for a dairy herd, first bringing in sheep, then dry cattle. Some years ago, it seemed there was no great profit in sheep, but the farm was perfect for fattening cattle, and that is how it had been since then. At first, the farm carried Herefords and Aberdeen Angus, but now there are more exotic breeds. Under the management of Murdoch's son, Warren, the cattle forage on eight hundred acres, running from the top of the Brynderwyns down to the flats where the farm began.

Warren has proved that the land can carry big cattle. These are not common in the north, and he goes seeking them as far south as the King Country in the centre of the North Island. They must be not only big animals; they must be top quality. They are three years old or more when they are bought. Some he may sell on in two months; others may stay up to a year on the higher parts of the farm. He brings in men to look to the fences and maintain the farm; ragwort and gorse are not allowed to get out of control. But the buying of stock is his task alone, and he loves it; out with the stock agents, talking to breeders, discussing the prices. He has done it all his life, ever since he left Waipu school. The exotic breeds do very well, but they need care in hot weather, unlike the Herefords and Angus cattle which can stand extremes. There is not much bush on the place now. "Bush doesn't earn money," says Warren. He makes no hay because big cattle, in his words, would be looking for it and wanting it six times a day.

Cattle and McLeans have always gone together and some good stories have survived. One of them, told by Bob Cullen, is printed in *This Valley in the Hills*, an entertaining and invaluable book compiled by Dick Butler for the Maungaturoto Centennial. It concerns Danny McLean — Danny Bridge, to distinguish him from Danny Birdgrove. Danny, who had leased a 3,000 acre property with not very good fences, was having a few mysterious losses of cattle. He decided to set a trap.

Among a large mob of cattle he brought in from Kaitaia was an 18-month-old broken coloured bull. It had no earmark and no brand. Danny burned a small brand just under the brisket where it could not be seen. He turned the animal out with the mob, and two weeks later the "bait" had been taken. He set out for the yards of the suspect. There was the same beast, with a brand and earmark, neither of them Danny's. The "rustler" claimed he bought it at a sale, but was silenced when shown the brand under the brisket. Danny claimed he had lost twenty-seven head of cattle in the previous year, and offered to sell them at a price well above their current market value. A cheque was produced very quickly. Danny went home admitting they were the best paying cattle he had ever bought, as nine of the twenty-seven missing had died — he found their bodies in a bog.

The story of the McLeans, ruthlessly condensed here, could be repeated with endless variations in many parts of the country inhabited by the Nova Scotian migrants. The love of horses crops up everywhere, from John McKay, in his nineties, riding to church at an unseemly speed, to Norman Finlayson who, it was said, built a stable before he finished his house. The horse was, of course, essential for working a farm, but its role went far beyond that of a beast of burden. And before the horse there was the working bullock.

Almost from the start of settlement the men from Nova Scotia were forming partnerships with the working bullocks; not only in clearing land for farming but to send logs and timber away to build houses in Auckland and as far away as Australia. The kauri became the basis of a highly special-ised industry. I remember Willie Kempt and Cockatoo McLeod, sedate farmers in later years, telling me about their life in the bush: the way in which several men, working as a team with their timberjacks, would move huge logs that had jammed when the water was released from a dam to take them down river; the engineering skill and inventiveness that went into building the dam itself; the excitement and danger of a drive, when a number of trees would be almost cut through and, held up by one another, remain vertical until the huge "key" tree, higher up the slope, was felled, and in its collapse brought all the others down with it. And somewhere in the scene would be the teams of patient bullocks, hauling logs along skidded roads or stretching their muscles to drag a timber-laden dray along a slushy track.

There were many fine blocks of bush across the Brynderwyn Range, with kauri chiefly on the higher land and a wide variety of other useful timber below. In all, a magnet to draw the enterprising young settler keen to test his strength in this unaccustomed setting. Pukekaroro, standing high on the right-hand side of the main highway going north, now delights the traveller's eye with its almost complete cover of young native bush; kauri, still in their graceful adolescent form, close packed down the spurs, rich in their vitality. Other native trees, not so easily recognised at a distance, help to clothe the mountain, a picture of undefiled beauty.

It is good to know that, given the chance, native bush can regenerate in a spectacular way. In six months, not long after the surrounding area had been settled, the Kauri Timber Company took over one million feet of timber from the Pukekaroro bush. The timber was prepared in many different ways. The logs would be squared with broadaxes, but it was found that, if they were absolutely smooth, friction when they were stacked in a ship's holds could cause them to catch fire. So the axe blade was twisted at each end; in this way ridges were left which allowed air to circulate and prevent any risk of fire. There are stories of huge trees, some perhaps owing their quality to the story-telling ability of an unknown bushman. There is, for example, the kauri which was twelve feet in diameter. The gang who cut it down blew it in half with explosives and camped on the two halves on the down-river journey to the mill. The final touch of truth: with all their gear on board, each half floated with three feet of freeboard above the waterline.

Huge timbermills were built. The Kaipara Harbour was alive with vessels picking up timber and logs to be processed further afield. One of the first involved was Isaac McLeod, who leased over 200 acres of kauri bush from Maori owners in the early 1870s. About twenty men were engaged, and for two years they took the marketable trees from the bush until it was worked out. On the riverbank nearby, Isaac had built his home, which was also a shop. The shop, in a few years, became also a post office; and so came the amenities of civilised life to the district of Maungaturoto.

While many of the younger Nova Scotian men crossed over the ranges to work in the timber camps and mills, others bought land in the valley and settled down to a farming life. Among them were Alex and Norman Finlayson, cousins, who married two sisters, Margaret and Annie McInnes. Their ties with Waipu stayed strong, although at the same time they became loyal members of the local community. Jack Finlayson, a son of Norman, married Madge Cullen, who died in 1994 when over one hundred years old.

The Finlaysons had taken up land early in the 1870s. Before long they were buying and selling at prices that seem strange today. In 1876, twenty store sheep were sold in December for £7 5s, and three hundredweight of potatoes fetched 5s. Horses were not easily obtained, and were consequently dear to buy and to service. Breaking in a filly cost 30s, and two draught horses, bought in Auckland, cost £100. In 1880, a drought year, there were bargains to be had. Durham, farming near the Waipu Gorge, sold 27 sheep for £9 4s.

The Waipu Gorge, for better or for worse, keeps cropping up in local folklore. A walking track at first, then a riding track that could easily be missed, it saved travellers many a weary roundabout journey; but it was narrow, steep, with hairpin bends that became a nightmare when cars first came on the scene in 1913, as one driver discovered.

"He heard a horn blaring round the corner," writes Dick Butler in *This Valley in the Hills*. "No time to think. A quick turn of the wheel and it shot up the bank, hanging there while the other car passed by beneath him. Then it slid back down on to the road with the passengers white-faced, shaken and bruised."

Stories without number tell of the way in which the new settlers moved to or from their homes. Angus Stewart, of Kaiwaka, supplied some of the first cows to Maungaturoto. "They would not drive but had to be led one by one," writes Dick Butler. "It meant a struggle for man and beast the whole way, with sometimes the man leading the cow and sometimes the cow leading the man."

Road signs in winter marked the depth of mud on the road, and indicated the most likely places for a vehicle to be bogged. There was a classic story of a wagon that disappeared; other factual stories would explain how a coach and its six horses, the passengers as well, would arrive at a village hotel covered in mud. When the coach was bogged, passengers had to help lift the wheels clear and set the coach on the road.

But it was necessary for journeys, long and short, to be made even in the most difficult conditions. Farmers anxious to improve the quality of their sheep and cattle would send away to centres in the south; the men with an eye for stock would follow the old precept of seeing before buying. I have already mentioned Danny McLean. One good story — one among many about Danny — tells of a drover who walked to Hawke's Bay with McLean. On the way he stopped for a drink of water from a stream and it was many hours later that he realised his gold watch must have slipped from his pocket into the water. Returning some weeks later, he found the spot, scrabbled around on the stream bed, and found his watch. A final proof of truth: the watch is still going all these years later!

Before communication by road improved, sea trading was all-important, and that brought with it an urgent need for wharves. It is not surprising that the humble wharf figures quite strongly in local folklore. One tidy little episode is preserved in letters which show, incidentally, how politicians are born, not made. It also shows how a simple innocence, masking a well-concealed touch of guile, can win through against the best efforts of Government civil servants.

On 7 September, 1894, the secretary of the Marine Department, Wellington, wrote to John Munro, coast waiter, Marsden Point:

> You report that there is another wharf at Waipu beside Mr Campbell's which has been erected without the consent of the Governor-in-Council. I have to request that you will ascertain definitely who has control of it and inform him that he must supply plans of the structure, prepared in

accordance with the requirements of the enclosed printed notice, and at the same time apply to this Department for a license to occupy the site. You should also point out to him that he is liable to a heavy penalty for erecting the wharf without authority.

John Munro to Mr Jos Abrams, constable at Waipu, 13 September (condensed):

Who has control of the wharf recently built at Waipu Entrance? It may be Mr N.J. Campbell, chairman of the Road Board, who has control of the wharf at McLean's bridge.

J. Abrams to J. Munro, 18 September:

I am unable to find anyone who claims to be in charge. Mr Wm Hart has one key of the shed on the wharf and the captain of the barge, Alex McKenzie, has the other. Mr N.J. Campbell is agent for the barge company. Mr Alex Mackay appears to have had charge of the whole job and I look on him as the person in charge.

A. Mackay to J. Munro, 22 September (this letter, a scene-setter, is quoted in full):

I beg to acknowledge the receipt of your letter and to state in reply that there is nobody that can be properly said at present to have control of the Waipu Wharf at Entrance, but as I have from the first carried on all correspondence in connection with it and acted a sort of superintendent over the job I expect I would be deemed to be the man having control. However, I have a short time ago written to the Hon the Minister of Marine asking him to give his sanction for the work. I am sorry I did not think of writing to you, you could have put me right at once. If what I have done is not in the right direction I trust you will still be kind enough to give me the required information and I shall be very much obliged. I remain, dear sir, yours very truly.

A. Mackay to J. Munro, 26 September (a touch of steel):

Your letter is to hand inclosing forms from Marine Department. I am very busy and cannot well attend to the work you point out to me at present. I will need to make a survey of the site and make plans which will take me a little time, but I will attend to the matter as soon as possible. We had no intention of committing a breach of the Harbours Act and thought the Govt would not trouble us so long as we did not do any harm.

Marine Department secretary to J. Munro, 28 September, concerning what is now a "proposed" wharf:

Mr A. Mackay has asked permission, on behalf of the settlers, to erect a wharf near the entrance of the Waipu River but he has been informed that proper plans must be supplied before the application can be dealt with. In the meantime I have to request that you will ascertain from him the exact position of the proposed site and the nature of the structure and let me know whether there is any objection to its being authorised, also state what you think would be a fair rent to charge for the site.

John Munro was frustrated. He asked A. Mackay for details on the 5th and 19th October; the reply came on 21 October:

The wharf has been built by voluntary labour and nobody receiving any pay there is no fund from which the Govt demand of £5 for the Order in Council can be paid, nor a fund from which I could be paid for my trouble. I may state, however, that the wharf is built where it will not obstruct navigation. It is open to the public free of charge, a great public convenience and I am of the opinion that instead of the Govt charging our settlers £5 and an annual charge for the site they will give us some help towards the cost of the structure. I hope the matter will soon be settled agreeably one way or other.

Marine Department secretary to John Munro, 4 December:

With reference to your letter of 25 October I forward herewith for your information copy of an Order in Council authorising Mr A. Mackay to erect a wharf on the Waipu River. Under the circumstances in which the wharf is being erected it has been decided to make no charge for the license and only a nominal rent of one shilling a year for the site, which amount it is not intended to collect.

Waipu wharf, when sail gave way to steam.

And so, quite a few months after it had been completed, the wharf at the Entrance became a reality.

For as long as ships of any kind — cutters, scows, small steamers — came up the river, the two wharves served Waipu well. Produce bound for Auckland would be stored in the wharf shed, alongside goods that would be collected by horse-drawn dray and displayed on the shelves of the store. But by the 1920s the sheds were standing empty on deserted wharves; except during school holidays and on long summer evenings, when a hopeful young fisherman, or fishergirl, would be carving up bait on the weathered planks and seeing what the river might offer.

"The sea was not their mistress. It was their partner, sometimes their enemy. It took them where they wanted to go, and enabled them to make a living." That was one pragmatic view of how the Nova Scotian seaman looked at the element that, for much of his working life, surrounded him. And, like anyone else who had to feed and clothe himself and his family, he left it behind without too much regret when the railway, and improved roads, robbed local sea trade of its profitability. Before very long, the erstwhile seaman would be running his little farm, or dealing in timber, or even finding a place inside a city office, preferably not too far from the waterfront.

But not all were as matter-of-fact in their attitude. For many, the sea was indeed a mistress — demanding, contrary, inscrutable, but always to be loved.

Keith Matheson, grandson of Duncan who, with his brother Angus, sailed the *Spray* out from Nova Scotia, became one of the most celebrated sea captains working from New Zealand ports.

I asked him: "What sort of vessel was the *Spray*? Would you have enjoyed sailing her?"

"She was a brigantine, a fast sailer, versatile, reasonably easy to handle in most conditions. Under full sail she would be beautiful." His eyes twinkled. "I know, because I've sailed vessels just like her."

He reached for paper and a pencil. "I'll show you." Quickly, deftly and lovingly he drew out the lines of a graceful hull, a long bowsprit and deckhouse, and two tall masts. He proceeded to draw in the sails, naming them as he went. There was a touch of nostalgia, understandably enough, in his voice. "Here are the jib and foretopmast staysail, sometimes called the inner and outer jib, especially if you were in a hurry. Coming down the foremast you have the foretopgallant sail, the foretopsail, the foresail, all of them square sails. Between the two masts are the main topmast staysail and below it the main staysail. Then you have the gaff topsail, at the peak of the mainmast, and below it the big working fore and aft mainsail."

His pencil was still busy, his voice soft. He marked where the reef points would be, and then with delicate strokes drew the stays, confusing to a layman; the foretopgallant stay, jib stay, foretopmast stay, forestay; then the main topmast stay and main lower mast stay.

"And there you have it," said Keith. "The heyday of the brigantine was from the mid-1860s until the 1880s. They ran up to the Pacific Islands carrying passengers and general cargo, up to 100 tons, sometimes more, with fruit on the return journey. Great days, but finished long ago."

Through all the sailing years the sea — mistress, partner or enemy — exacted its toll. The *Thistle*, under Duncan Prince, was driven by a storm on to rocks near Whangarei Heads, with two lives lost. Five members of the Kempt family were lost when the schooner *William Pope* disappeared without trace on the coast between Pakiri and Auckland in 1861. On a night so dark that the crew of the tug did not see what happened, the *Oban* (Captain Donald McKenzie) was being towed into Wellington Harbour when the rough sea washed the whole crew overboard. The *Rona* was wrecked on the west coast of the North Island and Captain Kenneth McKenzie went down with her. In 1875, the schooner *Ivanhoe* sailed from Auckland for Fiji. She never arrived and her crew, with Captain Donald Stuart, was never seen again. Fiji's reefs claimed the schooner *Coquette*, under the command of her builder, Captain Duncan Matheson. But this time the crew were saved.

The list could go on, but this is enough to show how, for wives and mothers at home, anxiety could be a constant companion. The Waipu main street points directly towards Flagstaff Hill, where, in the early days, a flag was hoisted to give warning that a boat was coming up the river. A tough life, but one that had colour, excitement and variety; that made Waipu and its sister settlements part of the big, bustling world beyond the horizon.

"I keep thinking about the old brigantines," said Keith. He sat quietly as we talked, the very model of a retired sea captain with his dark, immaculate suit, alert eyes and considering mouth in a face brown from sun and wind. "They were grand sailers, and with the wind in these square sails they could charge along. But suddenly the waters round the South Pacific islands were full of schooners, cutters and the like — lovely vessels, too, all fore and aft rig with not a square sail among them. They couldn't carry as much cargo, but that suited the owners fine. They were fast and could get the fruit to the Auckland market quickly." Keith paused and looked at me quizzically. "But do you know the real reason for the change? The schooner needed less crew to handle the sails than the brigantine. And in a competitive world, labour costs money, and it's money that counts."

Chapter Eleven

Dancing and Other Entertainments

"I HEAR THEY'RE OPENING UP land at Donnelly's Crossing for farming."
The speaker shook his head sadly. "Real gumdigger's country, sour
and sticky. Even the teatree's stunted. A man will need a good strong back!"

"And so will his wife," observed Long Jim blandly.

For many women in the Nova Scotian settlements, at least until well
into the twentieth century, life —and work — began and ended on the
farm. A good strong back would have been useful, but not essential. There
are tales of women carrying loads of horrific size, up to 300 pounds in
weight, and remarking that the hard part was getting it up on the shoulders. Once there, it could be carried easily enough for a good distance.

However, a woman's life on the farm had its compensations: lively social
contacts at church and at frolics, where men and women would gather to
carry out a common task; picnics on summer days, either at the beach or in
the bush; visits from relatives and friends, treasured all the more because
they might not happen frequently. And, above all for many of the girls,
there was dancing!

The Scottish Highlands had always been dancing country. Submerged
in places by Calvinism, dancing survived to achieve new vigour, not only in
Scotland but in Nova Scotia and New Zealand. Here and there, in homes
where it was seen as a tool of Satan, dancing was frowned on or prohibited;
but it was too powerful to be put down even temporarily.

"Beulah," I said to my ninety-five-year-old aunt, "did you go to dances
at Waipu as a girl? Did you enjoy them?"

Her eyes sparkled and the years seemed to fall away. "We loved it! Even
before there were any phones word would get around that there was a
dance, and everyone would be there."

Beulah was back in a different world, the world she knew eighty years
before. "The music, the movement, the laughing and talk! It was beautiful,
and what fun! I can remember my first dance in the hall. I was only little,
but I can still see Long Jim and his wife when they stood up. He looked as
tall as the roof, and they seemed to cover the length of the hall in two great
bounds. A schottische, I think it was. There was always the piano, and the
Shag (McMillan) played his flute.

"In our mother's time there were the dances on the bridges — piano
bridges they were called because of their rattling planks. Just think of it!

The fiddler or the piper playing, a lovely starry sky, darkness that was never quite dark in the summer, cool air and the silence that took over when the music stopped. Those must have been wonderful nights!"

But that was only one part of it. Dancing, as it came down from one generation to the next in the Highlands, and from there to Nova Scotia and New Zealand, retained a quality that was primitive, in some ways pagan. The men emphatically masculine, the women so feminine in their graceful movements. It is not surprising that Neil Gunn, from the depths of his Highland background, should go right back to the world of classic Greece to quote from a poem in his book *The Well at the World's End*. He wrote of the woman, eating her heart out in a suburban villa, dreaming of "flinging her high heels into the kitchen sink and hitting out for the dancing hills". When the wild rapture was over and hands leaned on the old washtub:

Will they ever come to me, ever again
The long, long dances,
On through the dark till the dim stars wane?
Shall I feel the dew on my throat, and the stream
Of wind in my hair? Shall our white feet gleam
In the dim expanses?

It might seem a far cry from the Maenads of Euripides' play, caught for modern readers in Gilbert Murray's beautiful translation, to the glowing faces of the young dancers in a little village hall; but perhaps it is not too fanciful to detect in the wild, skirling pipes, the pounding rhythm, the disciplined tramp of feet, something of an ancient ecstasy and fervour, homage to an unknown and forgotten god.

But for Beulah and her friends, there was no time for such thoughts. Dancing was excitement, dancing was fun, from the time when the horses and traps arrived until, with a jingle of harness and calls of farewell, everyone headed home. The men were the first to be busy, coats off while they swept up the sawdust spread on the floor. Then wax candles, guttering brightly, were made to spill wax around the hall. Next came the children's turn, pulled round on sacks to polish the wax into the dance floor. There was no babysitting on dance night. The babies were set down in lines, like peas in a pod, in a relatively quiet corner of the hall. A "wag" once changed them around. There was great confusion when a woman went to attend to her baby and, starting to change its nappies, found it was a boy instead of a girl.

After all the excitement it was back to the everyday routine; not necessarily drudgery, not necessarily a life built around the washtub and the kitchen sink. A different story could be told for almost every girl growing up in the young settlements. Here is something of the story of Myrtle

153

"Birdgrove" McLean, who was seventy-six when she was persuaded to be interviewed. Myrtle was modest and quiet-spoken. She faced up to the interview with typical courage.

Myrtle left school when she was twelve, having gained her proficiency, which meant she had passed the sixth standard. "I stayed at home and worked on the farm. Murdoch, our brother, had also left school at twelve. He was working like a man before he was seventeen. I can remember him ploughing on the terraces further up the hill. Other men helped, of course, and there were frolics for heavy farm jobs, with neighbours coming to take part and also enjoy working together. This happened especially with hay-making. Sometimes it would mean forking the hay into haycocks, which would be built into a stack, but our job as children, which we really enjoyed, was tramping down the hay stored in the barn."

The busy farm life suited her well. She had been introduced to it even before she became a fulltime farm worker. She had done her share of hand-milking the cows before and after school. When she was older, she would take the milk down to the factory, every day, with the horse and cart.

"Grandma had lots of hens. I can see her now, with her bonnet and apron, out feeding them. We'd help sometimes. They were the main money-earner at times.

"We learned to swim, not in the sea but in the creek near the Braigh School. Our teacher, Horace Hill, would take us there. He had his own special way of teaching us. He would put a belly band round a child, fasten it to a stick like a fishing rod and walk along the bank pulling his pupil beside him in the water. Ten years before, in Danny Ferry's time, the scene was different. The boys would swim naked in one pool, the girls in another further up the creek."

When her widowed mother moved from the Braigh to Waipu village itself, Myrtle "retired" with her. But retirement meant simply a new line of work. "The headmaster persuaded me to drive the school bus. I said I would see how it went. There were some terrible roads — a bit worrying at first, but I got used to it."

So much so that she continued to drive the bus for seventeen years, and before she gave up some of the children that she had picked up would be sending their own little ones to school under Myrtle's care. "Children on the most remote farms knew almost to the minute when Myrtle's bus would arrive and looked expectantly for it," I was told. "In her own quiet, smiling way she won the love of children and parents alike."

What would women talk about when they came together on social occasions, or to carry out tasks made easier with more than one pair of hands? They talked, of course, about other people, their foibles, the experiences, sad and humorous, that made up the cycle of their days.

One of the favourites was Mrs It, so called because, in the transition from Gaelic to English, pronouns and other words had become rather confused. One windy day she arrived at Murdo's, carrying a man's umbrella, wearing her husband's boots, her feet hardly touching the ground. "You must have been up and away early," said Murdo. "Ach no," she replied. "It didn't take long coming from Widow McLeod's because it had the wind in its behind!"

Another time, so the story goes, Mrs It was crossing a stream on a fallen tree when she slipped in. "You were lucky not to be drowned," said Murdo. "How were you saved?" She explained very concisely what happened: "It hooked its umbrella round a tree on the bank and it got out that way."

Some of the stories were enjoyed by the subject as well as by the narrator. There was a man who hated having three Christian names, so he gave his son and daughter three names each. But Catherine Nora Harvey MacKay achieved a quiet revenge. As a little girl she couldn't say "Good morning". Her interpretation, "Morna" became the name by which everyone knew her from schooldays on.

Conversation could range widely. It could tell of the boys, for example, who cut a track seven miles through the bush so that their mother, when well enough, could be carried out to talk and have company at the nearest neighbour.

Another brief one: "You're restless, why?"

"This is the time of year when we always made the candles but now with this kerosene I have nothing to do with my hands."

And, on a winter's night by the fire, tales remembered from Nova Scotia had a special effect. One came from Keith Matheson. Walking home after dark a man heard the subdued sound of animals on the road in front of him. "My neighbour's cattle must have got through a gate. I'll drive them home." He persisted for a while, with no success. It was only in the morning that he discovered the truth. On the road he saw giant, unmistakable footprints. He had been trying to herd a pair of bears! "Lucky they weren't hungry," was his succinct remark.

Ghost stories, or tales not easy to explain in a rational way, were favourites in evenings before radio and television changed our social habits. Another of Keith's stories, whenever it was retold, carried listeners back to a far different world. "When the river was deeply frozen, it was easier to drive the horse and sledge down the centre of the river; but the ice there would always break up earlier. Grandfather, this time, tried in vain to get his sledge out to the centre; and he swore that he saw his long-dead mother at the horse's head, leading it closer to the shore. Next morning he saw that the ice had broken, and he realised that, if he had gone further out, he would have almost certainly have drowned."

155

Not many of the stories that we can record today go back as far as that. The limit seems to be what the oldest living people can remember being told by their own grandparents. They can be plain, unvarnished tales, such as that of Louie McLean, born in 1877, married in 1901 to W.J. McLean who farmed near the Caves. It was an isolated farm — the road could quickly become a muddy track, so the grocery order had to be sufficient to feed the family for six months. She raised a family of eleven children before moving nearer to civilisation in the 1920s. Mary, the eldest child, had to be able to cope. Her mother was badly burned by a porridge spill when Mary was nine. She had to look after a bedridden mother and six other children, the youngest being nine weeks old.

The light and dark sides of life. How quickly the mind can switch from one to the other. Doris Ewen is one for whom life in all its aspects is a challenge and a delight. "I love my books," she once said to me. "I don't know why, but many people my age don't bother with them. I even bought two more last week. Not bad for one who's ninety!"

We talked of many things, but her thoughts were never very far from the farms, the bush, the cattle that had made up so much of her life.

This was the story she told us: "Have you ever seen the tiny little house all on its own in the middle of a field down the road? A woman from England called in here once and said she was sure there was a story around it. There certainly was," Doris said, and proceeded to tell it.

"He was just a young chap working on the family farm when he was kicked on the head by a horse, and part of his brain was damaged. This was a terrible thing. In those days, if you were mad you were hidden away and the family would pretend you didn't exist. So off he was sent to the lunatic asylum at Avondale near Auckland, and never talked about.

"A long time afterwards a man arrived at the farmhouse. He had brought three little presents for the family, but that was all he had except his clothes. This was the man who had been taken away. His brain had improved, and he had worked at the asylum growing vegetables and looking after the garden. But now he was old, they had kicked him out. His family built a little house for him. He put a fence around it to keep the opossums away, and before long he had another garden going. He worked happily there. Members of the family came to visit and to help him with anything he needed, and he in turn grew the vegetables for their farms." Doris paused, her face suddenly serious. "The English lady was right, I think. There certainly was a story in that little house."

Another story, far different from this, seemed to hold in it echoes of a blissful, uncomplicated time.

Emma and Mary McLean were sisters who lived together in a house on the way to the Braigh. To everyone in the district they were known as

Emma and Mary Ewen. No-one ever said Emma Ewen and Mary Ewen. The two names always went together, Emma first. She was the personality, a great one in the kitchen; and she knew how to look after everyone. In the front of their house they had a little shop with cottons and small dressmaking articles for sale. Emma was always the housekeeper. Mary, who was lame, did the dressmaking. Many's the dress she made for busy mothers in the village. "She was a very nice-looking person," one of the women told me, "but she had to drag a leg." Their brother, Alex Ewen, was a very public man. He owned a big sawmill and was at one time mayor of Whangarei. A busy man indeed, with no doubt his share of the stresses that come with a life in business. It was so different for Emma and Mary Ewen, one likes to think. The housekeeper kept house, the dressmaker made dresses, in the evening friends would walk up to their house for a chat. And so it continued, a serene, quietly fulfilling way of life. They both died at the age of 102.

There is one Waipu woman about whom more legends have gathered than around anyone else; and this is partly because the house where she lived still stands, ghostly in a setting that not even bright sunshine can make cheerful; solitary in a broad field, neglected and seeming to be crumbling into ruin. Kitty Slick has caught the imagination of writers; and it is not surprising that their writing has more of fiction than of fact in it. The same reaction came from some who were living in Waipu when Kitty was alive. I asked my Aunt Beulah (born in Waipu in 1902) if she had known

Kitty Slick, the witch that wasn't, lived in this Waipu house at the turn of the century.

Kitty, and what she was like. "She was a witch," Beulah replied. "At least that's what I thought until I met her. She lived on her own a little way out of the Centre, in Shoemakers Road, and if she saw anyone coming she would run and hide. Running across the field, through the scrub, her long dress streaming behind her. I had no real picture of her in my mind, just a sense of wildness, of a thin body and tangled hair and frightening eyes.

"I had never been really close to her; my imagination fed on stories I overheard. Every week, with my mother, I'd walk past her house, sometimes seeing Kitty flitting about outside. It was a four-mile walk to Granny McInnes's home, where the old lady lived alone, and mother would be busy baking, tidying the rooms, scrubbing the back steps and passing on any news. Then one day, as we walked home, Mum said in a most casual way: 'Come along, we'll go in and see Kitty.' We crossed the field and Mother walked through the open door. Kitty was in the kitchen at the end of the passage. Mother spoke to her, Kitty answered and a quiet conversation went on, with me hiding in Mother's skirts and too afraid, that first time, even to peep.

"Every week we'd call in. I would never have dared to speak to her, but I saw that, when she and Mother talked, she became quiet and at ease. I know now she wasn't a witch, but her face seemed crooked, her teeth needed care, her hair was rank and uncombed. No wonder people feared and avoided her. The poor, poor thing!

"I don't know what had made her like that. There had been no tragic event in her life, as far as I know, no disappointment or great shock. But there must have been some reason, who knows what? And once she saw the look in people's eyes she would turn away or run — except from someone like my mother."

The Kitty Slick legend grew, feeding on fantasy tales that were the creation of lively imaginations, ranging from childhood abuse to rejection by a heartless lover. But the truth seems to be much more prosaic, telling of a woman living on her own after her parents died, withdrawing gradually into herself, becoming more and more eccentric.

She was extremely houseproud, with everything in immaculate order. The stove — "You could see yourself in the high polish" — was never used. There was an old stove out in the lean-to on which she cooked. She was excellent at sewing. She would make dresses out of material that looked like window blinds so that they would rustle as she walked. She liked big hats. She was a good cook and, when butter sculpture was in vogue, she would exhibit her work at the local show, mounted on black velvet.

But the passing years took their toll and her eccentricity grew. If a motorcar passed along the road she would dive into the long grass. She never went off her property during the day, only at night. She loved working outside and could often be seen grubbing gorse in the fields. And the old house seemed to develop a personality that matched her own. Two stories help to keep Kitty's memory alive.

A visitor knocking at the door had no response. He looked inside and there, lying absolutely still, was Kitty, with no sign of breathing. Police, doctor and ambulance were summoned, but the doctor confirmed that she was dead. Then suddenly Kitty sat up, looked at the three men crowding the room and cried: "What are you doing here? Get out, all of you!"

The second story tells how a man found her lying motionless on the farm. The following story probably owes much to the narrator's sense of humour. The man got a bucket of water, some of which he sprinkled on her head, but there was no response. On his knees he cried out: "Speak to me Kitty — tell me are you dead!" Still no response, so he left the bucket beside her and hurried away.

The Waipu in which Kitty was an adult and in which Beulah was growing up, was a lively place, the true centre of the community. A different place altogether from what the visitor sees today. Along the main street, in unpretentious but visually pleasing buildings, a remarkably wide range of services was provided. There were, in vigorous confusion, a boarding-house, butcher, saddler, library, public hall, dressmaker, church, Sunday School hall, manse paddock and Masonic lodge. Fahy McKay's lolly shop was not far from the school paddock and the billiard room. The doctor's house was burnt down in 1926. Tom Butcher's shop became, in 1920, the National Bank. Until then the teller came in his two-wheeled gig, later in his car, from Maungaturoto, with his box of money and his revolver on the seat beside him. One day a passing local resident was startled to see that the teller had gone off, leaving the money and his revolver on the seat.

Waipu, in its pre-bridge heyday, had three ferries, one of them operating with an ingenious cable by means of which the little boat could be returned empty to the other bank when needed. All this might give an impression of hectic commercial activity, but that was not so. Life in the village moved at a gentle pace. The main street, or business area, was not one of those places that is locked up at night and deserted until morning. Private homes mingled with the shops and in most cases the storekeepers lived conveniently enough at the back of their shops.

Beulah's childhood was enlivened by conversation with neighbours and visitors, notable among them Abe McMillan who, in his later years, lived next-door to the store operated by Beulah's father and mother. Abe, a religious man, was once heard reproving his son for talking about the previous day's rugby football match with Maungaturoto. "You shouldn't do it," said Abe severely. "Such talk is not proper for a Sunday... What was the final score?"

The story that stayed in Beulah's memory was far less consequential. Gladys, her elder sister, was a great favourite of Abe, and she had been away at teachers' training college. Two days later he accosted her: "You haven't been in to see me."

"I have, but you were out."

"When did you come?"

"When were you out?"

"Between ten and noon."

"That's when I came!" The girls collapsed in giggles.

Not all the citizens would have approved of an item in an early report issued by the bowling club: "Two cases of whisky for opening day, and a keg of beer for the teetotallers." But even the most straight-laced would have smiled at the story of the decoy bag of sugar.

At times, so I was told, there was a "leetle" making of whisky in the mountain bush behind Waipu. It was noted by the authorities that, now and again, more than the normal amount of sugar would be unloaded at the Waipu wharf. An agent hid himself nearby to see where it went. Sure enough, a man arrived at the wharf that morning. He picked up one bag of sugar, loaded it on his shoulder and walked away, pursued at a safe distance by the watcher. He stopped for a rest; his pursuer hid in the ditch until his quarry picked up the bag and walked off again. It continued like this for a long time until, to his complete mystification, the watcher saw the wharf shed ahead. He had been led in a full circle. And now the bag of sugar was set down inside the shed. It was the only one there.

For Beulah, life behind the store was never dull. "Father liked to keep in close touch with his friends, and that included just about everyone who came into the shop. Especially if they had come on the *Ellen Lewis* with him from Nova Scotia. If it was near noon he would say, 'Come in for a bite.' There were times when Mum blessed him for it, but she became pretty good at stretching a meal to take in an extra diner, and they always had a warm welcome.

"One man in particular," Beulah said, "would always have a special place.

"Murdoch McGregor, an old bachelor, lived on the North River farm next to where Granny McInnes was living on her own. He was very religious. When we went up to see Granny he would be sitting there beside her, reading the Gaelic Bible to her. You could tell that she enjoyed the reading, and she enjoyed his company. Sundays he would be at church. Afterwards, before we could move, he would be out of his seat, down the road and in through our door, which was never closed. Then he'd sit down and wait for dinner. What's more, he would say grace, which went on and on and on. Mum would scold Gladys and me afterwards for giggling. She said: 'He's welcome any time he likes, because he's so good to your granny.'

"Two other regular visitors I can still see so clearly. Widow McLeod and old Mrs Finlayson lived in St Mary's Road, Mrs Finlayson at the very end. On pension day they would dress in their best black, with bonnet and shawl, two dignified ladies, and walk together down to the Centre to do a little shopping. There was never very much shopping done, but they would be invited through to have a bite with us. Then Mum would say to me: 'Take their parcels home for them, Beulah.' There might be only a packet of tea to carry, and off I'd go."

Beulah passed her proficiency examination when she was only eleven. She couldn't stay on at her school, and her father felt she was too young to go away to board in the city while she attended secondary school. However, at the Cove School the headmaster was a friend, and he was willing to take Beulah there for another year. But how did she get there? Six miles each way was too far for a girl to walk. The answer was a horse.

This is the story as Beulah remembered it: "Pa had a horse that he kept in a field by the store. An old horse, just how old I wouldn't know, but he was long past work, except sometimes to haul a load of firewood from the farm up the South Road. Pa said: 'He won't go fast enough for you to fall off, and he will easily find his way to school once you point his head in that direction.' So he found a bridle and a saddle and I could just reach high enough to put them on the horse. He stood as if he was asleep, head conveniently drooping. Auntie Annie Finlayson at Maungaturoto rode at horse shows all over the district. She sent me a divided skirt which she had grown out of. When I was ready to leave for school I would slip the skirt on over my dress, climb into the saddle and away we'd go. His ears switching slowly, his worn untidy mane, his big stumbling feet, his bony hips! In rain and sun, on the dusty summer road, through the mud of winter he carried me at the same steady pace past the cemetery, the few farm cottages, until we came to the bridge. This he refused to cross. He had to be led over and this I couldn't do, for if I got off his back I'd never get back again.

"I'd leave him in the school paddock until it was time to go home; and then he'd come walking up to greet me."

For Beulah, a horse to ride to school. For her friend Colin McGregor, a horse to ride to battle, a horse named Taipo — Maori for devil — that would win a measure of fame for himself in the deserts of the Middle East, where Colin was to fight.

Horses, and horsemanship, were an important part of a countryman's way of life in the years before the First World War, and afterwards until the motorcar consigned them to the back paddock. Colin enlisted in the North Auckland Mounted Rifles and joined the Main Body of the Australian and New Zealand forces in Egypt. The first convoy of transports from New Zealand had carried 9000 men and over 3800 horses. No tanks or armoured vehicles. It was Bobbie Finlayson from Purua who pointed Colin in the direction of Taipo. Horse and man became a closely knit pair, and a successful one in contests between battles. Speed, from his partly thoroughbred inheritance, also gave Taipo an extra edge in the field. "When we heard the drone of the German fighters approaching," said Colin, "we'd ride like hell out into the desert, scattering widely so that the bombs wouldn't find a concentrated target. And in quieter times there were always the keen contests with the Canterbury Yeomanry Cavalry — the CYC — who rather fancied themselves as the best. They knew differently when we had finished with them in the mounted wrestling matches, and the tent-pegging!"

Colin was lucky to escape unscathed in the ebb and flow of the Turkish campaign, except when a bad bout of malaria laid him low. Taipo was not so fortunate. Shot through the neck, he was sent off to the veterinary hospital, but that didn't deter him for long. After two months he was back with his partner again and, as Colin said, running like the devil. There was plenty of running to do, under conditions that could not have been less suitable for horses. It was a constant struggle to bring water to the horses; there was one time when they were seventy hours without it.

In 1916, the New Zealand Mounted Brigade, along with Australian Light Horse and English Yeomanry, turned back the Turkish advance on Egypt with what has been styled the last great cavalry charge in military history. The men did not carry sabres or lances, but they galloped knee to knee in tight formation with their bayonets fixed. When Colin returned to New Zealand he could not bring Taipo with him, but he was spared the fate of most of the other horses, killed to keep them from a wretched life in the desert. Taipo ran in a number of races in Palestine, allowing his rivals a good view of his heels.

In my last conversation with Colin, not long before his hundredth birthday, it was not easy to get him to talk about the past, let alone his own activities. The joy of living shone from his eyes; the war, his years of farming that followed it, might receive casual mention, but it was the present, his family and the chain of his friends that held his interest. He and his younger brother Rod had been good companions and he enjoyed his visits to Waipu, where his sister Bella was married to Gus McKay, and where he had close links with families that had been brought even closer together by wartime experiences.

If some of his friends were coming over to the Whangarei Heads for tennis matches, there was time to go out the night before and catch fish to be boiled — with potatoes — for lunch on the beach. Colin was a lucky man. His energy, his lively mind, his warmth and humour seemed undimmed by the passing years.

The Bobbie Finlayson mentioned earlier, who introduced Colin to Taipo,

162

was also known as Lt-Colonel A.C.M. Finlayson, M.C. and bar, three times mentioned in despatches. He was Trooper McGregor's commanding officer in the Mounted Rifles. The Finlaysons, cousins to those at Maungaturoto, were grand horsemen. They had big farms at Purua, and later bought land near Whangarei. Bob Finlayson had a younger brother, Beb, who married Rita, another sister of Colin.

Bobbie had joined the North Auckland Mounted Rifles before the war began. "As a young second-lieutenant," I was told, "he had a go at the trick-riding contest at a circus, and was ticked off by senior officers. If he had been thrown, they said, he would have lost the respect of his men. But there was no chance of that ever happening with Bobbie!"

He went away with the Main Body of New Zealanders and took part in the desperate fighting at Gallipoli, an ill-starred campaign in which the Turks beat off every attack. Chunuk Bair was a name written on many Waipu hearts, for it was there that four young men from the settlement, three of them cousins, were killed when a shell from a British naval vessel fell short among the attackers. Reinforced in Egypt, the Mounted Brigade went to Palestine, and it was there that Bobbie came into his own.

He was not strong on theory, but as a practical man there were few to match him. And he had one marvellous talent, apart from the qualities that made him an outstanding leader: He could read the stars and unravel their secrets. Out in the desert, he quickly learned the differences between the star charts of the Northern and Southern Hemispheres, and put this knowledge to good use. Colin told me the story.

"The brigade was to move at night, in absolute darkness and complete silence, round the wing of the Turkish positions so they could be attacked from the rear in the morning. Bobbie had the job of leading the whole brigade on this night march, navigating by the stars, three miles this way, three miles that way until they were in position. Then we waited for the morning to come."

For many of those who took part the war had begun as something of a light-hearted exercise, but Gallipoli changed all that. Even in peacetime there were poignant reminders of tragedy surfacing everywhere. I discovered one just recently: a handsome Oxford edition of Robert Burns' poems, with an inscription that read, "To Mr Norman Durham with best wishes and earnest hope of a safe return from the war. From Dr Russell, Waipu." Norman was one of those who didn't come back.

But men are resilient, and there were stories that even in deep gloom could raise a smile. At Hakaru, not far from Waipu, the gumdigging fraternity would gather for refreshment at the public house run by the celebrated Mrs Sara. A gumdigger who had gone to France with the New Zealand Division, on leave in England, was given hospitality at a very aristocratic home. Asked where he came from, he replied: "A little place called Hakaru. You'll never have heard of it."

His host stroked his beard thoughtfully. "Ah, yes," he replied. "And how is my old friend Mrs Sara?"

Chapter Twelve

Enter the Law

A TIGHT LITTLE COMMUNITY, self disciplined, ready and able to organise itself without outside help. That is how many of the early citizens of Waipu saw their home in the Northland wilderness. If a new wharf or road were needed, who better than themselves to decide on the site and carry out the job? But inevitably the law, and bureaucracy with all its trappings, intervened.

The appointment of a police constable was one of the first signs of a changing order. He was welcome enough, even if he was coming to a district that liked to abide by the law, as long as it did not infringe on their personal rights. There were features of village life that, in the view of many, fell well outside the authority of the law, but more of those later.

As early as 1860, when the settlement was still a baby, a tragic accident brought Waipu under the eye of the larger, outside world of officialdom. A boat carrying five women and five men, one of them the eighty-year-old Norman McLeod, had left Whangarei Heads and, under the power of sail and four sturdy oarsmen, had reached the landing-place on Waipu beach opposite the road to Donald McLean's home. Roderick McLeod told what happened:

> Took down masts and sails and stowed them in the boat — put out our four oars and pulled in until we got outside the breakers. We waited there some time to get a favourable chance to pull into the shore. When we thought we had it we pulled with all our strength, all four of us, till we got into where the breakers were breaking. The sea suddenly rose and caught the boat on the quarter and slewed her right round, broadside on, filled and capsized her. All got underneath her.

It is not difficult to visualise the confusion that followed: the upturned boat wallowing in the foaming sea; desperate efforts to free those who were still trapped; the shock of the waves, breaking in white foam, that still kept pounding in. One man floated in on an oar; Dolina Harnett, born a McGregor, was saved from drowning by her crinoline filling with air and acting as a lifebuoy. Many of those in the water could not swim, but they clung to the keel as the boat was slowly washed up the beach. Norman McLeod, having been helped from the water, found the body of Mrs Catherine MacDonald some distance away, but the corpse of Thomas McLeod was not discovered until late in the night. Donald McGregor, then sixty-seven, was near collapse when Roderick McLeod brought him from the water.

Two days later there was an inquest conducted by H.R. Aubrey, JP, as coroner. Witnesses were sworn in and their evidence noted by a jury of twelve, who found that the two victims came to their deaths by the accidental upsetting of a boat on the Waipu Beach. Foreman of the jury was Murdoch Captain McKenzie. Duncan Prince was there too. The other ten were Roderick and Duncan McKay, John Fraser, Angus Morrison, James Sutherland, Donald McDonald, Kenneth Campbell, Roderick Campbell, John Finlayson and John McLeod. It would have been a solemn and painful time for them. Most of the jury had travelled on the *Margaret* and *Highland Lass* and all of them, including the two who had been drowned, were closely linked by ties of family or friendship. It is interesting to see the words "his mark" against the names of two of the signatories.

In the course of her research into her family Jeannine Henry, a great-great-granddaughter of Donald McGregor, located the coroner's report from which this information has been taken. Donald McGregor, she writes, was not the owner of the boat, as was stated by N.R. McKenzie and others. John McLeod, named in the evidence as owner, would be the minister's son, John Grant McLeod, McGregor's son-in-law. Nor is there any suggestion that Norman's preaching distracted the oarsmen, as has been said, causing the boat to be overturned within the line of the breakers. Jeannine's task was not made easier by the year 1862 being given in *The Gael Fares Forth* as the date of the accident, exactly two years after it happened.

Jeannine writes:

The report was very moving for me as I visualised my great-great-grandfather Donald McGregor, then sixty-seven years of age, struggling to get ashore. He was lucky that Roderick McLeod managed to assist him with a second oar. Norman McLeod would have been eighty years old at the time so the experience would have shaken him up somewhat. Not to mention his parishioners!

My own particular interest, apart from my family ancestry, relates to the maritime life of the Nova Scotian settlers and their descendants. My great-grandfather, Capt. Kenneth McGregor, of Whangarei Heads, owned (mostly as part owner) numerous sailing ships. Some of them were in partnership with Capt. Alex McGregor (for whom my grandfather was named), founder of the McGregor Steamship Co. and later the Northern Steamship Co. Capt. Kenneth's first ship, the *Raven*, was built by him when he was a shipwright at Russell in 1853. He was joint owner of this with his brother-in-law, George McLeod Snr. Both were settlers at Whangarei Heads soon after this date.

My father, Philip McGregor, like his brother George, was a marine engineer for many years. Dad came to Australia in 1928 to work for the

Melbourne Steamship Co. Capt. Donald Urquhart, formerly of Craig Shipping Line fame and then, in 1928, harbourmaster/pilot of Port Philip, Victoria, was responsible for my father obtaining this position. Donald was Capt. Kenneth McGregor's nephew, therefore a cousin of my grandfather. Thus they, like many others, maintained the seafaring tradition.

The law, in its formal guise, gradually became part of the Waipu way of life. Thankfully, it did not always appear in a gloomy or tragic setting. The influence of Whangarei on Waipu, as the county town, was strong. And Whangarei being what it was, and lawyers — or some of them — being what they are, many good stories of the law in action have survived to entertain the modern reader.

One of the most colourful and talented lawyers operating in Whangarei was Ralph Trimmer; and in the course of a long and lively career he appeared for, or against, a number of the Waipu residents. Here is one story, told in Trimmer's cheerfully individual style:

The Courthouse [in the 1930s] was immediately across the road from the old Settlers Hotel. It was the accepted practice for the Clerk of the Court and the Bailiff to take turns in slipping across and having a few

The caption for this pre-1914 photo, probably of the Caledonian committee, shows why nicknames were necessary among the Nova Scotians. Standing (left to right) Robbie (Yomax) McKay, Alec (Little Bukau) McKay, Fenton (Butcher) McKay, Johnny (Jack) McKay, Rob Durham, Rory (Butcher) McKay, John (Acko) McKay. Seated (left to right): Jimmy (Slick) McLean, John R. (Bokko or Johnny Ackie) McKay, Gussie (Ferry) McKay, Danny (Hector) McKenzie, John N.I. (Ferry) McKay, Willie Fraser, Norman (Bear) McLeod.

167

spots which they believed were justifiably free. As journalists, Spud Murray and Davy Jones had somewhat similar views. On some occasions, this resulted in colourful but inaccurate reporting, as for example, when Beb and Charlie Finlayson sued their uncle, Long Jim McKay, over a fencing contract. Spud Murray's published report had McKay as plaintiff instead of Beb and Charlie, and it also showed McKay as losing instead of winning.

I had appeared in Court for Long Jim, and the following morning I called at the *Northern Advocate* reporters' room, and tried to persuade Spud that he should correct the report. I was backing out of the room under the whiplash of his volubility when I collided with the owner of the newspaper, Hugh Crawford, who had heard the high-pitched altercation from his office. He asked what the rumpus and the language was all about.

At this stage in strode Long Jim McKay, six foot five in height. He was normally a peaceable, quietly spoken man, a man whom the public respected and chose for many years as chairman of the Whangarei Hospital Board and chairman of the Whangarei County Council. As a young man, Jim had grown up in the environment of bushmen and bullock drivers.

He had heard some of the performance as he walked in from the street and, stretching over me, he grabbed Hugh Crawford and Spud Murray by their coat-collars and appeared to lift them both off the ground at the same time, expressing some views about them that were not printable here. I thought it time to disappear and, as I did so, I could hear the voices fifty yards down the street.

That day the *Advocate* contained a suitable correction.

In the next few years, Ralph Trimmer was to see more of the Finlaysons. "One morning," he recalled, "my office door opened and a hat landed on the middle of the floor. Half a minute later, Beb and Charlie Finlayson walked in and sat down. Then Charlie said: 'During the last year or two the Finlaysons have been involved in quite a number of Court cases and you have been against us. We have lost each time. The other night we had a meeting of the clan and Beb and I have been appointed to call on you and see if we can make an arrangement with you that, if at any time in the future somebody wants you to act against a Finlayson, you say NO at once, you are already acting for them.'

Ralph Trimmer agreed, as long as none of the clients who already retained him would suffer.

"'That's okay with us,' Charlie replied. 'Here's the first job, and we want you to win it. It's a charge of dangerous driving against our sister Etta.'

"In those days," Ralph explained, "the train for Auckland left at around noon, which meant that weddings were often held in the morning to allow the newlyweds to travel south by train. Etta had been attending an important wedding reception in the Whau Valley at Worsp's home, next to which was the dairy farm of old man Bindon. The reception over, everyone took off by car to escort the bride and groom to the station. Etta, with a few friends on board, drove off in her car, and swung round a corner to find, immediately in front of her, Bindon in his horse-drawn cart going in the same direction with his milk cans all around him.

"Etta's car picked up the tail of Bindon's cart and pushed it, Bindon, milk cans, horse and all diagonally across the road and through a fence. The horse's head ended up looking in the bay window of a house. Quite an achievement. The speed limit in Whangarei in those days was fifteen miles an hour. The traffic inspector, Wilcox, collected all the facts, but under cross-examination the situation became confused. It was not clear whether the car pushed the cart and horse across the road or whether the horse bolted, dragged the cart and car across the road and was only stopped by the bay window.

"However, there were some other questions that needed to be put. Beb and Charlie had schooled me up on them. The dialogue went something like this:

Trimmer: How long have you been traffic officer for the borough, Mr Wilcox?

Wilcox: Five years, Mr Trimmer.

Trimmer: How many driving licences have you issued?

Wilcox: Hundreds.

Trimmer: What kind of car do you drive?

Wilcox: A Ford.

Trimmer: No Dodge, Rugby or other geared car?

Wilcox: No.

Trimmer: How long have you been able to drive a Ford car?

Wilcox: Three months.

Trimmer: So for four-and-three-quarter years you have been testing applicants although you yourself could not drive at all?

Wilcox: That is so.

Trimmer: You have a driver's licence. Who tested you for it?

Wilcox: I did.

Trimmer: Who issued you the licence?

Wilcox: I did.

Trimmer: By the way, Mr Wilcox, have you had a collision or an accident since you gave yourself a driver's licence?

Wilcox: Certainly not.

Trimmer: Did you not have a collision with a boy on a bicycle in Kamo Road?

Wilcox: Oh yes. Is that what you mean?

Trimmer: I do. Tell us about it.

Wilcox: Well, I honked but he wouldn't get out of the way.
Trimmer: Was he going the same way as you? Was he ahead of you?
Wilcox: Well, I honked and he wouldn't get out of my way.
Trimmer: So you ran over him?
Wilcox: He wouldn't get out of my way.

Trimmer sat down. Felix Levien, the magistrate, said: 'I do not need to hear any further evidence. Case dismissed.' "

In Waipu, in Nova Scotia before that and right back in the Highlands there had always been those who delighted in argument, in proving their superiority in words, in putting down a fancied slight. Some, like Beb and Charlie, saw a Court case as something as exciting as a clan battle in earlier days. For others, recourse to the law, in the shape of the village constable, could provide a painless answer to a petty problem which otherwise might fester. Two stubborn Nova Scotians, one driving his horse and cart, the other a car, meet in the centre of the Waipu bridge. Who gives way? The Waipu constable is summoned to give a decision that allows each man to retain his dignity.

For the Highlander of old, there was a vast difference between laws — or customs — that had developed locally, and those that were imposed by strangers from somewhere down south. Local custom remained strong, often surviving migration across the Atlantic and even down to New Zealand.

The Customs officer, eventually in all three countries, represented a law

The pioneer memorial, the war memorial and the old church — at the centre of the tight little community of Waipu, as seen in 1933. But the world soon moved in.

that many, even the most law-abiding, found intolerable. Holding an honoured place in the House of Memories in Waipu, contrasting sharply with the homely propriety of most of the articles handed down from the past, are the copper parts of a still that was operated by Captain McKenzie at Omaha, near Leigh, from 1858 to 1878. McKenzie instructed a young Maori chief of the Ngatiwai tribe in its use. The still operated on the Great Barrier Island and then in the forest on the mainland, between Whangaruru and the Bay of Islands. Until 1882 the fiery spirit produced there found a ready market in the port of Russell, but in that year the Maori chiefs declared the area "tapu", thus prohibiting a profitable operation. Many years later the head and worm of the still came into the hands of William McKenzie Fraser, man of many parts, engineer for the county and then for the Whangarei Harbour Board. And it was Bill Fraser who marked the centennial of the migration from Nova Scotia by presenting the still to the museum.

Bill's grandfather, M.T. McKenzie, had been an early pioneer; his father, Simon Fraser, had gone to New Zealand directly from Assynt and in 1861 discovered two of the richest goldfields in Otago. He was a magnificent piper, giving the name Piper's Flat and Piper's Hill to two of the areas where he worked. Bill Fraser had no formal education beyond primary school, but his far-sightedness, shown notably in the dredging of the Town Basin, the reclamation of mudflats, the building of roads and bridges, ensured that Whangarei and its district could move confidently ahead. There was usually an excuse for Bill, with a few of his convivial cronies, to go down the harbour at weekends in the harbour board launch to inspect the lights or check some other problem. The sight of the launch going on its way, with Bill standing in the stern and playing a selection on his pipes, gave pleasure to those within hearing but also resulted in letters to the *Advocate* questioning his use of the launch at this time.

I have warm memories of my last encounter with Bill Fraser. Arriving for the Highland sports one New Year's Day, I asked a committee member where I might find him. He smiled. "There's only one place," he said, and pointed down to where the piping competitions were being held. Not many people were there, for the sound carried satisfactorily across the grounds. But there, sitting alone on a bench beneath the platform, listening to the pibroch, the classical bagpipe music that stirs the blood like nothing else, was my friend. In a world of his own, his head down, his eyes fixed on something far beyond the little village. I hesitated to approach him, for reveries, dreams if you will, are treasures to a man of Bill's years. But he saw me and we talked quietly while the music swirled around us.

Bill was a mine of information on many subjects. "At various times, stills were working all through the hills back of Waipu, down towards Mangawhai in particular. My one was probably the best of them," he said.

"Were the people concerned about breaking the law?"

"It all depended on what kind of law it was," he replied. "On some subjects there had to be laws — at least that's how they thought — but in most instances people liked to judge for themselves and act according to what they thought was right, or sensible." He laughed. "We're back now to the job the Customs officer tried to do. I remember old Captain McKenzie saying that just about everyone brought some goods back from a voyage. No-one thought anything of it. The law, it would seem, shouldn't refer to such activities as that!"

Most tales of smuggling, in Waipu folklore, seem to be centred on Langs Beach, a beautiful stretch of sand about seven miles south of the village. Hector Lang, whose home stands along the beach from the old Lang homestead, was ready to tell me what he knew about it.

"I don't know why it should be," said Hector, "but no subject seems to rouse the same interest as smuggling — especially what is supposed to have happened down below us here on the beach. There was always a bit of whisky made back there in the hills, but what interests people is the stuff brought into the country. How was it done? Looking back, it all seems fairly simple.

"For the trading vessels coming in from the islands of the South Pacific, the most convenient port of entry, complete with Customs officer, was Marsden Point at the entrance to the Whangarei Harbour. It was quite easy for a few cases of rum or whisky to be hidden on one of the nearby beaches when the coast was clear, before the vessel was inspected. Once the inspection was over the cargo could be picked up and away they would sail to Auckland, with documents saying they had passed an examination. And then the illicit cargo could be safely sold. I imagine the Customs people had a shrewd suspicion about what was happening.

"Now at the southern end of Langs Beach," said Hector, "there were stockyards where cattle were held before being shipped to Auckland. A flat-bottomed scow would come in at high tide and wait until it was grounded as the water went down. Then the cattle would be driven down the beach and loaded on the scow without anyone getting his feet wet.

"One day — this was before my time — the stage was perfectly set for action. The cattle were in the yards, in comes a boat from the Islands, they row ashore and bury a case or two in the sand. Suddenly, round the point comes a revenue boat. An uncle of mine, quite a young chap, was at the yards. The captain said to him: 'Here's half a sovereign. Now let the cattle out and drive them up the beach.' By the time the revenue men came ashore, the sand had been trampled by many hooves. They realised there was no chance of finding the booty and away they went."

Hector paused, looking out over the glittering bay, past the Hen and

Chickens, past craggy Bream Head to the north. "There was another time," he continued, "when things didn't work out quite as planned. Once again there was rum to be buried; but a sail was seen out at sea bearing down on them. Those folk could recognise a sail as easily as a modern youngster can tell the make of a car from one glance. They saw it was a revenue vessel; there was no time to act, so they hauled up their anchor and off they went, their cargo still on board. The cattle were already moving along the beach.

"Out of the revenue boat came a gang of men armed with kauri gum spears and they probed the sand from one end of the beach to the other. They found nothing, for nothing was there.

"And that," said Hector, "was the start of a story that is still believed, that under the sand there is a cache of rum that no-one has succeeded in finding.

"By the way," he added. "Remember the half-sovereign given to my uncle? That proves something. The Langs could have had nothing to do with that particular cargo. If they had, of course there wouldn't have been any payment made for turning the cattle loose."

It is a quality of human nature that stories remembered from the past should, in many cases, be either humorous or bearing their own strange innocence. Certainly, among the anecdotes that I have heard, there are few that deal with the type of violence encountered today in newspapers or on television. Indeed, there is only one that comes to mind: a householder in Baddeck had been murdered; the murderer escaped by making his way down a snow-covered street to a boat at the wharf, foiling any pursuit by wearing his snowshoes back to front.

Language itself could have little quirks that, in later times, would be remembered with a chuckle or two. If a Gaelic word had two consonants coming together, a vowel would be inserted between them. Or so a Cape Breton friend told me. Thus, "pregnant" became "pregerant". Also, a girl might be warned not to shake hands with a strange man, or the worst could happen. A girl, let us call her Jane, went down to Boston to work. On Sunday she attended church. It was a grand Baptist church; there was an organ and a fiddler and trumpets. Everyone sang loudly and the preacher urged them to repent their sins. Jane was overwhelmed. Then a man in the pew in front of her turned round, grasped her hand and cried: "You are my sister!"

Jane pulled her hand away. "No, I'm not," she said. "I have only one brother, his name is David, he lives in Cape Breton and I'm going back there before I get pregerant!"

A final anecdote for this chapter goes back not to the law but to its near relation, local government. The Waipu River Protection Board is in full session. Bricky Campbell rises to his feet to complain about the way the watercourse had been allowed to silt up and shrink. A man of direct speech, he declares: "The way it is, I could piss halfway over it!".

The chairman: "Mr Campbell, you're out of order!"

Mr Campbell: "Yes, and if I wasn't out of order I could piss right over it."

Chapter Thirteen

Mathesons, Meiklejohns, McKenzies and Others

T HEY HAD A SAYING IN Nova Scotia that if you stood three Mathesons side by side they would black out the light in the hall. And, looking at the picture of Angus Matheson, you would have felt that was no exaggeration. He was one of a group photographed about fifty years after they had sailed in the *Spray* from Cape Breton to New Zealand. It was Angus who immediately caught the eye. Tall, lean, loose limbed, big framed, he sprawled as much as the chair and available space would allow. His eyes were sombre; his face long, with high cheekbones, shaggy hair and a handsome beard. He seemed, as he sat there, to be harbouring secret thoughts about other times and distant places.

Angus was a hard man, a tough disciplinarian. The better that a man knows the sea, the more he realises that he can never safely relax with it. Before he was thirty Angus had learned all this and more: building sturdy craft at Baddeck, the little Cape Breton port, sailing them along the storm-lashed Atlantic coast from Newfoundland to Pictou, around Cape North to New Brunswick, Maine and Bermuda. There was pride in being a good seaman, but seafaring was a tough, cruel business, with few second chances offered. There was no room for softness — with his crew, his family or himself.

But for Angus and his brother Duncan — of whom more later — there was as much pride and even more in building a vessel that was swift, strong and beautiful; a vessel designed to suit the work that lay ahead and which they then owned and sailed. Angus and Duncan were conservative — they did not discard thoughtlessly what had served well in the past.

"I went back to Lochalsh to see whether I could find any Matheson relatives," Captain Keith Matheson, grandson of Duncan, told me. "I found more than Mathesons there. Along the coast there were boats whose lines were the same as those built by my people in Nova Scotia and New Zealand. No-one had seen any real reason for making drastic change.

"The lines, the design, were in their heads and at their fingertips. And they transferred them to half-models to give them physical form. I've still got half-models of some of the vessels they built, lovingly shaped, beautifully finished. Little works of art in themselves."

A ship's log may be no more of a human document than, say, an accountant's ledger. But, just as the Matheson half-models reveal something of their makers, so, I hoped, would a study of the Matheson logs tell us something about the men who made the entries one hundred and fifty years ago and more. Isabelle ("Belle") Matheson, grand-daughter of Duncan, allowed me to look through the logs kept by Angus on trading voyages in Canadian waters, on the epic journey from Cape Breton to New Zealand, and again, twenty years later, on the New Zealand coast.

Details of the first voyage from Halifax to "Quebeck" in October, 1853 are brief. For most of the time *Vistula*, the little brig, would have been near the coast as they sailed north to the Strait of Canso. The route followed was busy enough: vessels they encountered, the sails they were carrying and the courses being followed were noted in the log, as were sail changes and wind directions on their own vessel. Seven days after leaving port they were about two miles off East Point, Prince Edward Island, on a NNE course out into the Gulf of St Lawrence, with the Cape Breton Island coast rising to the east. Through these same waters the little *Ark* had sailed thirty-three years before, with her crew looking for the home they found shortly afterwards at St Ann's. It took the brig two days of fog, light rain and less breeze to come abreast of Bonaventure Island tucked in against the Gaspe Peninsula. They spoke with a ship from Glasgow and saw a steamer. With the Madelene River entrance to the west, they made across the Gaspe Passage to the northern shore: "At half past five A.M. seen the land and wore ship Bay of Seven Islands." A fortnight after departure, they received the pilot on board. He would take the brig up the St Lawrence River to Quebec, about three hundred miles away.

Around this time the Matheson brothers would have been deeply involved in their most ambitious venture to date — the building of a brigantine of 106 tons, big enough and roomy enough to carry ninety-three passengers around the world to New Zealand a few years later. But first the *Spray*, as she was called, had to be proved on local seas, and also earn some revenue for her owners. Belle Matheson has pages of a log covering part of a voyage to St John's, Newfoundland, and back to Baddeck in May, 1856. The *Spray*, described as a powerful, fast-sailing vessel, was also employed as the mail packet between Halifax and Bermuda. Belle has another document dating from 1842 — the certificate of registry for the *Richard Smith* of fifty-two tons, built at Arichat, Nova Scotia, and owned nine years later by Hugh Matheson, of Baddeck, mariner.

"Who was he?" I asked Belle.

"No doubt he was Ewen, father of Duncan and Angus," Belle said. "As far as the Highlanders were concerned, Hugh and Ewen were the same name. You'll be wondering what became of him... When I was small his name was only spoken in whispers. I think he must have gone looking for greener pastures or other harbours! Anyway, Widow Matheson came out to New Zealand with her sons and died thirty-four years later at the age of ninety. That was before I was born but I remember being told that she was a tiny little woman who smoked a pipe — she said it helped her asthma." Before he went away, Hugh had left his mark on the settlement, having commanded one of the boats that brought the first party from Pictou to St Ann's.

Angus Matheson, in the log of the *Spray* as elsewhere, was no waster of words. The entry for Saturday, January 11, 1857 reads: "At 2 p.m. weighed anchor from Calves Cove and proceeded out the Brasdor to sea at 4 p.m." I had read the entries for several days before I realised this was the start of the great voyage to New Zealand. There was a good excuse for brevity. Almost immediately the *Spray* was battling big seas which damaged the davit of the ship's boat. "A fearful gale," wrote Angus. "Stowed the top-sail, main staysail, foretopmast staysail and hove to under double-reefed mainsail." Add to this a few crew problems. On the first day out, the cook and steward were off duty. Next day, the steward "noct off duty without any notice" and was replaced by one of the passengers. The cook was still off duty. After a week the gale eased, but the Sunday morning calm was shattered early.

"Hugh McLean the cook came on deck and made use of the most pro-fane abusive language and refused to do his duty went below until 7 o'clock he then came on deck and went to his duty absent two hours. The second mate was obliged to light the fire and cook the breakfast." After that, the voyage settled to a more predictable routine. By January 27 Angus could report: "A clear and pleasant morning with appearance of settled weather." But the steward was in trouble. When a cask of pork was opened, the stew-ard "through negligence has lost a piece of pork weighing 18 pounds for which the captain intends to charge him". Two days later the steward ab-sented himself from duty without any previous notice and "not to be stew-ard any longer". Now for a few days the *Spray* was flying, helped along by a fresh easterly. Under dark skies with a "heavy dash of rain" she covered nearly 200 miles in a day, making around eight knots.

Exactly a month after leaving Cape Breton, an event occurred which would have excited the passengers more than it did Angus. A calm day, "with seven sails in sight to the eastward". Then a light wind took them to a latitude of 0° 31'N of the equator. Next day, the reading was 0° 26'S. Thus did the passengers discover the hemisphere in which most of them would spend the rest of their lives.

By now they had settled into beautiful sailing weather. Something of the exhilaration they must all have been feeling creeps into the log: "Fresh breeze and fine weather with all sail set by the wind... At 5 a.m. the topsail runner carried away — got it repaired and set the sails again. N.B. at 9.30 the cook lost the draw bucket overboard through carelessness, for which charge him 5s."

They had not sighted land since leaving Nova Scotia; now the ocean seemed even emptier. They were making good speed, six, seven and eight knots listed in the log. Keith Matheson had some interesting comments to make. Never far from Angus's mind as he sailed down the Atlantic, said Keith, would be the importance of making a fairly precise landfall at the Cape of Good Hope. In the 1850s, many vessels were navigated without the aid of a chronometer and, even if one was available, there was no guarantee of its accuracy in determining longitude and the vessel's position. Latitude could be established by observing the sun's maximum altitude with a sextant and checking with the tables in the current Nautical Almanac. But how to find the correct longitude? The answer lay in the remote Tristan da Cunha islands, halfway between the Cape and Argentina, on about the same latitude as the Cape. Being well to the west of Tristan because of the weight of the South-East Trades, Angus knew that, if he got into the latitude of the group and steered east, he would raise the islands sooner or later. Unless, of course, the *Spray* by some mischance was east of the islands when the navigator thought she was west. Then, after realising the error, Angus would have had to turn round and sail back again, sticking to the same latitude until the landfall was made.

Running the latitude down, they called it, and that is what the *Spray* did for only a day or two until, on March 13, the high volcanic peaks of Tristan appeared to the south-west. The time was four in the morning. By eight o'clock the south-east end of the island was about twelve miles distant. As he wrote: "Took from there a new departure." Angus could have been well satisfied with his navigation. But there had still been room for error. Keith, checking Angus's calculations, found that his great-uncle had made a simple subtraction mistake which put the ship three degrees too far west. This mistake had been carried forward for a week until Tristan was sighted.

Confident now in their position, they carried all possible sail with a wind that for the most part was blowing fresh or strong from the south or south-west. At midnight on March 23 they had all sail set: "A fresh breeze and cloudy... At 2 a.m. hove the ship to, the distance being nearly run up. At 5 a.m. saw the Cape bearing east by south. Set sail and steered for the land. At noon abreast of green point. Blowing hard from the south-east. Working into Table Bay under double-reefed topsails and mainsail. At 2 brought up with both anchors 30 fathoms cable. Furled sails and cleared deck. Set anchor watch."

In this way Angus brought to an end the log of the first half of the voyage to New Zealand, a voyage which he described to the shipping man on the Capetown newspaper as "tedious". Perhaps that is how it seemed to him, although the fact that his wife gave birth to their second child off the Cape might have been excitement enough. For many other unseasoned travellers, the voyage seemed an almost endless series of storms. For all of them, passengers and crew alike, a break of ten days on shore at Capetown would have given welcome relief.

Perhaps Angus was characteristically underplaying his feelings when he used the word "tedious" to describe his first voyage of any magnitude. The log gives few indications that they were carrying nearly one hundred passengers. The ship was described as "in ballast", which is an unusual way of saying that her cargo was people. There are scattered references to opening casks of meat and broaching casks of water. Before reaching the Cape the empty casks in the "hole" were filled with salt water, possibly to give the vessel more stability in heavy seas. There is no reference to passengers helping with manning the ship in times of stress. It is very likely that this would happen, for most of those on board were linked with ties of kinship or community, and many of the men were experienced seamen in their home waters.

Captain Keith Matheson grew up in sail under conditions not too far removed from those enjoyed or suffered by the men of the *Spray*. He felt that, if satisfaction comes with a full use of one's senses, then many seamen of that time would have led reasonably satisfying lives.

"I think the seamen of those days had a much keener appreciation of the value of the senses of sight, hearing and even smell than we have in these days of radio time signals, radio direction finders, echo sounders and radar; also meteorological information which would have been so helpful in sailing ship days.

"Many a ship," Keith said, "has been saved from disaster by a good lookout observing the 'loom of the land' — a darkening through fog or haze — the sound of the surf on the shore or even the smell of vegetation.

"On the sailing ship, without the roar and vibration of the machinery, the faculties of observation were very keen and well developed. Another good reason for this was that the preservation of the ship, and often of your life, depended on it."

There are vessels on which it is possible to make a leisurely passage with no great pressure on officers or crew, but the *Spray* was not one of them. The smallness of the ship, the number of passengers, the length of the voyage made it essential to use every puff of wind that would help them on their way, and a study of the log suggests that the *Spray* was worked as hard as a modern racing yacht. She carried all possible sail by night as well as by day, and the crew had to tend sails meticulously. On February 1, for example, the log reads: "P.M. Fresh breeze and cloudy with all sail set by the wind… At 1 a.m., heavy squalls. Handed the topgallant sail and main topmast staysail." Not the most relaxing work in the dead of night. Another entry: "At 8 p.m. strong breeze, took in all light sails. At midnight reefed topsail and mainsail, stowed the jib. At 2½ a.m. wind increasing with heavy squalls. Clewed up foresail and topsail and hove to. At 8 a.m. a regular gale with heavy sea running. At 10½ flying jib boom went by the board." There would have been little sleep for passengers and crew that night.

Among the crew, a bunch of independent Highlanders, tensions would build up. Not when conditions were severe — everybody was too busy then — but, as on March 3, when the weather was "moderate and pleasant". That was the day when, at 2 p.m., "Kenneth McKenzie refused to do his duty; when ordered to releave the wheel he would not. At 6 p.m. returned to duty." There is no mention of any action taken against him — the Mathesons would have known him for a long time as they all grew up together. It was this same Kenneth McKenzie who, in a violent storm off the Australian coast towards the end of the voyage, volunteered to go over the ship's side to secure a boom that had gone adrift and was threatening to damage the vessel. "Kenny Omaha", as he was later called from the place where he settled in New Zealand, became a celebrated sea captain in the South Pacific, and father of Captain George McKenzie, even more famous in the Tasman trade as master for many years of the fast and beautiful topsail schooner *Huia*.

In the early 1850s, when the *Spray* first took to the sea, what sort of pay did the seamen receive, and what were the conditions of employment? Some other documents in Angus's logbook give a clue. The Articles of Agreement between Angus, as master of the *Spray* while trading from Cape Breton and his crew (a mate and four seamen) covered a period not to exceed six months: "From the harbour of Lewisburg to Halifax and any other North American coasting voyages as required, to be discharged at the harbour of Baddeck, Cape Breton."

Under the articles, "One hour's absence before cargo is discharged warrants forfeiture of one month's pay. One hour's absence from ship 24 hours before intended departure to be deemed a desertion."

The temptation of the harbour grog shops was great. Kenneth McDonald chose his time well to celebrate on the night before the *Spray* cleared St John's, Newfoundland, for Baddeck on an early voyage. The log records that Kenneth was "absent from duty and drunk", but he was at least on board.

The crew list included in the articles would make a modern seaman marvel:

Name	Age	Birthplace	Quality	Wages per calendar
Angus Matheson	30	Scotland	Master	£8-0-0
Duncan Matheson	32	Scotland	Mate	£5-10-0
Kenneth McKenzie	30	Scotland	Seaman	£4-0-0
Donald McAulay	22	Scotland	Ord. seaman	£2-10-0
Kenneth McDonald	28	Scotland	Seaman	£4-0-0
Archibald Stewart*	41	Scotland	Seaman	£4-0-0

* signed on at later date

The log for the rest of the voyage has disappeared. On board the *Spray*, however, was Hugh McKenzie, school teacher, farmer and, in the manner of the Nova Scotians, just about everything else. Hugh kept notes which recorded the *Spray's* progress. Stormy weather continued as they were driven eastward round the south of Australia. On entering the Tasman Sea, a truly ferocious storm forced them north up the coast. It was then that Kenny Omaha showed his drive and courage in securing the rampant boom, before they sought shelter, and time for repairs, in Twofold Bay.

New South Wales welcomed the battered, sea-weary travellers. A customs officer came on board and they asked him what news there was. His reply: "Nothing much. Only that a dozen convicts were hung up to dry this morning." Perhaps, even as early as 1857, the characteristic Australian sense of humour was emerging.

A comfortable crossing of the Tasman Sea, a narrow escape in the Bay of Islands when the *Spray* scraped over a submerged rock, a frustrating delay in that harbour for eight days because of unfavourable winds. Then Auckland at last and reunion with relatives and friends. Decisions had to be made quickly. Although most of the folk who had arrived earlier were in the Waipu area, Auckland had already become the centre for the shipowners and seamen. The *Spray* arrived on June 25. Within a month she was advertised to sail for Sydney: "Accommodations equal to those of any vessel in the trade." She was now under the command of Captain H.F. Anderson, formerly second officer on the *Margaret*.

To us today it might seem incredible that a hundred people, many of them speaking only Gaelic, could be absorbed so painlessly into a very different kind of land. The tight structure of their Cape Breton community, however, had not loosened with the move to New Zealand. Hospitality was offered and accepted as a matter of course. Accommodation had been organised close to the wharves, there was advice on what land was available within the community area or — and this was particularly important to the Mathesons — where boatbuilding and farming could be combined. Three years of settlement at Waipu had shown that its potential as a shipbuilding centre was limited, and in addition much of the convenient land had been taken up. But there were many other possibilities, north and south of Waipu.

Trading up and down the coast, the Waipu men would have noticed the beautiful sheltered water of Omaha Bay, halfway to Auckland. But before the Mathesons went to Omaha, or even decided that would be their chosen home, there were adjustments to be made, new conditions to be accepted. To Jessie Matheson, Angus's wife, with her little baby born on the *Spray*, release from the ship must have felt like stepping from prison into the bright light of day. Restricted movement and the lack of privacy were the chief disadvantages. There could have been few complaints about the food — the basic ingredients for their meals had been flour, corn, potatoes, corned meats, dried fish — for they had known what to expect and, after all, it was not very different from what they would have had during a Cape Breton winter. There may also have been dehydrated vegetables; and great store was set by onions. But now, in a mild green land with fertile soil waiting to be tilled, there was an urgency about sowing and planting, harvesting fresh vegetables, acquiring a milking cow so that they could make their curds and butter.

For Duncan Matheson there were two important steps to be taken. The first, the disposal of the *Spray*, owned by him and Angus. The second, and even more important, his marriage to Catherine Finlayson. Catherine's mother, Christina, had been a passenger on the *Spray* with four of her family, but she herself had come to New Zealand earlier on the *Highland Lass*, probably to help an over-burdened mother with her children. In Auckland she had lived with a missionary family, the Maunsells, helping with sewing and other duties. The family still have a keepsake that Susan Maunsell gave her. So now she accompanied her mother to Waipu, where she and Duncan were married. The following year, Duncan, Catherine and their baby daughter, just a few weeks old, arrived at Omaha. Their son Roderick would be the first born at Little Omaha. The first girl born in the district was Christina Matheson, daughter of Angus and Jessie, who moved there in 1859.

By that time the passengers on the *Spray* had gone to at least six different localities, all of them settled by Nova Scotian kinsfolk or friends. Although they were widely dispersed, the communities were still, paradoxically, closely knit. Keith Matheson remembered the impressive assembly of "survivors" at his grandmother's house fifty years later. All talking in Gaelic, they would refresh their minds with memories of Nova Scotia, of the great voyage, and discovering where everyone had gone in the years between; the intricacies of family relationships. Once there was a serious purpose behind this research; in Waipu a young couple were engaged to be married when they discovered they were first cousins. The marriage did not proceed and the man remained a bachelor for the rest of his long life. And in Omaha, Keith Matheson once confounded a second cousin sailing with him on the New Zealand coast: "Did you know that your grandfather's sister was also your great-grandmother?"

It was true pioneering for the Mathesons down at Omaha that year of 1858, and for many years more; just as primitive as what their parents had endured in Cape Breton, though under a warmer sun. A tent was their first shelter, close to the beach. Then as soon as sufficient space had been cleared in the bush, they moved into a Maori-style hut made from the fronds of the nikau palm. As time allowed, they built a house of rough-sawn timber which, unlined as it was, seemed like a palace in comparison.

Farming had to be no more than a part-time occupation for Duncan and Angus. Sailing was the natural way to earn money for improving their land. Voyages kept them from home for long periods — even coastal trading could extend over many weeks. The log of the *Kate McGregor*, under Angus's command, covers one such voyage in the 1870s. The *Kate McGregor* left Auckland on February 26, 1877, for Lyttelton. They put into Hicks Bay to repair a split foresail and reached Lyttelton on March 7. Cargo was discharged by March 12, chiefly timber and draining pipes, and several hundred doors. Discipline was just as firm in New Zealand as in Nova Scotia. John Hunter, ashore without leave, was "apprehended and sentenced to forfeit two days' pay and one month hard labour".

There were frustrating delays in loading cargo but on March 17 the good ship *Kate McGregor* was on her way to Auckland again. No spectacular distances were covered up the east coast, with mostly light and baffling winds, and ten days passed before they were discharging cargo in Auckland. Two days later they were loading again; shipped the cook on April 7 and left port on the next day on the way to Oamaru. On April 22 the pilot came on board and they moored alongside the Oamaru pier. For several days heavy seas allowed little or no cargo to be landed. They were hauling off and alongside every day for a week before they finished discharging and began loading. At last the weather improved, and on May 4 they were under way, this time for Waikato, through Cook Strait and up the west coast of the North Island. Two days passed and they were abreast of Stephens Island and could well have thought they were clear of the notorious strait; but instead a great gale came at them from the north-west, tore sails to ribbons and forced them to run south, past Stephens Island again, and into Wellington Harbour to repair their sails. They were now a week out of Oamaru, and must have wondered when they would get anywhere. On May 14 they joined four other vessels waiting for a chance, the weather squally and thick with rain, the barometer down to 29.70 and falling. Their opportunity came after two days, with fickle Cook Strait presenting light winds and occasional calms. Slow progress around Cape Egmont, then the gales came at them again. The forestay carried away, the mainsail damaged. On May 29 they crossed the bar at the entrance to the Waikato River: "Closing on the South Spit put the ship about fell suddenly calm and in less than a minute struck on the Spit." Until June 2 they were discharging cargo, lightening their vessel so that they could heave it off into deep water. Then they made fast at the wharf and took in ballast.

More than most people, sailors need patience. From June 7 to June 28 they lay in the river with the log recording, "Heavy break all along the bar; no chance to get out", or words to that effect. But everything comes to an end and at last, on June 29, they were able to sail up to the Manukau Harbour, cross another bar and, on June 30, come to anchor in the port of Onehunga.

Over eight weeks from Oamaru to Onehunga, with only one scheduled stop, would probably have been a record rarely beaten. And that may be the reason why this log survived, while those of Angus's many other successful trading voyages have disappeared. Presumably Angus was able to get home to Omaha after these two long months to see how his family was faring, how the farm was developing. But right through from the 1850s there were these long periods of absence for Duncan as well as Angus, when the weight of responsibility rested on the shoulders of wives and growing children. They seemed, from upbringing, temperament and sheer necessity, to have carried it successfully. Both brothers sailed deep water as well as on the more testing coastal ventures. Indeed, Duncan returned to Nova Scotia to buy a vessel, the *Oceola*, which he sailed back to New Zealand. His chief officer was Hugh Ross, a grandson of Norman McLeod.

From the recollections of their children and grandchildren it is possible to gain some idea of the life that Jessie and Catherine Matheson led. Babies were born, crops were sown, cattle and poultry provided milk, eggs and meat, eventually in sufficient quantities for the surplus to be sold. But women on their own developed special qualities. For months on end there might be little communication with Auckland, and supplies could run out. Catherine Matheson, her family recall, had sown wheat on cleared ground among tree stumps near the house. One time, when there was no flour left to make bread, she reaped wheat with a sickle, threshed it and ground it with a handmill. And the bread was excellent!

There were many more calls on their time, made more demanding by the lack of transport of virtually any kind — unless by boat. Thus, when a trading vessel called at Big Omaha, some miles south along the coast from Matheson's Bay, stores had to be collected on foot. Catherine, on one occasion at least, carried a hundred-pound sack of flour home on her back. She also had an arrangement with the captain of a cutter that called at Big

Omaha. When she carried a box of eggs from home to meet the cutter, he would sell the eggs in Auckland for her, keeping a dozen eggs as payment. Money played no great part in life in the distinct. As more settlers arrived, and cattle became more plentiful, farmers would take turns in killing a beast and sharing the meat. But, as in Nova Scotia before and in Scotland even earlier, fish, potatoes and milk dominated the family diet. Lacking the taste-titillating rubbish of today, this seemed to provide most of what was needed for survival. Strong in body, strong in mind, with a cheerful, forward-looking disposition, Catherine lived on into her eighty-ninth year.

Was life dull? It seems they were too busy to be bored. It was good to have a little time to share congenial company while the spinning wheels turned or the knitting needles clicked. The climate was mild, and even in winter the grass grew and the gardens kept producing. How did the children like it? As one of Angus's daughters, the future Mrs Christina Smith, put it: "When we wanted a holiday, we went down to the beach for the day and ate periwinkles." Few children could have been brought up in a more beautiful environment: white sand, craggy headlands, islands of a fantastic blue; and inland streams running clean through lush undergrowth and forest trees that stood like great colonnades. The houses soon gained a comfortable, settled feeling, with gardens and irregularly shaped fields around them, but farming remained a secondary employment. With the men spending so much time at sea, there was only a slow output of sailing vessels, most of them under Duncan's direction. Stories have gathered around all of them and around the men who sailed them. First in the list was *Saucy Lass*, a schooner 60 feet long, built in 1864 for D.H. McKenzie and Kenneth McGregor, whose vessels sailed the world from China to New York. The contract laid down that the deck should be planed, but for some reason most of it was dressed with an adze. When the owner objected, he was invited to point out which part had been planed and which had been adzed. He couldn't do so.

Three years later came *Coquette*, of 43 tons. She was wrecked in Fiji in 1870 while under the command of Duncan Matheson, her part-owner. His report was terse and to the point: "I beg to forward this to inform you that the schooner *Coquette* was wrecked on Frenchman's Reef, near Suva, on the 14th September. All hands saved with difficulty."

In 1873 the brigantine *Ryno*, significantly bigger than the others at 83 feet, was launched. She started down the ways before a bottle could be broken on her bows, and Duncan called her name as, in desperation, he threw an adze at her bow. In 1876 Angus designed and built the cutter *Rangatira*. Last of all was *Three Cheers* which in a tragic way signalled the end of an era. Keith Matheson gave me some of the details.

"Duncan spent three years building this schooner. Even more than usual

185

he lavished his skill and care on her. He was nearly sixty, and perhaps accepted that he would be building no more like her. She was all ready to be masted when a spar crashed down, pinning grandfather to the deck by his leg. They did what they could, which wasn't very much for the leg had been destroyed, with bones projecting in all directions. Grandfather stayed conscious and when the doctor came said to him: 'Do the best you can.' He died soon afterwards.

"He would have been proud of his last ship. At the Auckland Regatta in 1883 *Three Cheers* won the champion trading vessels' race, with a prize of £75 and a cup valued at £10. *Rangatira* completed a double for the Mathesons when she won the big cutter race. In the hard world of commercial trading, where fast passages meant better returns, *Three Cheers* was equally at home. We had a family story that she had, on one occasion, raced with an intercolonial steamer on the Tasman crossing and beaten her."

Duncan's son Roderick had served his time at sea. He had also been one of the team that built *Three Cheers*, camping at Tutukaka, north of Whangarei, while he cut frames and timbers for the new vessel. Thirty years later he showed Keith, his son, the stumps of the kauri trees felled for the job. The shock of his father's violent death would have been great; and now he turned away from the sea and the shipyard to concentrate on farming and gardening. But the break was never complete. Working on the farm, he suffered from hay fever. He confessed to Keith that the only way he could get relief was to be three miles offshore.

"When I was about five years old," Keith recalled, "father had two rowboats which he would load with watermelons and kumaras. Towing one with the other, off he rowed to Leigh cove. By that time — about 1900 — little steamers were calling to pick up goods for Auckland."

The rowboats were only a start. "I noticed that Dad was always on the lookout for special pieces of wood. These, he told me, would be used for crooks and knees for the boat he planned to build for himself. He already had the model and a pohutukawa stempost put aside. Soon he had finished a shed in a secluded spot up the river near the waterfall. Whenever he had the chance, Dad would disappear up the bush track and get to work. It was a long, painstaking task and, as far as I know, he had no help save what I as a six-year-old could give him.

"This is how it went. She was planked with battens one inch square, hand-sawn out of twelve-inch by one-inch heart kauri planks. Imagine the work entailed for each plank: ripping, tapering, bevelling, planing true to make a perfect fit; clamping close to moulds, boring and nailing. There was no caulking to fall out and a true form could be maintained. I have seen shipwrights sight along her bottom and remark that she looked as if she was pressed out of a mould.

"It was a great day for us all, including mother with two-month-old Ronald, when our 23-foot cutter took the water and the mast was stepped under a big pohutukawa tree. I remember father and mother talking one night and deciding on *Endeavour* for her name. The next thing was, would she be ready for the New Year regatta at Big Omaha? A dry summer meant that the river mouth was blocked with a sand bar, but that was not going to stop father. We found later that he had worked nearly all night cutting a channel through the sandbank. The enclosed water went with a rush and the next high tide opened a channel down which the *Endeavour* sailed to her moorings. No, we didn't win our regatta race. Father had Duncan Knaggs and Johnnie Williams as crew — I was there too — but the other craft, with much less draught than *Endeavour*, were able to take short cuts over the sandbanks!

"Father had designed *Endeavour* so that she could carry produce from the farm to Auckland. Her model was like that of the larger coastal cargo cutters with a straight stem, full forward and of ample bilge, a fine, high run with a short counter so that she did not drag water, however deeply loaded. She was kept happily busy during the cropping season, and when that ended Dad started fishing for the market. Before very long, fishing became his main occupation. This suited me very well. Even before leaving school in 1909, at the age of fifteen, I had spent Saturdays and school holidays out with him; and once free of school I became a full-time fisherman. For variety there was an occasional trip on a coastal scow, on the schooner *Orete* trading to Gisborne and on the ketch *Will Watch*, but fishing, especially when the harvest was good, satisfied me completely. Then in 1915 my father died, after being ill for a year, and my life changed."

When I first met Keith Matheson he was in his early seventies, but still likely to go overseas in a ship heading for Australia, the East Indies or the sub-Antarctic islands far to the south of New Zealand. He was of medium height, conservatively dressed as were most sea captains of his vintage when ashore, in a tidy navy-blue suit. His face was deeply tanned and, as he walked, his massive head was thrust forward as if his eyes were searching the horizon. His face was serious in repose, but it could crinkle with humour as he warmed to a conversation. A modest man, he nonetheless enjoyed recalling incidents from his fifty years at sea, although he was careful not to give too much prominence to his own experiences.

"A trip or two on a coastal scow, a spell of a year on the *Huia*," was how Keith dismissed his sea apprenticeship. "And just about everyone was on the *Huia* at one time or another!" Later on he was back on the *Huia*, New Zealand's most celebrated topsail schooner, as second mate.

"I liked the *Huia*, though she was a hard ship — fast and correspondingly wet, diving deeply under the slightest provocation. There was plenty

Captain Keith Matheson, a modest man, conservative in manner and style, one of the great seamen of his time. PHOTO: C.W. HAWKINS

of sail drill, many times under water hanging on for dear life as one hauled on the head sheets, braces and halliards.

"Jim Drummond, later to become master of the *Huia* but at the time an A.B., could have been thought a very lucky man, washed off the jib boom when the vessel dived unexpectedly into a swell. I was forward also but clambered up the forestay. There were several men out on the boom making the jib fast. It was pitch black, but they couldn't feel Jim next to them, so knew he had gone. Captain Lane, standing aft, heard their yells and, guessing what might have happened, threw a line overboard. As we went aft, sure enough Jim was hanging on to it, about 80 feet astern. Could he retain his grasp? Yes, we got him aboard safely, none the worse. Then we had time to marvel at the chance that a rope happened to be there, and that it was thrown over the right side to come within Jim's grasp as the ship went plunging on.

"Another time we were on a voyage from Melbourne to Dunedin. In the South Tasman we struck a southerly gale and the ship was taking such a battering hove-to that Captain Lane put her before it and ran to the north. I was on watch about 2 a.m., standing on top of the house gripping the main boom when I saw a mighty breaking sea astern. The vessel ran down the face of it at terrific speed then, like a surfboard out of control, ran her bow under and rounded-to while the sea threw her completely on her beam ends. I remember as I hung on to the boom seeing the foreyard go in the water. I thought the man at the wheel was gone, but he had jammed himself under the wheelbox and had met the gripe with the helm so that the vessel was off before the wind immediately. That was Wally Cole, one of the best of helmsmen. Such was the catapulting effect of that sudden broach-to that every movable object in the ship was fired toward the lee side, mattresses out of the deep bunks, bolts and nuts in deep boxes on the weather side of the engine room flew across the engine and the engineer and landed on the other side. But most remarkable to me was what happened in the sail locker, how she completely pancaked our stow of sails in a confined space so that the sails originally on the bottom were now on top. There was some damage around the deck but nothing very serious. A man went through the lee rigging but hauled himself back on a trailing halliard. The sea remained very heavy for another day, but there was nothing again like that freak sea. If the vessel had not been loaded to the deck beams she surely would never have recovered."

The year 1938 saw a big change in Keith's way of life. He joined as sailing master the *Vanora*, a 73-foot auxiliary ketch owned by an American woman, Mrs Harte, who was sailing around the world. This was to be the last lap of a voyage less common then than now: destination New York, via the Magellan Straits. Years later Keith remembered vividly the wild, grand scenery of the Patagonian channels, with glacier-fed waterfalls splashing down almost on the deck as the willy-waws swung them around in a snug anchorage. There were memories of great, surging seas in the Roaring Forties and sudden unpredictable squalls up the South American coast, but for Keith one of the most anxious days came on July 6, the day after the *Vanora* reached New York. Following the excitement of arrival, with photographers and reporters thronging the yacht basin, the newsreel people persuaded Mrs Harte to repeat the arrival next day.

"With friends on board showing my crew more hospitality than was good for them in a crowded harbour, we proceeded down past the Statue of Liberty to return under full sail — square sail and square topsail set with the visitors sitting on sheets and halliards and generally distracting my well-lubricated crew. A day to remember, with small craft and larger ones too crossing our bows. But we berthed again without incident."

Keith's North American wanderings began in a very appropriate way. He joined another yacht sailing to Nova Scotia up the New England coast. The sailing of the *Spray* and the other migrant vessels was still fresh in the minds of the people and, when it was reported that Keith was planning to buy a Nova Scotian vessel to resail the course of his grandfather to New

The topsail schooner Tagua, *"queen of the South Pacific", captained for six years by Keith Matheson during the Second World War, setting up coastguard and meteorological stations from the sub-Antarctic to the equator, a line of defence against enemy raiders.*
PHOTO: C.W. HAWKINS

Zealand, many applied to take part. But then, in September, 1939, the war began and his plan was scrapped. Getting back to New Zealand was not easy. Before seeing Auckland again he had shipped as chief officer on an American freighter taking, ironically, a cargo of scrap metal to Japan. One wonders how much of this might have been fired back at Allied forces when Japan came into the war a little later.

Keith was now in his late forties; the most exciting period of his life was about to begin. The *Tagua* was an American-built vessel of 209 tons and, Keith considered, "as fine a trading schooner as has been seen in the South Pacific". He joined her as first mate and in 1941 became master, a post that he held for six years. *Tagua* became queen of the South Pacific, her domain extending from Christmas Island in the north to the Auckland and Campbell Islands in the south; from Pitcairn and Henderson Islands in the east to the Solomons in the west. A vast expanse of ocean, in which she made her purposeful way from just north of the equator to the sub-Antarctic, from coral islands to the heavy jungles of the west. On board *Tagua* at various times were coastguards and meteorologists to set up stations in remote and hazardous areas, a line of defence against enemy raiders. Then there were engineers and construction gangs to establish aerodromes. There

190

were surveyors, doctors, nurses, missionaries, geologists, authors. The list was endless. Their enthusiasm, Keith said, was remarkable. After twelve months in the windy, fog-bound latitudes of sub-Antarctica, some were eager to offer themselves for another term. The *Tagua* was under charter to the New Zealand Government but, when her story could be told, her deeds became celebrated far beyond that little country. She, her captain and crew were fortunate to have no direct contact with the war that was ravaging the world around them. Keith retained a grim memory of sailing through a mass of dead bodies, left after a vessel had been sunk by a Japanese submarine. Another time they went to Suwarrow Island because no radio report had been received for some time from the party stationed there. Had the Japanese taken over? "We couldn't know until we got there," said Keith. "But it was only a radio failure."

With the war's end there was still work to be done: resettling Gilbert Islanders in their own villages; collecting bodies of the war dead and bringing them to the New Zealand war cemetery at Bourail in New Caledonia; transporting "war leftovers" from the Solomons battle area to Auckland or Fiji.

"On the voyage to Fiji I had my brother Ronald as mate; having not seen much of my home for a number of years I signed on a new mate and Ronald took *Tagua* away from Suva. I had fixed my relief, but not my means to get home. There was no passage available but there was an American-built yacht for sale in Suva. I admired her lines. She was a double-ended marconi-rigged auxiliary ketch, 38′6″ by 12′2″ beam, once owned by Errol Flynn the actor. She was luxuriously appointed and I thought this would be something to bring home instead of wasting time waiting for a passage. So with a three-man amateur crew we sailed her to Auckland. My family and I got a lot of pleasure in the *Barbary* cruising up and down the coast, but I had to go to sea again, so after three years sold her."

To sea again meant trading voyages to Japan, to Borneo, to Cambodia, mostly in smallish cargo vessels or tankers. The *Nukulau* sprang a leak in the Tasman, the *Fiona* heard their distress call and picked up the crew two minutes before the *Nukulau* sank. In 1961 the *Verao*, deeply laden, developed a heavy list as she struggled into big seas. She was likely to go down without warning; the fifteen men on board, with only what they were wearing, took to the one 18-foot lifeboat, which shipped more and more water as the seas increased. On her beam ends, the *Verao* stayed afloat through a stormy night and in the morning was sighted by a searching plane which dropped a life raft. A rescue ship arrived that evening.

As master of the *Taranui* in his seventieth year, Keith took a party of scientists back to his old haunts in the Auckland Islands, visiting the old provision depot, the weather reporting station in Perseverance Harbour, on Campbell Island — a much more elaborate place than the one he had known. He continued to relieve as master on the *Taranui* through 1966. He died suddenly in December, 1969, at the age of 75.

I make no apology for covering his career in a fairly detailed way, though there is much more that I would like to have included. In Keith, one could see the durable qualities of his forebears as seamen and as men. Like many who had been raised in sail, he was a deeply thoughtful man who did not thrust his opinions at a listener but let them emerge quietly. He enjoyed good company and good food, and never lost the thrill of making port in strange or familiar lands. But the beautiful *Tagua*, queen of the South Pacific, held a big share of his heart; never more so than when he took her into Maryborough, Queensland. There, they had not seen an Island schooner with an Island crew since the old days when it was a favourite port for Island trade — which meant the landing of labourers to work the sugar cane — and they gave her a royal reception.

It would be incorrect to say that Captain Duncan Keith Matheson typified the Nova Scotian sea captain. There were many of that breed both before and after him, and they were personalities in their own right; but there were recognisable characteristics that linked them together. And, in any such gallery of seamen, Keith Matheson could stand proud and straight.

When Kenneth Ainslie was a lad, he was much too busy making his way in the world to spare more than a passing thought for his Nova Scotian ancestors; going to sea at thirteen and being away from home most of the time gave little chance for curiosity about the family. But history kept crowding in on him, almost in spite of himself. He served his time aboard the barque *Louisa Craig*. "She was not due for around a month," Kenneth told me, "so I pestered the marine superintendent until he found me a berth as a cabin boy in the barquentine *Ysabel*, sailing to Noumea and Surprise Island and back to Auckland. Among the ABs there was a real old shellback who, upon learning I was a nephew of Captain George McKenzie, said: 'You must then be a grandson of Smuggler McKenzie'.

"A bit taken aback, I denied I was the grandson of any smuggler. When I next saw my mother I scandalised her by asking if my grandfather was known as such. She was quite shocked and wanted to know who could have told me such a terrible thing. Briefly, the old sailor's story was that McKenzie, on his return trips from the Pacific, sometimes brought back unmanifested rum and tobacco in small quantities, landing these at Omaha before making his entrance at Auckland. Just how long this went on I don't know, but apparently McKenzie, who had a quick temper, had trodden on the toes of a neighbour. This chap decided to get his own back; which he did by getting on his horse, riding to Devonport, crossing to Auckland and reporting the matter to the Customs. Two men were sent post haste to Omaha and caught him with the goods partly unloaded. The skipper said: 'Well boys, you have me this time. I suppose you'll impound the ship... Well, if you like I'll sail her up to Auckland for you.' On the way up, so the story goes, McKenzie got the two men drunk on the contraband rum and then removed the evidence by dumping it over the side. I don't know how true the story is, but like most sailors' yarns there may have been a suspicion of truth somewhere."

There were a number of McKenzies with the first name of Kenneth involved in the migration, and among those who went to sea confusion was likely to develop. But we have already met the Smuggler as crewman on the *Spray*, later nicknamed Kenny Omaha. Kenneth Ainslie, named after him, said his grandfather had built himself a small craft in Nova Scotia and sailed her back to Scotland, where he married Margaret and returned to Nova Scotia. Margaret had also been born a McKenzie.

Like many others only a generation away from the personal rule of a clan chief, Kenneth McKenzie had a healthy disrespect for imposed external authority. Strong minded, independent, unwilling to suffer fools gladly or sadly, he was busy carving out his own road into the new world of the Pacific. It seemed reasonable enough for a man to bring in a few contraband goods. Win or lose, it gave a pleasant excitement to life.

The Pacific Islands offered plenty of opportunity to a man of enterprise. Copra, pearl shell, cotton, oranges, bananas and pineapples were carried one way; a great variety of manufactured goods on the return trip. Before long, other avenues opened, notably the transport of islanders to work on the plantations of Queensland, Fiji and New Caledonia. The labourers came chiefly from the New Hebrides and the Solomons. Kenneth Ainslie mentioned three vessels that his grandfather had commanded — *Borealis, Saxon* and *Talisman*. Of the three, *Borealis* achieved the most notoriety.

The man who set Nova Scotian eyes towards the Pacific was Captain Hugh Anderson, son-in-law of the Rev. Norman McLeod. The *Borealis* was built for Anderson and McKenzie by John Darrach and Sons, of Mahurangi; the price for "hull and spars complete" was fifteen hundred pounds. She was launched in December, 1879. Within three months she was in Fiji where she was chartered for labour recruiting in the New Hebrides, under McKenzie's command. Kenneth Ainslie told me this story:

"Dropping anchor off one of the islands, McKenzie, together with the mate, put off in a small boat and pulled round a headland to where the native village was. On landing they found the place deserted but saw some women and children scampering into the bush. Apparently McKenzie was already suspicious that things were not as they should be. He and the mate started to pull back to the ship. Rounding the headland they saw a collection of canoes alongside, with natives swarming everywhere; and they heard yells and other sounds coming over the water. McKenzie was all for getting back as fast as they could. But the mate realised that, were they to do so, they too would be massacred. So, as McKenzie insisted on rowing back to his ship the mate had to knock him senseless with an oar.

"He pulled out to sea and after dark returned to the ship.

"They found carnage in the fullest sense. Every member was cut to pieces. In fact, very little of the second mate was found — only a few parts and his Bible. He was McKenzie's son and my uncle William. An hour or so later they heard groans coming from a water tank on deck and, on investigating, found the cook who, after being cut about a bit, managed to get into the tank and thus save his life. Well, McKenzie, the mate and the cook sailed the vessel to Australia. It seems that Bully Hayes, the infamous blackbirder, or slaver, had visited the island a few weeks before and shang-haied most of the men. Those who remained, upon sighting McKenzie's vessel, thought Hayes was returning, and that was the cause of the violent attack. *Borealis* was painted white, and similar in appearance to the schooner owned and operated by Hayes."

Several years before this shattering experience, McKenzie was already deeply involved in the blackbirder's world of kidnapping, murder and often bloody retaliation. In 1871 the crew of the schooner *Fanny*, visiting the island of Nguna to collect labourers for the cotton plantations of Fiji, were killed as "man-stealers". In its efforts to quell the barbarous labour traffic, HMS *Rosario* reached the island a little later and found that "the massacre was committed in consequence of one of their women, an albino, the wife of a chief, having been stolen by a white man named McKenzie, in the schooner *Donald McLean*, taken down to Tanna and there sold for labour."

Commander Markham of the *Rosario* assured the husband that he would seek and find the kidnapped lady. This he did and, when he took her back to Nguna, there were "exclamations of approval and gratification" at her restoration. The story did not end there. On entering Noumea, they discovered the *Donald McLean* at anchor; but McKenzie was not on board. "Our second lieutenant found that she had no papers whatever to give her authority to hire workers. Her master, one Donald McLeod, was made to sign a paper acknowledging the illegality of his proceedings."

MeLeod and McKenzie had been crew members on the *Spray*. Others of the McLeod family, who became as highly respected in New Zealand as they had been in Nova Scotia, were passengers on the *Breadalbane* and settled at Whangarei Heads. Donald, however, made New Caledonia his home. He succeeded in amassing wealth and land and, in after years, a reputation as a worthy pioneer in the south-west Pacific. Contact with his New Zealand kinsfolk stayed strong; between 1876 and 1891 he had at least five ships registered in New Zealand.

The captain who served as a model for Jack London's "Sea Wolf" was supposed to have been a Nova Scotian. Was he from the Waipu migration? a friend wonders.

Kenneth McKenzie died in 1902 when he was about 76. He had had time to see his son George, following his example, become a captain of ships trading through the South Pacific, some would say the greatest seaman of them all. But the dynasty was not concentrated on one line. Lilian, one of George's sisters, married Captain Murdoch McKenzie, of Waipu, who commanded the barque *Kathleen Hilda* and was described by a knowledgeable contemporary as "one of the best shipmasters I ever sailed with". Then there were the young ones: William, killed on the *Borealis*, and Danny, drowned off North Head in the Auckland Harbour. If they had lived, what might they have become? The sea, its beauty and its savagery, fascinated all the family, from one generation to the next.

George McKenzie was a good businessman as well as a great seaman. He linked up with Captain Jimmy Smith, who also traded to the islands and who had married Kitty, daughter of Donald Campbell, a passenger on the *Gertrude*. Smith and McKenzie, in partnership, were a powerful force in young Auckland. They owned merchant ships, they ran the Devonport Ferry Company, the North Shore steam tramways, a coal mine in the Waikato district sixty miles south. George was also a director of the Northern Steam Ship Company. Smith's Bush, a landmark on Auckland's North Shore, keeps Jimmy Smith's name alive. He had no family, but he and Kitty brought up one of Kitty's nieces. There was always warm hospitality from Mrs Captain Smith, as she was called, for visitors from the north. The "tower house", where they lived in the suburb of Grey Lynn, still stands.

Kenneth Ainslie himself had a career as remarkable as any of his forebears. "I served my time in sail," he told me, "later went into steam and when World War Two broke out acted as water transport officer in North Africa to December, 1941, when the Yanks asked for my transfer to them. I joined them in Sydney in January, '42 and stayed with them until June '46 as superintendent of navigation for the Southwest Pacific. I was then in charge of marine operations for UNRRA in the Philippine-China area, later becoming general manager of a shipping corporation till 1949 when, having been away from my family for ten years, I decided to go to England to see them. I did salvage work in UK waters till being sent for to go to Melbourne. The job there was to blow up the old *Terawhiti* which had sunk in the fairway. Then, in May 1951, it was back to the Philippines."

When I heard from him last, Kenneth was thinking of returning to New Zealand. There were difficulties, however, over getting his capital out, and over finding a suitable shore job connected with shipping when he was not on the spot. He was obviously very tired when he wrote to me. In 1956 his book, *Pacific Ordeal,* had been a notable success, published in the United States and Britain and translated into half a dozen other languages. "Have been designing one or two ships lately," he wrote. "Such work calls for much concentration and fine calculations, and at the end of the day and sometimes late at night, all one wants to do is pack off to bed."

It is typical of Kenneth Ainslie's style that he made no mention in his letters to me of two of his greatest adventures. They are vividly described in *Pacific Ordeal.* The first of them, which he covers in little more than two pages, would have made a book on its own. In 1918, Kenneth was acting second mate of a barque taking coal from Australia to Peru. After two months at sea they were bowling along one murky night, under full sail through big seas, when the lookout spotted breakers ahead. It was too late to react; the ship crashed headlong on to rocks and the masts came down, killing the captain. The rest were swept shoreward on great rollers, finishing up on what was little more than a bleak, outlying rock of the Galapagos Islands; barely a mile across, devoid of vegetation, with its highest point about ten feet above sea level. There were, fortunately, two freshwater springs. They built a crude shelter and a signal mast from the wreckage, and lived on turtles, turtle eggs and the few fish they could catch by hand.

"At the end of three months," Kenneth wrote, "most of us firmly believed we would never be rescued. Our minds were decaying under the strain. I found myself writing long letters home with a stick in the sand."

Their only hope was an Ecuadorian Government vessel which made a six-monthly tour of the islands looking for castaways. It arrived a few days into their fourth month and took them to Valparaiso. It was like coming back from the dead to families who had abandoned all hope.

The second adventure came thirty years later when he was serving with UNRRA in the Philippines shortly after the end of the war with Japan. The company acting as agents for UNRRA, he was told, had bought an ex-US Navy rescue tug. Would he like to go over to the States and sail it back? It should, he hoped, be a pleasant voyage and something of a holiday. But it didn't prove quite what he had hoped. When he arrived, he was told that the tug would be towing four ex-US minesweepers to Manila; thirteen thousand miles across the Pacific with a largely inexperienced crew, through the emptiest part of a great ocean. It proved, as Kenneth described it, a most eventful voyage. He had to control a crew unused to discipline who at times threatened mutiny. At least a dozen times one or more of the minesweepers broke away and had to be reharnessed to the mother ship in storm and darkness.

It became a nightmare that was endlessly repeated, a nightmare that would have drained the spirit of a lesser man. Tow lines wore out, fuel was exhausted before they reached Palmyra, halfway to Manila. Calling on his early experience, Kenneth rigged makeshift sails contrived from leaky tarpaulins, blankets, any clothing the men could spare. The tug crawled west at one or two knots. When a fireman developed a gangrenous thumb that would have killed him if left alone, there was nothing in the primitive medicine chest to help. Kenneth amputated it with a hacksaw blade from the engineers' stores. The climax came when the tug made a one-day dash to Palmyra for extra fuel, leaving three volunteers in charge of the unpowered minesweepers. Before they could link up with the tug again, a current had carried the sweepers far east of the estimated rendezvous. Enter the US Navy from their base in Hawaii. An admiral was placed in charge of their biggest exercise since the end of the war and, seventeen days after they had been left on their own, the sweepers were back in the fold.

Kenneth Ainslie was the third generation of family sea captains to have sailed the Pacific. What different worlds they had known since young McKenzie had signed on as a seaman at four pounds a month on the *Spray*, away back in the 1850s. George, his son, had seen the golden age of sail, making the topsail schooner *Huia* a familiar name through Australia and New Zealand with her exploits on the Tasman. Kenneth Ainslie saw the change from sail to steam, from the power and simplicity of wind-driven vessels to the complex machinery of the 1950s. A century separated him from the other Kenneth, his grandfather, but they were linked together by changeless qualities: an inborn sea-sense, skill that built on painfully acquired knowledge and, above all, sheer guts in facing the worst that could be thrown at them. Kenneth Ainslie was proud of his grandfather and his uncle. They, too, would have found much in the Ainslie career to fill them with a similar pride.

It would be impossible to write about the Mathesons and the McKenzies, and their Omaha country, without introducing the Meiklejohns. Two years after the Mathesons had settled at Little Omaha, James Strange Meiklejohn bought a thousand acres for five hundred pounds at Big Omaha, a few miles away. They were now somewhat closer than when the Meiklejohns were living on Prince Edward Island and the Mathesons across a narrow strait on Cape Breton Island. They were to grow even closer when Duncan Matheson's son Roderick married Captain Meiklejohn's grand-daughter, fusing in their sons two remarkable bloodlines. As Keith Matheson once said to me: "My brother Ronald and I couldn't help becoming sea captains."

If one was looking for a central figure for the Meiklejohn story, a story packed with the exploits of a virile seagoing bunch of men, it would still be difficult to go past Catherine. Physically she was tiny, but she was big in everything that matters — in spirit, heart, humour and family loyalty. And, at one time or another, she needed all these qualities in double measure. In

197

addition, she had an endearing "fey" quality, part perhaps of her mixed French and Highland ancestry. Fairies and "little people" were never far away from Catherine, but there was also a strength and determination that sat strangely on her slight frame.

Catherine left her Ross-shire home for Pictou around the year 1830, travelling in a migrant ship that had James Meiklejohn as carpenter and second mate. James made a sensible decision when, on arriving at Pictou, he jumped ship to marry Catherine. Shortly afterwards they settled across the water from Pictou on Prince Edward Island, where they farmed, built the occasional ship and raised a family of seven sons. The ships, loaded with timber and island produce, were sailed to Liverpool and sold. But the Meiklejohns were farmers as much as sailors or shipbuilders, tending their land with skill and care. Blue mussel mud from the estuary was spread on the red soil to maintain fertility. Many crops, other than potatoes for which the island was famous, were raised; and at the centre of all this activity was the little figure of Catherine Meiklejohn.

She was certainly kept busy. Her seven sons were born between 1832 and 1847: James, John, Alexander, William, Robert, Lemuel and Septimus. There was a seven-year break between Robert and Lemuel, but the others arrived with remarkable regularity. They entered a home where their parents were well matched in their contrasting characteristics. Les Meiklejohn, eldest son of Septimus and deeply involved in the family story, summed them up in this way:

"As a youngster, James had been kicked around a bit, the only son of a second marriage. In a shipyard at Leith and then at sea, he was tyrannical, enthusiastic, religious in his own way, hard yet affectionate. Proud of his sons but careless of their future, except inasmuch as it concerned him. They went straight to the yard with little or no schooling, and they learned to do well what he wanted them to do. James himself was quick to learn, dogmatic, easily disappointed in others but loyal to his friends. After leaving the migrant ship, *Industry*, in 1831, and getting married, he never sailed under anyone else's command again. The sea was no place for a man — meaning himself — unless in command of a ship that he owned himself."

There was a different note in Les's voice when he spoke of "Granny": "She was the one who reconciled the boys to their father as much as anyone could. I like to picture her there at Georgetown on the Island. She was fond of good clothes but not of housekeeping. Of the outdoors, rather than wrapping herself in the normal preoccupations of mother and housewife. Highly intelligent, interested in novel things and new people. But she was involved most of all with her boys, watching them grow and, when they were old enough, looking out suitable girls for them to marry. In spite of that, they all loved her!"

Twenty-four years after their marriage, the decision was made to move on. James had been appointed an immigration agent for the colony of New Zealand, and this may have influenced his decision. He would have known that three shiploads of migrants had already reached there from neighbouring Cape Breton Island, and that another one was due to leave. James's most ambitious vessel, a brigantine significantly named the *Union*, was launched in May, 1856, and cleared port for Britain in June with a cargo of deals. Crewing was no problem. The boys, ranging from twenty-three to eight years, were big enough either to help with the work or to keep out of harm's way. There was, apart from the family, a black cook; and, of course, there was Catherine to make sure everything ran smoothly. The careful plans James had made suffered only one failure. John, his second son, the master shipwright, didn't want to go, for he was engaged to a local girl, Cordelia Alley. His father got him on board to do some work down below and, when John came up on deck, he found the ship had moved quietly down harbour. Telling his father what he thought of him, he dived overboard and swam a mile to the shore through water still carrying winter ice, under a bitterly cold wind. The *Union* sailed on and eventually word reached the family that John had made it to the shore and married the girl. Family ties were still strong: John and Cordelia, accompanied by two little daughters, reached Auckland by way of London in 1861 and rejoined the others.

The Meiklejohn master plan worked well. The deals — blocks of pine plank used for flooring — were unloaded in Liverpool; a cargo of coal was taken on in Cardiff for Alicante, in Spain. Then wine was loaded for Rio de Janeiro. James had been in Rio before — in 1829 in the brig *Rachel*, also with wine; a visit made memorable when one of the crew, George Main Prize, fell overboard in the harbour while drunk, being rescued only with difficulty. This time, however, the cargo was unloaded without incident, and *Union* proceeded to Montevideo with a cargo of salt, doubtless to process the beef that Uruguay produced in vast quantities. From there, the vessel went up the river to pick up an unusual cargo — marrow bones and bone ash: great tubs of bones, 18,000 in a day, which had to be broken and settled down on a bed of bone ash. A delicate cargo unless properly stowed but *Union*, though light, handled it well through fierce storms off the South American coast on the way back to Britain. One entry in the log records: "Gale most terrific. Stove pipe washed away. Struck in the stern with a heavy sea. Stove in bulwarks binnacle glasses and filled cabin with water. No cooking this day."

This would have been the storm that figured in family legends when James ordered all the family below while he took the helm. Catherine said that, if he stayed on deck, so would she. So James lashed himself to the wheel, Catherine to the mast, and together they saw the storm out. They reached Liverpool safely; but now Catherine's mind was set on finding a permanent home. A round mahogany table and chest, that stayed in the family, were some of the things bought before the *Union* sailed away again, to Cape Town, where the Governor, Sir George Grey, urged them to settle in New Zealand; to Mauritius for a cargo of sugar carried to Brisbane; then to Sydney, where the *Union* was sold. On her first voyage for her new owner, *Union* was wrecked on the notorious bar of the Kaipara Harbour, seven miles of shoaling sands on New Zealand's west coast. The Meiklejohns, fretting at the slow speed of the vessel in which they were passengers, crossed to Auckland, and a new life.

Having made their choice of Big Omaha as their home, the Meiklejohns were quickly on to the land. Les Meiklejohn created the scene for me, and through his words I saw vividly the little procession as it moved up from the beach: father and mother, six of their seven sons, a milking cow which Catherine insisted should be bought, and a little ten-year-old girl, Susan Dodd, whom Catherine had brought for company. There was another possible reason.

"On the boat from Australia," Les told me, "Susan's stepfather and mother had other children of their own and didn't seem to need her. So Granny said she would take her. I think she had her in mind for her son Robert when they grew up. But much had to be done before they built castles in the air.

"They must have been goers," said Les. "In the first year they had finished a big house which they called Unionville — four rooms below, stairs winding round the chimney, bedrooms above — and had also built their first schooner, the *Pioneer*. The cow thrived in the bush, but they had to start ploughing and sowing pasture. They built a lot of vessels and did an awful lot of ploughing.

"My uncle Sandy was the great ploughman, a big cheerful man of great strength. He had an old Scotch beam plough, drawn by six bullocks. It had no wheel but balanced itself. The depth of the ploughing came from pushing down or lifting on the handles. Sandy, when he ploughed the flats, left it all in five-yard ridges. Harrows made of large bundles of teatree were not of much use. It was terrible to drive over them with a horse and cart. He must have ploughed about six inches deep. When I ploughed it about fifty years later I brought up the heavy fern that he had buried. It was only by cross-ploughing that I got rid of the ridges. The fern just fell to powder when I touched it.

"Granny was involved in everything that happened," said Les. "She made up names for all the headlands and valleys surrounding her. There were Sinbad and Sunburn — Sinbad a little round knob of a hill, Sunburn which had a dry patch that was always bare. Turkey Spur recalled the old turkey hen that got away and raised her chicks there. Other places still carry names from Granny's time. Further back is Kauri Spur. Then there's Major's Flat, where Major the bullock grazed. Tea Tree Spur had teatree on it from the earliest times and was never cleared.

"But Granny's favourite was the Enchanted Point, down across the creek in the heavy bush on Viv Meiklejohn's side. It fascinated her, but she was never quite sure about it all. Catherine was wandering about down there one day. In one place the creek does a big loop, and where it comes back on course the gap is less than a chain wide. In she went through the heavy bush, admiring the plants and trees, not realising that she was now on what was almost an island. Every way she walked, she came to the water. Again and again it happened like that, the creek was everywhere. This was the one time Granny was really flummoxed. She decided the fairies had lifted her up and put her down in another place. 'Now stop teasing me, you little creatures,' she scolded.

"After a while the fairies took pity on her and Granny found her way back to the world she knew."

There was plenty there to keep her busy for the women, in this society, were fully involved in work that aimed at acquiring that rare commodity in country areas — cash. For the men, shipbuilding was the obvious means; and under the control of John, the expert shipwright, a steady stream of vessels left the Omaha yards. The routine was possibly less rigorous than it had been on Prince Edward Island. The timetable for the building of the schooner *Success* on the Island in the 1850s gives some interesting details. James, John, Alexander and four other men worked through the summer to August, when work stopped for the harvest. There were also days off in November for pulling turnips and for the potato digging, at which William and Robert also assisted.

The women were good providers but also developed an eye for a profitable sale. Les Meiklejohn always referred to his wife as "She", with a capital S. "She made more from seventy-five ducks, with eggs at two shillings and sixpence a dozen, than I made from nine cows," he said. "There was plenty to do — wood ash to be bagged, corn and wheat grown on Canoe Hill to be thrashed. Pears and apples to be picked and packed. They'd bring a pound a case when sent to Wellington. It was handy having close contacts in the shipping business! Later, there were thirty cows to be milked by hand and sometimes She did most of them herself. If we were rafting timber out, we had to work when the tide was right; no stopping for the milking."

The sea and the forest, over the years, exacted a toll from the Meiklejohn family. Robert, the fifth son, was the first victim. He and his father were working in the bush felling a leaning tree. A scarf was cut into the top side instead of the under side. The tree split up the middle and launched itself back like a great spear straight at Robert, pinning him down and killing him instantly.

Three years later, in March, 1864, big, gentle Captain Sandy, a Viking of a man as his nephew remembered him, was returning to Auckland from Mercury Bay with a load of timber. The schooner *Rapid* that Meiklejohn built had another of the family on board; Lemuel, the sixth son, was on his first New Zealand voyage. His parents were not happy about him going. Catherine, perhaps with her gift of second sight, urged Sandy to look after him; and "Don't come home without him" were James's last words to Sandy. All went well until, late on Sunday, a sudden fierce storm hit the schooner, throwing her on her beam ends and drowning three passengers with shocking speed. For three days and nights the derelict schooner was driven about the Gulf, the survivors, with no food to sustain them, holding to the rigging as best they could, while the waves washed through the horizontal masts. On Monday another man was washed from the rigging. And on Tuesday, after saving his brother three times, Sandy watched in anguish as Lem was swept away into the waste of waters. Stupified with cold and exhaustion, he had been speechless for five hours. A wind change at last carried the waterlogged vessel towards the Great Barrier Island, where it struck on rocks off an uninhabited, desolate shore. Sandy, the only one of the four still alive who could swim, carried a line ashore and two more men were saved. Then Sandy, barefooted and fighting off exhaustion after a three-day struggle, crawled five miles along the coast until he found a native whaleboat that rescued the other two survivors. Sandy came home to be cursed by his father. He never went to sea again.

This double tragedy hit James and Catherine hard and James never really recovered from it. The sequel had an ironical twist. Just after Robert's death, John Meiklejohn's first son, Heber, was born.

"Old James begged John to name him Robert," said Les, "but from sheer contrariness he wouldn't give him that name. In much the same way James tried hard to have Milton, born in 1865, called Lemuel after the boy drowned on the *Rapid*, but with no more luck. However, the old man had the last word. In his family Bible, the two names appear as Robert and Lemuel."

Sandy built a small schooner, *Daydawn*, after the tragedy, but mostly devoted himself to the land and its produce. He died suddenly in 1868, only four years after he had renounced the sea.

"John Meiklejohn, a fine shapely man, heavily built and strong-willed, was a different sort from Sandy," Les said. "Old James, who had always rather liked his drink, went to Auckland to sell a vessel and buy some gear for the shipyard. Some of the waterfront sharks filled him with grog. Robert who was with him, and just a lad, could see what was happening. He pleaded with his father to come home and leave the vessel, but he was too far gone to agree. When he came to, everything was gone. He didn't have enough money to buy the stores. When he got home John set up a council of war. 'You're disrated,' they told the old man. 'We must pension you off. You'll have no more to do with the business.' And so they built a house for him in Auckland, and he lived there with Catherine until he died in 1876."

By the time he died, his son William had also come ashore. He had a deep-water ticket and was also described as the most weather-wise captain on the coast, but he had become over-fond of drink. He couldn't trust himself in command and refused to place himself in a position where his impaired judgment could cause an accident. He retired to Omaha, and his widowed mother came back to keep him company. Before that, however, he had achieved his greatest ambition — the command of a vessel as handsome and as swift as the *Union*. The *Omaha*, an 83-foot brigantine of 132 tons, made some profitable voyages under his command. After he went ashore, another master had her on the run between Lyttelton and the Chatham Islands. She was ready to sail on her last trip at 11 one morning, but did not leave until after noon. One short hour made a big difference to William and Septimus, who each had a quarter-share in the *Omaha*. Working out of port in the Chathams, she was mishandled and became a total wreck. It proved that the Lyttelton agent had overlooked renewing the insurance cover, which expired at noon that very day.

Right through to the end of the century the Meiklejohns kept on building ships, concentrating for about twenty years on developing the scow, which became the most important trading vessel on the New Zealand coast and across the Tasman. The scows made a rather inauspicious start. The first of them, the *Lake Erie*, had lee-boards which were awkward to handle and a flat bow hopeless in a head sea. Keith Matheson said the Mathesons scorned them at first. When the *Lake Erie* left on her first voyage to Auckland they said she would never get there. She did, but it took her two nights and a day. After that, things could only improve. The later scows had centreboards, while bow and stern were given shape. The scow could now sail like a keeler but, with centreboard raised, could navigate the shallow tidal estuaries or lie aground while sand or timber were loaded into her.

The scow saw the end of the commercial sailing era around the New Zealand coast. Incredibly, before the twentieth century had run for long, a fine fleet of ships would be rotting for lack of use. Railways and roads would serve all the needs of the settlers. The Meiklejohns were realists. They didn't cry over the passing of a time that had been good to them. Instead, they turned to the land and to the trades associated with it. Or else they went away, specialised in education and sought a living in the

Scows, often loaded with logs, like the Ida, *shown here, were the last commercial sailing vessels to work the New Zealand coast.*

academic or commercial world. But those who remained still had many of the qualities of their forebears, not least a "folksy" humour, a dry and expressive way with words that often relied for its effectiveness on understatement. They had a staunch religious upbringing — if the boys whistled on Sundays they had to repeat the Shorter Catechism — but they would repeat with relish the old Island story of the man who thought so much of his dog that, when it died, he wished to have it buried in the family plot. The minister was unwilling. The old man, therefore, buried it just outside the churchyard fence. While his wife attended the service he would sit quietly by the dog's grave and read his Bible.

And there was the reproof by Uncle William that the family chuckled over years later. William, having retired from the sea, immersed himself in work on the farm and in the orchard. Wherever he went he was followed by three adoring nephews, one of them Leslie, who told me the story. On this day he was doing some grafting in the orchard. One of the boys was learning to whistle, but could only blow through his teeth. He kept it up all day until William, his patience for once exhausted, said quietly to him: "Can ye not stop that, boy? It's worse than farting!"

Nor did certain ironies escape them. After the Waikato wars of the 1860s, a party of Maori prisoners who had been working on Kawau Island, escaped and took refuge on nearby Tamahunga Mountain where they lived quietly.

One Sunday James and John, with their wives, climbed up to the Pa on the mountain top, arriving in time for church. They were interested to note that the Maori congregation, with typical generosity, prayed for themselves, their friends and their enemies; and also that the bell which was rung for church had last been seen at the neck of a Meiklejohn bullock which had gone missing.

I spent many pleasant days in the green land of Big Omaha with Keith Matheson, Les Meiklejohn and Sylvia Moore, the family historian through whose care and energy much of the Meiklejohn story was preserved. This was land that they had made their own, through toil and service. The older people may have called Prince Edward Island "home", but now it is Big Omaha that holds the family's love. They often think about old James, hard but affectionate, impatient, argumentative, but a man among men; his quick and lively wife Catherine, who loved fine clothes and the outdoors, with a dislike of housekeeping and a housewife's routine chores, who brought a soft Highland lilt to everything she did. They think, too, of the seven sons who all, in different ways, added a phrase or paragraph to the story of a new land.

This is their homeland today, just as Leigh, not far away, is home to the Mathesons and Waipu, thirty miles north, has a special place in the minds of Nova Scotian descendants. They showed me the old cemetery by a steep cutting in the hillside, with the weathered stones standing together, one with a little brigantine carved above the names. I saw homely things: the mulberry tree where Unionville, the old house, had stood; the kauri hand-rail on the bridge. After the hurlyburly of the past there was a great quiet-ness, made even more emphatic by the sound of running water. There were personal things, too, reminders of the past: sextant and revolver; pretty shells brought from the Island; a branding iron, a serving dish, a walking stick whittled by William after he left the sea; the sabre which the boys found old James sharpening — "To strike a blow for the Presbyterians" when news of the Disruption reached him. And there was Catherine's old shawl, and a teatowel made from flax grown on her Highland farm 150 years before, cared for on the Island and brought around the world to Big Omaha. Such things make the past seem very near.

Perhaps the same thought was in Les Meiklejohn's mind when, after a long silence during which his brooding eyes were fixed on bushclad Tamahunga, he began to speak.

"Across from the old house there was a shallow, rather swampy stream and beyond it, on rising ground, the family cemetery where Robert had been buried after he was killed in the forest. Sandy lay there too, and when Catherine died, she joined her sons.

"But a new cemetery had been opened at Matakana and my uncle William, when he felt his time was coming, decided he should be buried there. 'But we all should be together,' he said. 'I can't do it myself, but after I'm gone I want you to collect your granny's bones, and those of Robert and Sandy, and bury them properly up there. And I'll leave some money so that you can put up a proper headstone and a fence.'

"William died and it was time to carry out his wishes. My father Septimus would not go near the graves, but my brother and I decided we should do the job. My uncle made some coffins and we went down one day to the old cemetery.

"There was not much left of Robert — only a few broken bones, for he had been badly knocked about when the tree killed him. And Sandy was just a jumble. However, we collected what was left and then turned to granny's grave. We dug down carefully through the soil, cutting the roots of the willow tree, and soon came to the rough coffin which had held her. I had never realised what a tiny wee thing she was. The top and sides had fallen away, but the bottom board was as sound as when she was buried. And there her bones lay neatly in place.

"But this was the strangest thing. The roots of the willow tree had taken possession of her body. Soft roots curled through her skull and along her ribs, like knitting wool in a loose ball. The bones lay there peacefully. Granny had loved the earth, and the earth had taken her back fully into its keeping."

Not far from the Meiklejohns there lived the three MacLean brothers. Tall, gaunt, long-boned men, high in the cheekbones, lean in the temples, shaggy-browed over solemn, considering eyes.

They were farmers, and their home a slab-sided shack of hand-split vertical boards, with small windows, two rooms, a huge wooden chimney that held their colonial oven and a crane festooned with kettles and iron pans. There was a table of rough-sawn, pale scrubbed timber, a sturdy mahogany dresser, grey blankets thrown back from beds mattressed with springy creeper pulled from the forest trees.

A fence laced with dry bundles of trimmed teatree scrub, like a housewife's old broom, surrounded their home. Beyond it stretched the raw acres of their farm. Flat land with the tall ghosts of dead, burnt trees, swamps choked with reeds, low, drab rolling hills scorched by the clearing fires and scratched by the plough.

In summer the MacLeans sweated under a pitiless sun which took the bright colour from their beards and burned their bare arms and necks to brown, tough leather. The hills danced in the heat. The harsh soil smoked in eddies of dust. In winter they squelched through spongy mud. Rivers ran yellow, the swamps spread. They dug drains in the stubborn clay, put

206

up fences to control their few head of cattle. And all the time they dreamed of the gentle, misty glens, the soft, tolerant rain and the kindly sun that they had known before.

There was a piper, a commercial traveller whose business took him at intervals past the farm. Like a rabbit in the haunts of a harrier hawk he would try to slip by, but subconsciously he knew each time that he was doomed. Cowering on the seat of his trap he would speak kindly to the mare between the shafts: "Put your feet down softly, lass!"

And he would shiver as the iron-shod wheels crunched over an extra large stone.

"Come on, lass, quietly now. Or should we be making a wild dash for it? Let's hope the dogs and a-all are down the back of the farm!"

But even without the warning of a bark, as he approached the little house, a dark-clad MacLean would be greeting him cordially with no trace of surprise.

"Ah there you are, Tammy. You'll be stopping as usual, no doubt. Bring the pipes along in. The boys will be here soon. They were expecting you.

"Here then, just a wee taste to get the dust of the road out of your throat." From a black bottle on the table whisky splashed into two tin mugs. "You have no cold? Your chest is strong? Man, it's good to see you again.

"And now, a tune to bring the boys along!"

Poor Tammy, no more master of his fate than a sheep held by a good eye dog, found himself blowing a bag full of wind, making a few hasty adjustments under the tender watchful eye of his host and tapping one foot outside the doorway, while the drone and skirl of his barbaric music filled the broad valley.

"You're in rare form tonight," MacLean says with deep satisfaction, watching his brothers approaching in the distance. "What a grand night we'll be having! Just like the o-old times!" And in the midst of his happiness a shadow crosses his face at the reawakened memories.

Dusk falls, the horse still stands between the shafts, one rear leg fretting against the flies. The dog moves away from his place below the axle of the trap and looks nervously in at the door. The three MacLeans are sitting at the table, the gloom settling in their beards, their eyes glowing as if from some inward light. The music echoes up the great chimney.

"Now don't you be stopping, Tammy. One of us will get a meal together. Chops would be quickest."

The ashes in the fireplace come to life under a frying pan, the dog edges in, belly to the floor, until a word from one of the masters sends him scuttling outside again. His household duties done, the youngest MacLean sits down once more.

Reels, strathspeys, marches; the sadness, the glory of men striding away to war, the joys of reunion with old friends and wives and sweethearts; the revelry and sensual delight of the harvest gathered, the cattle in from the hill, the fishing boats back from the sea.

By now Tammy, too, is possessed. His feet keep moving, his chest and cheeks heave and deflate, his fingering is firm and clean. Someone has thrown a rata log on the fire and a lantern flickers on the dresser. The three MacLeans sit at the table, heads propped on long forearms, their eyes dreamy but intent. Fat congeals around the chop bones on four plates. The black bottle is empty. The dog, at his post by the fire, unregarded now, watches his masters with questing, devoted eyes.

Outside, a great wind from the south has cleared the sky. The dying moon emphasises the dark mass of the hills, the emptiness that spreads to the edge of vision.

The brothers, cramped and muscle weary, rise from the table and, at a decent distance from the house, arrange themselves along the teatree fence. They sigh, shoulder to shoulder, and look at the sky and breathe the cold keen air.

"Twill soon be morning," says one of them. "Perhaps we should be letting Tammy get some rest."

"Ay, perhaps we should at that," another one replies, his shaggy head shaking in sympathy.

Inside the house, almost in answer to their thoughts, the sound of the pipes has died away, as if the piper had marched over the hill, or fallen asleep.

"Och, it's early yet," says the third one. "Tammy would not be wanting to disappoint us like that, and him here so rarely."

Their boots sound on the floor, and the piper starts guiltily. "I was just coming to look for you."

"Go on, man, have a wee bit of a spell. Over by the fence out there. And while you're away I'll recite a bit of verse that the minister learned me last time he called."

His eyes darken with thought and feeling, and he begins in a deep, resonant voice that becomes even deeper with emotion. His brothers listen attentively.

Land of brown heath and shaggy wood,
Land of the mountain and the flood;
Land of my sires, what mortal hand
Could e'er untie the filial band
That knits me to thy ...

His brow wrinkles. "Damn it, I forget. What was it the minister said now?" He thumps his chest in an effort of recollection.

Triumphantly, but with a challenging look: *That knits me to thy coral strand!*

"I don't think you're right there. They had no coral in Scotland, as far as I'm knowing. Doubtless the minister was thinking of the hymn about Greenland and India's coral strand when he was talking."

"I'm not so sure," his brother answers stubbornly. "These strands can be strange things. Do you not remember how they used to say that the Bluenoses decided to settle here because, as they sailed down the coast, the white beaches looked like the burghoo they were eating at home in Nova Scotia? And the beaches in Scotland could be the same — coral or flint or porridge or anything, just as the poet fancies!"

He stands up aggressively, the quiet one, the youngest brother who cheerfully does what his brothers tell him, and works his heart out on the harsh gumland soil. He is ready to fight for his poem, for the images it brings to his mind. But one of his brothers says softly: "A beautiful poem indeed; we must learn more of it… But now where's Tammy? Come along Tammy, you're wasting the good night. Give us some more of that lovely music."

The wind dies with the dawn. Pale golden streaks show through the cloud that lies heavily on the eastern horizon. The brothers still sit at the table and Tammy, that gallant man, dishevelled, distraught but unconquered, plays a lament for the departing night. He wipes his mouthpiece with a grubby white handkerchief and works the tense muscles of his face.

"Well, it's been grand indeed," says the eldest brother, speaking for all. He looks at the drab landscape outside the door, the blackened trees, the half-hearted grass, the unfinished fences. "It brings back memories."

"But now there's a day's work to be done, and doubtless you'll have something to do also, Tammy. We'll be having breakfast. Chops will be quickest, and maybe an egg."

Obediently the youngest brother moves to his chores. Tammy packs away his pipes and, as though mesmerised, goes out to prepare his horse and trap for the road. He shakes his head sadly at the patient animal, which flicks an ear in sympathy, and he looks about him for a moment before entering the house.

In the whole valley, on the broad gentle slopes of the hill, there is no movement, save the soft, slow climb of the smoke from the MacLeans' reawakened fire.

Chapter Fourteen

Scotland, Nova Scotia, New Zealand:
A Personal Odyssey

FROM THE HOTEL AT SLIGACHAN, on the island of Skye, we feasted our eyes on the Cuillins, rising in their awesome majesty beyond the long valley down which, more than two hundred years ago, Prince Charles Stuart had walked to meet his destiny. Sligachan presented a picture of an age, which perhaps we could call Edwardian, when leisurely gentlemen came from far afield to enjoy the pleasures of fishing, shooting and good food and drink.

How different was the feeling as we travelled north to Portree and then to Dunvegan, home of Clan MacLeod. Next day, a quiet road took us along the southern side of Loch Dunvegan. Mist clung to the sea and the sky, and we drove through a pale, mysterious land with few features to be recognised. It seemed indeed like the last road, with nothing ahead but a scatter of islands on the dim horizon and the ocean stretching away to the Americas. The road climbed a little and then quite suddenly the sun burned the mist away and it was a bright summer morning. Below us lay Glendale, a green valley, smoothly contoured, spreading down to the sea. At first sight it was in no way spectacular. A croft, deep in roses and green trees, lay below the road to the left. This had been the home of my Campbell ancestors until they sailed to Nova Scotia. One of them had been born there in 1805. Other family members stayed there after so many vanished to North America; and there were still cousins farming the croft until after the Second World War.

We followed the road to Loch Pooltiel and the wharf where the fishing boats would shelter. Millstones were a sign of old activity. On this quiet day the silence was profound. It reached inland like the mist that had finally disappeared, enveloping valleys and hills. No voices, no calling of sheep or cattle, no sound of movement. A pearly sheen on the sea. The seagulls standing in their own reflections and the waves lapping so gently that you couldn't hear them break.

Up from Pooltiel, with its sheltered waters reaching across to the beetling cliffs of Dunvegan Head, the road ran south through green, gently sloping farmland, with always the deep channel of the Minch below and, out to the west, the shadowed islands of the Outer Hebrides, North Uist and its neighbours. When the car stopped and the motor died, there was a silence that could be felt, an empty silence that struck deeper when we saw, not far away, signs of an activity that had once brought with it the sound of voices, the bustle of domestic life, of children playing: the broken remnants of abandoned homes that had faded into the soil. I was reminded, standing there deep in reverie, of a sentence that I had read not long before in a short story by A.E. Coppard, referring to a far different landscape but equally applicable here: "There was about the ground the very delicacy of solitude."

A little further along we spoke to a young man by the roadside. His name was Campbell, and he was a descendant no doubt of the Glendale folk who, in the 1880s, defied the Government forces and won for the crofters the right to do what they wished with the land they farmed. But there was nothing harsh or defiant about him; rather a quiet strength and a serenity in his soft voice that was in tune with the land. He himself, he explained, was farming three of the original crofts in order to make a living.

In the old days, crofting never provided the Glendale men with a full livelihood. Most of them would take their fishing boats out from the loch, past Dunvegan Head into the uncertain waters of the Minch, sometimes meeting with success, sometimes harassed by the frequent changes in the weather.

We said goodbye to Skye, and to our hospitable friends at Loch Awe, knowing that there was much more to see, more friendly people to meet in the Highlands, and determined that we would be back again.

The Scotland I discovered on this first visit was vastly different from the country I had imagined. How much more so was this with Nova Scotia! In my mind was a land of endless winter, of snow and ice; I soon learned the truth. We had driven through from Ontario to Halifax, and one more day on those long Canadian roads would see us at Baddeck. My diary recalls what we found:

> Along the coast road, in regular succession, came beautiful, cleanly designed churches commanding the eye from their special place on a knoll or beside the sea; cottages, bigger houses and barns, the barns shingle-walled and roofed, sometimes with half-collapsed beams that made them sit awkwardly; mile upon mile of firs and other forest trees, many of them stunted by fierce winter weather; occasional meadows bright with wild flowers and vividly green with fresh spring grass; at the roadside, rich splashes of colour from self-sown Russell lupins; and above all the sight and sound of water — sparkling down rocky streams, sliding in surges from the sea, contrasting with the acres of swamp with quiet pools and reaches as bright as glass under a grey sky.

There were wide fields in the valleys near Antigonish, bales of hay just made to be stored for winter; occasional sheep and cattle near the big barns. But as we drove down to the Bras d'Or lakes, the work of man no longer dominated the eye — the hills close at hand were in many shades of green; but further away, as a soft rain fell, it was the flowing curve of the mountains, purple against the sky, austere in their form and fascinating in their pure simplicity, that captured the heart and mind.

Rod MacInnes, of Air Canada, after he had visited Waipu, had invited us to stay at his home on Boularderie Island, across the water from Baddeck and St Ann's. When we drove through the gate towards the house, there was a skirl of pipes, and out through the door came a great surge of men and women to meet their "cousins" from New Zealand. A truly Cape Breton welcome! By the end of the afternoon we felt as comfortable with everyone as if we, too, had grown up in St Ann's or Baddeck. After that, nothing was ever quite the same. It was holiday time, and we encountered a high-spirited group who had returned home from Boston where, like many Cape Bretoners, they had gone to find work. To qualify as a true man of Cape Breton, I was told, I had to "down" a glass of a colourless liquid which proved to be neat gin.

Among those who had not migrated, however, there was a blend of cheerfulness and sadness, not easy to define, in moments when they looked back. John MacAskill telling, with pride, how self-sustaining the communities had been; Alan MacLeod recalling how, even in the 1930s, you could look across the whole of the MacLeod and Macaulay farms — all in pasture.

Certainly, for those who had preferred to stay rather than seek work elsewhere, memories must have become overpowering at times. We drove up into the hills where once there had been farms, but now the forest had virtually taken over. One man said to me: "When the dog died, the white-tailed deer would be down eating Mother's flowers around the house."

Instead of farms, there were tourists. The Keltic Lodge, one of three hotels run by the provincial government, achieved an occupancy rate of over ninety percent while we were there during the two months of high summer, and that figure could well have grown since then. The lodge has a commanding site on the cliffs above Ingonish on the Cabot Trail. We delighted in its comfort, and also in the opportunity it gave to enjoy the beauty of a unique countryside. The trail took us past remote little fishing villages and others, like Cheticamp, where old Acadian crafts survived. The pastureland was shrinking, and we saw ancient shingled barns that were disappearing in new forest growth. There were magnificent beaches and long estuaries with sandbanks and shining water. These were sights to stir the visitor's mind, and tourism was obviously of major importance to Nova Scotia, just as it was to the Scottish Highlands. "Frankly," said the Keltic

Lodge manager, "I don't know what we'd do without it."

But, as later visits have confirmed, there is much more to Cape Breton than tourism, important though it might be. First and foremost, it is a place where people can enjoy living and working. I think of those we met on our first time there — men and women confident in their background, fulfilled in their lives. People like Alex and Norrie MacLeod, on a farm that had been MacLeod land for six generations; John Sam Nicholson who, having seen much of the world, wanted nothing more than his home at Middle River; Isobel Macaulay Jones, who told me how the *Aspy* would come round in the 1930s with the winter supplies for the community. The potatoes were already stored, the fish sundried.

And it was people like Isobel who helped to develop another important side of Nova Scotian life, seen today in the historic Highland Village at Iona and the Gaelic College of Celtic Arts and Crafts at St Ann's. Although they bring visitors to Nova Scotia, these are far from being tourist "baits". The summer school associated with the college draws nearly three-quarters of its students from outside Nova Scotia. A large number are from the United States and the rest of Canada, but many are from Scotland, England and New Zealand. The range of activities is wide. Efforts are made to revive the Gaelic language itself. There is instruction in the bagpipes and the fiddle, as well as in Highland dancing. St Ann's Gaelic choir performs. Weaving, and other crafts such as spinning and dyeing, have their place. There is accommodation available for a considerable number of visitors.

It does not end there with Sam MacPhee, the energetic and enthusiastic executive director. In a recent newsletter he wrote: "For those of you who have not been here in winter — it's a beautiful spot, and we certainly should be striving to make more use of it and enjoy it through one of our prettiest, and certainly longest, seasons." With its 350 acres of wooded hills, with trails that can be used for biking, hiking, skiing and snowmobiling, the property could be a busy place even in the depths of winter.

When I think about Waipu, New Year's Day is one of the first things to come to mind. My diary, so irregular in most ways, had recorded New Year's Day, 1992, in more than normal detail. Here is what it says:

> We had driven up during the morning from Campbells Bay, near Auckland, passing through regular bands of rain sweeping in from the west across our path. But there was sunshine at Waipu, the farms still green on the flats, but the hills brown from an early summer drought.
>
> There is a bitter-sweet taste for many in the Caledonian Society's "annual gathering and sports", as an early poster called it: pleasure at reunions with old friends and kinsfolk, sadness at the absence of others who have died during the year that has passed. And all the time there is the

The executive director of the Gaelic College, Sam McPhee, and his wife Sandy, in full regalia.

skirl of the pipes, a voice on the loudspeaker announcing sporting events, the tapping of the dancers' feet as they take part in competitions. It is a friendly ground, right in the centre of the township, close to the Church, the House of Memories, the hall; and providentially left in fern and scrub by its first owner, Murdoch Governor McGregor, until it was bought for development by the society over 120 years ago.

All around the verge, cars had been marshalled into tight lines, picnic baskets were out, men and women with a questing look in their eyes were ranging the grounds in search of those they hoped to meet. For many, indeed, it was a social gathering rather than a sports day.

And that's how it was for me. Skirting the crowd that watched a Highland dancing contest, I met a relaxed Hector Lang, not long back from a visit to Nova Scotia and enjoying a break this year from official duties. In the secretary's office I found Ian McKay, not looking quite as relaxed. Ian is more familiarly known as Ian Johnny Jack, which means that his grandfather was Jack McKay and his father Johnny McKay. We had known each other for forty years but recently had met only rarely, so it was a happy meeting.

"What are you doing today?" I asked him, "apart from meeting a few dozen McKay relatives."

He grinned wryly. "I have to open the show in a few minutes." He

A young competitor makes last minute adjustments
to her pipes.

pointed to his suit. "Why else do you think I'd be wearing all this?"

In his speech Ian suggested that, in spite of claims that the early Nova Scotians had been harsh, humorless and puritanical in their outlook, the community had members with a well-developed sense of fun. And he gave some examples.

For every one that I met there would have been a dozen that I missed. I spoke briefly to Norman Kempt, over ninety years old and up from Auckland for the New Year. And also to Hugh Griffin, another member of the Lang clan who had served the society well for many years. He was enjoying the day because usually, he said, he had his head down over the money.

There had been no tradition of piping among the first Nova Scotian migrants — the pipes as well as the tartans had been banned after the '45 — and it was not until the 1880s that the settlement produced its own pipers, largely because of Simon Fraser, who came to Whangarei from the Otago goldfields and married into the McKenzie clan. He was a grand piper, a great teacher and he passed on his love of the pipes to his son, William McKenzie Fraser. Once they had been introduced to Waipu the pipes flourished. I was delighted to meet again one of the great pipers that Waipu has produced — Bain McGregor. Bain, all six foot six of him, was a resplendent figure in full Highland regalia. His pipes, with their intricate silver mountings, had been the pride of his father, Cook McGregor, and Bain had brought fresh honours to them all over the world. But times had changed. "This would be my first competition in about three years," he said. He is a serious man and he spoke with a touch of regret. "Once the pipes meant just about everything to me — I couldn't get enough of them — but now, I suppose because of the pressure of other things on my time, the farm, marriage, the baby, my enthusiasm has gone." Later in the day Bain was photographed playing a pibroch while an old friend, a master of piping for over fifty years, listened to the music which has no parallel anywhere. Let's hope that Bain one day will have the time to regain his enthusiasm for his lost love.

The day slid slowly towards dusk. Many of the country visitors had gone, for there were dairy herds — stern taskmasters — waiting at home to be milked. We walked slowly across the grounds to a house where some of our friends had gathered earlier in the day. We talked to Flora Long Jim whose grandson, Ian Jones, would have been as tall as old Long Jim himself, and whose skill combined with an imperturbable good humour made him one of the most popular as well as the most talented of recent All Black rugby players. Miriam McKay was there too, widow of Don Gussie, also known as Sir Donald McKay, Minister of Health in the National Government. Miriam was in reminiscent mood. We talked about Epsom Presbyterian Church which we had both attended, about the Rev. Dr William McDonald who had married Mary Fraser from Waipu; and of their two brilliant sons, Alex and Hector. Alex excelled at classics, gaining first-class honours in both Latin and Greek, becoming a Fellow of Clare College, Cambridge and professor of Ancient History at Sydney, and Fellow of the British Academy.

"He came up to see me once at Waipu," Miriam said. "I was in the cowshed helping Don with the afternoon milking, not the most elegant of jobs at the best of times. Alex looked around him and said: 'You know, Miriam, if you had married me, you would never have had to put up with this sort of thing.'

"I smiled and told him, so truly, that there was nowhere else in the world I'd want to be."

Celebrations continued that night in the hall, but that is where my diary ended. It didn't touch on many of the most important events of the day. Sheer physical strength, as an example, had been an essential of life in the early settlement, as it had been in Nova Scotia and in the Highlands before that. And there were events at the sports, traditional events, to test the power and the toughness of modern man. Foot races, too, and jumping contests. But for many there, these things were a lively backdrop to a day of reminiscence.

Two other places in Waipu attract many visitors on New Year's Day: the cemetery with its old, weathered headstones, and the House of Memories, filled with old portraits, farming implements, household goods, items of clothing that help bring the past to life. Many of the visitors are looking for more than that, however. The fascination of family trees has captured them and the quest for ancestors becomes as exciting as a treasure hunt. For many, the search reaches a happy ending in the House of Memories, thanks largely to the help that comes from a remarkable woman, Betty Powell. Ask Betty about an early relationship, however complex it might be, and there is an instant reaction. Her hand goes to her forehead, a look of intense concentration, and in almost every case an answer will come through. When I tell her she is better than a computer, she shakes her head modestly, but many people would agree. Betty's correspondence file reveals two things: letters from many parts of the world show just how widespread the Nova Scotian network has become; and also, it underlines the fact that genealogy is one of today's flourishing growth industries.

On my last visit to Nova Scotia, the same enthusiasm was evident. There was talk of "twinning" between Baddeck/St Ann's and Waipu, which later came about; and a number of people suggested that it was time for me to write some more about the migration, and the way the communities in the Highlands, in Nova Scotia and in New Zealand had developed.

Now, suddenly, the connection had become real, chiefly because of the efforts of Norman MacAskill and a band of helpers in Assynt, and Barbara Weiskrantz, descendant of a first cousin of Norman McLeod and an energetic delver into the story of the McLeod migration. I first learned about

Caledonian sports day at New Year. The village en fête, farms tidy under the sun, and Bream Bay sweeping round to Whangarei Heads.

the plans being hatched at Lochinver in Assynt, in a letter from Barbara. She had just met Norman MacAskill while on a visit to Lochinver seeking information about McLeod, and he had shown her where McLeod had been born and had lived as a young man at Clachtoll.

A very relaxed man with a firm sense of purpose, Norman told Barbara about his plan for a memorial to McLeod at his birthplace. It would consist of a "rough-hewn, craggy piece" of ancient rock, erected on the bluff at Clachtoll Bay, with a suitably worded plaque. He had set up a local working party, and sought Barbara's help in involving the people of St Ann's and Waipu. This was quickly coming. Norman explained, in a letter to the *Scotsman*, the background to the project.

> Roger Hutchinson, in his excellent article on the voyages of the Normanites in the 19th century, led by the Rev. Norman McLeod, may be excused for claiming that "Assynt, and, therefore, the remainder of Scotland, has largely forgotten this historic hero of his time".
>
> He is remembered in Assynt through handed-down oral tales of his youthful exploits, and also through the annual visits of descendants seeking traces of their ancestors. They have expressed surprise that a man who has memorials erected to his memory in Nova Scotia and New Zealand has none in the place of his birth. The people of Assynt, enthusiastically supported by societies in Canada and New Zealand, are actively taking steps to rectify this omission.

The project came together with remarkable smoothness. Thinly populated though it might be, this corner of Assynt had not lost its talent for producing people and committees that could work harmoniously, either collectively or as individuals. The craggy gneiss rock, which was originally to be used in the memorial, was replaced by a block of local marble; a suitable inscription for the plaque was arrived at after consultation across the world. The date for the unveiling was changed from the possibly bleak month of March, McLeod's birth month, to August, when sunshine — and midges — could be reasonably expected. There were good reasons for the change. Not only would it suit the visitors expected from other parts of the world, but the St Ann's Gaelic College Pipe Band, having become champions of North America, would be in Edinburgh for the world championships, accompanied by the college executive director, Sam MacPhee, and a goodly crowd of supporters. And as the day approached, it was obvious that the presence of the band on unveiling day at Clachtoll would be a big attraction.

Preparations, and the planning of the finer details, brought people together in delightful fashion. Even after nearly two hundred years, Norman MacAskill told me in one of his very entertaining letters:

Back in the Highlands, horned sheep interrupt their grazing to watch strangers approach

The mention of the Rev. Norman is good for a mild argument among the right people. A wry octogenarian here said, "The world requires everybody. If there weren't good and bad, we wouldn't know we were perfect ourselves."

We have had pockets of Campbells in these parts too, as well as in Skye. Last month Ken Campbell from near Waipu, now resident in New Jersey, traced his ancestors' homes at Lochinver and made a contribution to the Norman McLeod Memorial Fund. His people sailed on the *Margaret.*

Another who found intense pleasure in discovering the Assynt of her ancestors, and cousins of varying closeness who still lived there, was Barbara Weiskrantz. She wrote to me:

Sutherland was absolutely magnificent this trip. My second cousin Alec Menzies, now 92, was recovering from a heart attack but insisting that he had to keep six of his remaining 22 sheep. He was sitting by the window with his binoculars at the ready and I was later amused to read the following in Alasdair Maclean's book *Night Falls on Ardnamurchan,* apropos of Highland gossiping: "Good fieldglasses were an important item of furniture in the old-style Highland home and were usually among the first purchases of newlyweds, giving precedence only to the female calf, the dozen point-of-lay pullets and the framed sampler of The Lord is my Shepherd. One regrets their passing for they were cheaper than the television sets that have replaced them and vastly more entertaining." Alec has both!

Barbara Weiskrantz, descendant of a cousin of Norman McLeod, unravelled the story of the migrants and those who stayed in Assynt. Seen here, flanked by her husband Larry (right) and the author.

It was only as the unveiling came nearer that a direct descendant of Norman McLeod, available to perform the ceremony, was discovered. Carolanne, born in Waipu and living in England with her husband, Captain Ron Brownbill, had accepted the invitation with, she told me, some trepidation. Norman MacAskill, seeking someone to speak for the Nova Scotian descendants now in New Zealand, had put the hard word on me; and I was devoured by nervousness thereafter.

My diary takes us from Heathrow to Inverness, and on to Assynt, a journey into an unknown county, a journey looked forward to with expectation and self-doubting:

What a contrast when we landed at Inverness! Chaos and confusion, with hundreds of travellers, mostly families starting their holidays, at Heathrow; here, a kind of rustic, cheerful simplicity. Two sturdy young men hurled luggage on the moving band; the car rental office had disappeared and the girls did their office work squatting against a wall. But the car we had ordered was there, although the keys were back in town!

Eventually we were on our way through a tidy, prosperous landscape, past signs that said "Inverness — Gateway to the Highlands," though any hills seemed a long way off. The miles flowed away like the frequent streams we skirted and suddenly the mountains were there: big, massive, rounded mountains with forest planted sometimes to their tops, sometimes leaving bare, rocky faces above the trees. The valley through which the road passed was broad and fertile. It was easy to imagine how the ice had, long, long before, ground the mountains away to make a path to the sea. There had not been much rain. The lake behind the hydro dam had shrunk down stony margins; we watched ragged clouds drape themselves over the mountain tops, breaking up before any rain came. The road climbed a long pass, empty of life. There had been sheep before, and occasional cattle. Now there was heather, brilliantly bright, green bracken and the bones of the mountains showing through thin layers of soil.

Now the road signs said "Ullapool", which proved to be a cheerful town on a long, deeply indented loch. Houses of stone, nearly all of them well-tended, with gabled windows emphasised with bright new paint. About twenty miles now to Lochinver where we would be staying. We could only imagine the full shape of the great mountains of Assynt, threatening us through awesome veils of cloud. Darkness seemed to be coming prematurely, the land steeped in gloom. Then suddenly, in late afternoon, the sun broke through. We drove through Elphin, and then down to the coast. Two hours after leaving Inverness we were in Lochinver, almost as far as one could get, in Britain, from the frenetic pressure of people and cars.

Lochinver stretches along the waterfront, with a Gothic hotel — ex duke's home — looking out on a giant fish processing plant. Inver Lodge Hotel where we stayed is up a private road and overlooks the whole loch. We sat at our window and watched fishing boats in succession wrinkle the smooth water and come into the wharf, with hosts of gulls feeding on the waste thrown overboard. Suilven, the mountain we longed to see, was hidden; the atmosphere was so restful it was hard to imagine the outer world. After dinner we went down to see Norman MacAskill and be briefed for the next day. We were in bed early.

August 2 was the day! What an awful morning. Slept lightly, and woke to a deep mist down to ground and sea level. We were due out at Stoer community hall at 11.30. Drove through the most desolate country imaginable; then suddenly at Clachtoll there were flat expanses of grass, crofts in fair numbers, stone walls neatly maintained and flocks of sheep. Also, in two big camping grounds, caravans and tents galore. At the hall, a grand welcome, made all the better because, just as we arrived, so also did Roland and Bonnie Thornhill from Nova Scotia. An exciting reunion. We were delighted also to meet the group of local women who laid on lentil soup, sandwiches and tea. The hereditary Highland talent for organising a warm welcome along with supplies of food and drink was as strong among these women as ever. It was no small party, for the St Ann's Pipe Band, plus supporters, were also there to add to the general conviviality.

After that, off to the unveiling. A remarkable number of spectators, seats for the speakers, a marquee in case of rain. Norman MacAskill congratulated himself on the way the misty rain switched off just as proceedings

Norman MacAskill

began. Everything went well. Roly Thornhill raised some laughs when he spoke about the epic film that Hollywood should make on the migration, with Robert Redford producing it and, as climax, the *Margaret* sailing up on Langs Beach at Waipu. Which all made it easier for me speaking after him.

It was good to meet a lot of the locals, a delightful bunch: Iain MacRae, of Maidenloch, who passed the vote of thanks in a witty and informal way; Mrs Flossie MacPhail, who someone described as "the community"; an old Highlander named Macaulay, in full regalia and quite unselfconscious of the effect; and the effervescent organiser, Mrs Ishbel Macauley. Her story is a signpost on the way the Highlands could go. A widow, she runs Cheviot ewes and hogs on her ten-acre holding. She was one of the Assynt women who combined with their menfolk to buy the 21,000-acre North Lochinver Estate and set up a trust including over one hundred crofters. Ishbel was appointed the crofting trust's director for the township of Stoer. The hope is that, instead of the land being the playground for the landlord and his friends, the crofters themselves will be able to run it in a businesslike way and no longer see their young people going away to find work. "I just cannot imagine Ishbel in her previous job," Carolanne told me. "She's such a lovely softy!" Ishbel's first career, until she retired ten years ago to become a crofter, was as a CID police inspector in Glasgow.

August 3: I looked out over the water, with one red-hulled fishing boat moving out gently past the breakwater to the Narrows. Not a sign of movement in the great fishing plant. Someone said: "The big fishing boats catch fish we don't eat here; their catch is sent untouched and fresh

Ishbel Macauley, former Glasgow CID inspector, now a crofter and devoted worker for her people. Photo: Willie Shand

in forty-ton trucks right through to Spain. The fish? Something called orange roughy." There are certainly conservative attitudes to fish. The orange roughy, recently discovered in huge numbers in very deep waters south of New Zealand, is so popular it is in danger of being fished out. But it hasn't enough flavour for the Highlander.

We drove to Elphin in cloudy weather, Suilven still frustrating us, showing only partly behind cloud, and stayed that night at Birchbank. Tom Strang, the owner, is a very experienced hill-walker, taking parties all round the area, and has written several guide books. We had a nice plain dinner: soup, crumbled haddock, potatoes, cauliflower, carrots. We are sharing a rental car with Barbara and Larry Weiskrantz, and enjoy meeting some of Barbara's local relatives. Signs on roadside: "Watch out for lambs." Larry's comment: "The fences are designed to keep the sheep on the roads!"

We're sorry not to have had more time with Norman MacAskill, and also with Sam MacPhee, but both are very busy men. Sam with the pipe band, and Norman who was leaving for Canada, and Nova Scotia, in a few days with his little Gaelic music group. I hope the band does well.

Looking back over the last few days there are pictures in my mind of the memorial stone, with Carolanne unveiling the plaque; and the playing of the band as they marched up to the memorial — music, against the soft surge of the sea. The pipers played their part nobly. When refreshments were served in the marquee, a few of them sang Gaelic songs, the man a former gold medallist at the Mod.

The barren hills of Assynt look down on the green fields of Clachtoll and the McLean memorial.

But above all there was the friendliness and warmth of greetings between people with a common bond, even though they had not met before.

Before leaving Birchbank, I woke early and looked out the window. And there, marvel of marvels, was a beautiful blue sky and Suilven clear all over! I dressed quickly, took my camera and managed to photograph Suilven, Cul Mor, Cul Beag and Stack Polly, four magic mountains, before the midges discovered me and forced me inside. The mountains stayed clear all day and, driving down to Ullapool, we were able to delight in the many faces they present to the world.

The road north beckoned. Here was country familiar to the ancestors of the migrants, many of them victims of the Sutherland Clearances. Near Lochinver a Mrs MacKenzie had pointed out to me the place where mothers would watch the ships taking their sons away. We set off in the morning, with the wind strong and clouds heavy. Over the road, sheep were lying against the fences, hens searching the field and bright washing dancing on the clothesline.

North to Kylesku over their grand new bridge, the loch steep-sided and threatening. There was major reconstruction for several miles; sign of greater tourist pressure, perhaps? On to Durness on the north coast where we froze as we looked at a craft village. Out to the north-west was Cape Wrath, a name that came not from the angry seas but because it was the "turning"

The unveiling completed by Carolanne Brownbill. Among visitors, the Hon. Roland Brownbill, former Minister of Culture and Tourism in Nova Scotia, on the right.

(Norse *hvarf*) for the Viking ships on their way to the fat lands further south. The grave of a Viking warrior had been recently found near Durness, and we let our imaginations drift over the fact that the Vikings had dominated Sutherland, and much of Britain and Europe, for over three hundred years. Going back that long from today, we would be back in Stuart times.

There are still echoes of the quality of timelessness that the Hebrides, and the Western Highlands, would once induce. One anecdote tells of the man researching the word *mañana*, and finding its equivalent in French, Urdu and so on. Eventually he came to the Hebrides and asked: "What would be the Gaelic equivalent of these words meaning tomorrow?" The Hebridean thought hard and finally said: "I can't recall any word conveying such urgency."

Through a timeless morning we drove on past sandy beaches, enlivened by occasional sunshine; a long way down Loch Eriboll, then in the afternoon along a one-way road where we met only two vehicles. The art of driving on one-way roads is to look ahead for a passing place, usually marked by a tall pole, and gamble on getting there first. The narrow road, running now to the south passed between Loch Hope and Ben Hope, over 3000 feet high. We paused to marvel at a 2000-year-old Iron Age brock before stopping for the night at Altnaharra. We were now at the head of Strathnaver which had been cleared of its inhabitants, in favour of sheep, by the infamous Patrick Sellars in the 1810s.

225

There was light rain, a fairly reliable companion when we set off in the morning, heading north again toward the coast. We were amazed at the fertile beauty of Strathnaver — bales of hay in hundreds, fields green and well-tended, climbing the hills to the barren upper slopes; ewes and lambs, big and bouncy, being mustered for the lamb sales. Bettyhill, a pleasant village on the coast, has a museum which we visited, housed in a former church, and melancholy for its reminders of former tragic events. Amazingly, we sat in warm sunshine at a Melvich restaurant, further along the coast, looking across to the Orkneys and east towards John o'Groats. The clouds lifted, mentally and physically, as we walked along a splendid beach beneath sturdy cliffs and eventually reached a lighthouse out on Strathy Point. We drove back to Altnaharra, this time up the great valley of the River Naver. No wonder, we thought, that Sellars and Company were ready to go to extreme lengths to clear Strathnaver of all human settlement, seeing it as a great sheep farm and reminding us of a run in back-country New Zealand.

Now, sadly, our journey of exploration and discovery in a fascinating area was coming to a close. We roused ourselves to another beautiful day — the Highlands had done us proud! Through Lairg, strategically placed for tourists and also for the sale of lambs; down to Bonar Bridge at the head of the Dornoch Firth; finally back to Inverness; and there we said goodbye to our friends Barbara and Larry, who had added so much to the pleasure of our travelling but who now had to hasten home to Oxford.

Only a week before, we had been standing on a mound above the water at Clachtoll, which now seemed part of a different planet. The great marble

The McLeod memorial looks down on a restless sea.

stone, with its inscription to Norman McLeod, son of Clachtoll and a leader who left his mark far across the world, is now part of the Assynt landscape, as fitting to the eye as the other stones which the Vikings, even greater travellers, raised to mark their presence in the lands they occupied and held for so long. No doubt, in centuries to come, travellers will study the stone, wondering who this man McLeod could have been and what strange venture had been commemorated. Legend takes over but, for a while at least, the name of Norman McLeod will raise echoes, sometimes strong, sometimes faint, in the minds of men and women living far different lives in lands a long way from Assynt. As will his last words: "Children, children, look to yourselves. The world is mad!"

Before returning home to New Zealand we saw other places which draw visitors to the Highlands: the tower at Glenfinnan, where Charles Edward Stuart raised his standard in 1745; and the field of Culloden where, a year later, Butcher Cumberland destroyed his army. A dramatic place even after 250 years; and how plainly one can see the way the Highlanders were manoeuvred into a hopeless position from the start: attacking uphill, across a marshy burn, with the enemy strong in artillery and mortars which cut them down before they could come to grips. Mounds where the dead were buried were their memorial — a memorial to the futility of war.

Even after all this my mind kept returning to the craggy memorial stone beside Clachtoll Bay, looking down on the site of the croft where Norman McLeod was born. An enigmatic figure. A fiery leader, but one who led his people in ways of peace, not war. I wonder what he felt when he read letters such as that from William McKenzie, who wrote from Clachtoll to his brother Donald at Waipu in August, 1858; a man who could write: "Norman McLeod, whose tender caressing of me when a boy I still freshly recollect." Norman would have memories of Assynt and Clachtoll, some pleasant, some harsh, but what would he have thought when he read on:

> The prospects here for young are somewhat obscure and discouraging, even young parties are strictly prohibited from marriage by the Soil owners, whose Property rules are in strict accordance with the old Egyptian depopulating code, even the stance of a Hut for young parties are utterly unobtainable in any condition.

That "desperately poor and oppressed period in Assynt and elsewhere" is not forgotten. "Before the Crofters Act 1886," Norman MacAskill writes to me, "the land-owners could evict people as they chose. When extra hands were no longer required for kelp-making, they discouraged marriages. When young couples married secretly and shared the parents' home, mealtimes had to be staggered and the same fire used. 'Two smokes' could mean detection and eviction. I remember the old folk talking of this."

227

Betty Powell, expert genealogist at the Waipu House of Memories, in the building she knows so well.

All this indeed happened and is part of a people's story. Norman McLeod would surely have remembered it. But what would he feel today, in contrast, if he could see the hills of Assynt, where new hope is growing among the crofters, along with far-reaching power to make decisions on the future of their land; if, too, he could see St Ann's and Baddeck, quieter now than when he was there, but still possessing a deep strength and unique charm; and Waipu, still in many ways a place apart, in spite of the pressures of a modern world, holding its quality in the face of change.

The Nova Scotian connection, back to the Highlands and the Hebrides, forward to New Zealand, still prevails.

Appendix 1

Ships and Passengers

The following is a list of vessels that brought the migrants to New Zealand from Nova Scotia, the names of heads of families, the number in each family, and the places from which they hailed.

The barque Margaret, 236 tons, Capt. Matson, from St Ann's, Nova Scotia, 28 October, 1851. Arrived Adelaide, South Australia, 10 April, 1852.

H.F. Anderson (1), Aberdeen; Donald Campbell (7), St Ann's; Kenneth Dingwall (1), St Ann's; Donald Finlayson, Baddeck; John Fraser, Esq. (7), St Ann's; Donald McGregor (8), St Ann's Glen; John McGregor (3), St Ann's; Roderick Matheson (1), St Ann's; Roderick McGregor (2), St Ann's; James McGregor (3), St Ann's; Hugh McInnes, Alex. McInnes, James McInnes (3), St Ann's; John McKay (14), Baddeck; Roderick McKay, Jr (3), Baddeck; Miss Martha McRae (7), Middle River; Roderick McKay, Sr (11), Baddeck; Donald McLeod (9), St Ann's; John D. McLeod (10), St Ann's; George McLeod (3), St Ann's; Rev. Norman McLeod (8), St Ann's; John Kerr (1), St Ann's; Thomas McLeod (1), St Ann's; John McLeod (1), St Ann's; Donald Ross, Esq. (10), St Ann's; Roderick Ross, Esq. (7), St Ann's; Hector Sutherland (9), St Ann's; Mrs Matson and family.

The brig Highland Lass, 179 tons, Capt. M. McKenzie, from Big Bras d'Or, Nova Scotia, 17 May, 1852. Arrived Adelaide, 6 October, 1852.

Catherine Finlayson (1), Baddeck; John Finlayson (4), Baddeck; Roderick Finlayson (4), Baddeck; Roderick Gillis* (3), Baddeck; Napoleon Gibbons† (1), Sydney, C.B.; Donald McDonald (10), Boularderie; Donald McDonald* (11), P.E. Island; Neil McGregor (2), St Ann's; Angus McKay (1), Baddeck; Duncan McKay (5), Grand River; Duncan McKay (11), Baddeck; Jonathan McKay (1), Baddeck; Duncan McKenzie (7), Baddeck; Murdoch McKenzie (7), Baddeck; Hector McKenzie (4), Baddeck; John McKenzie*(8), Baddeck; William McKenzie (3), Big Harbour; Donald McKenzie (5), Big Harbour; Murdoch McKenzie‡ (5), Big Harbour; Roderick McKenzie* (1), — ; Donald McLean (9), Baddeck; John McLennan (7), Big Harbour; John McQuarrie (1), Middle River; Alex. McRae* (6), Middle River; Duncan Matheson (1), Grand River; Thomas Orman* (1), Halifax; Colin Simson§ (1), Sydney Mines; Kenneth Stuart (7), St Ann's Glen.

The brig Gertrude, *215 tons, Capt. Rose, from St Ann's, 24 June, 1856. Arrived Auckland, New Zealand, 25 December, 1856.*

Alexander Buchanan (8), Big Glen, Baddeck; Donald Campbell (7), St Ann's; John Campbell, Esq., Middle River; Mrs John McRae (3), Middle River; Neil Campbell (8), St Ann's; Roderick Campbell (10), Middle River; John Gillanders (11), Middle River; Robert Haswell (9), St Ann's; Robert McDonald (5), St Ann's; Roderick McDonald (10), St Ann's; William McDonald (10), St Ann's; Donald McGregor (2), St Ann's; John McGregor (2), St Ann's; Murdoch McGregor (4), St Ann's; John McInnes (6), Big Glen, St Ann's; Ewen McInnis (4), St Ann's; George McKay (5), Laordois, Cape Breton; Alex. McKenzie (3), Middle River; Alex. McKenzie (5), St Ann's; John McLennan (4), Middle River; Alex. McLeod (5), St Ann's; Donald McLeod (10), St Ann's; Kenneth McLeod (5), St Ann's; Neil McLeod (3), St Ann's; William McLeod (4), St Ann's; Donald McMillan (3), St Ann's; Ebenezer McMillan (2), St Ann's; John McMillan (4), St Ann's; Norman McMillan (2), St Ann's; John Morrison (4), St Ann's; Aeneas Morrison (4), St Ann's; John Munro, Esq. (8), St Ann's; Donald Munro (1), St Ann's; Angus Nicholson (8), St Ann's.

The brigantine Spray, *107 tons, Capt. Duncan, from Big Bras d'Or, 10 January, 1857. Arrived Auckland 25 June, 1857.*

Neil Campbell (1), Kenneth Campbell (1), Middle River; A. Cameron (6), P.E. Island; John Duncan (2), Aberdeen; Alex. Finlayson (5), Baddeck; G.H. Horne (1), Antwerp; Alex. McKenzie (5), St Ann's; Alex. McKenzie (5), Big Harbour; Donald McKenzie (8), St Ann's Glen; Alexander McKenzie (2), St Ann's Glen; Hugh McKenzie (3), St Ann's Glen; Kenneth McKenzie (6) — ; Ewen McLean (1), St Ann's Glen; Farquhar McLennan (1), Middle River; Donald McLeod (2), St Ann's; Robert McNab (2), Baddeck; William McMillan (2), Baddeck; Angus Matheson (3), Baddeck; Duncan Matheson (3), Baddeck; Widow Matheson (5), St Ann's Glen; Ann Munro (1), St Ann's Glen; Alex. Stuart (3), Big Harbour; Archibald Stuart (3), Big Harbour; James Stuart (6), St Ann's Glen; John Urquhart (1), Boularderie (returned to Gairloch); Donald McMillan (1), Baddeck.

The barque Breadalbane, *224 tons, Capt. James, from Big Bras d'Or, 27 December, 1857. Arrived Auckland 21 May, 1858.*

Roderick Fraser (9), Boularderie; Roderick Fraser (2), St Ann's; Kenneth Ferguson (2), Boularderie; Charles Lewis (1), Prussia; Alex. McAulay (2), Bras d'Or; Colin McDonald (12), Boularderie; John McDonald (11), St Ann's; Norman McDonald (3), Boularderie; Widow McDonald (7), Big Harbour; Mrs Roderick McDonald (7), Big Harbour; John McInnis (2), — ; Donald McInnis (3), St Ann's; Malcolm McInnis (2), St Ann's; Roderick

McInnis (4), St Ann's; Alex. McKenzie (7), Boularderie; James McKenzie (3), Boularderie; M.T. McKenzie (6), Boularderie; William McKenzie (2), Boularderie; Roderick McKenzie (5), St Ann's; Donald McLean, St Ann's Glen; Roderick McLean (8), Boularderie; Murdoch McLennan (5), Boularderie; Norman McKay (1), — ; Mary McLean (1), St Ann's Glen; Alex. McLeod (10), St Ann's; Donald Morrison (9), St Ann's; Choan Stuart (2), Big Harbour; James Sutherland, Esq. (5), Boularderie; Hugh Sutherland (2), Boularderie; Mrs John McInnes (6), St Ann's.

The barque Ellen Lewis, *336 tons, Capt. Ross, from St Ann's, 1 December, 1859. Arrived Auckland 11 May, 1860.* [Owned by the Hon. William Ross and others.]

Alex Campbell (4), St Ann's; Donald Campbell (3), St Ann's; Hugh Campbell (7), St Ann's; Samuel Campbell (5), Broad Cove; Joseph Elmsley, M.D. (7), Baddeck; Mrs Jane Ferguson (5), St Ann's; James Fraser (8), St Ann's; John Fraser (6), Boularderie; Hugh Fraser (2), St Ann's; Peter Fraser (4), St Ann's; Allan Gillies (1), Broad Cove; John Gillies† (1), Broad Cove; Alex. Kempt (6), Boularderie; Duncan Kempt (5), Boularderie; Gregor Kempt (9), Boularderie; John Kempt (2), Boularderie; Donald McAulay (3), St Ann's; Murdoch McAulay (1), Baddeck; John McBeth (4), Middle River; John McDonald (4), St Ann's; Ewen McGregor (9), St Ann's; Alexander McIsaac (11), Broad Cove; Angus McIsaac† (1), Broad Cove; Hector McKay (5), Lake Ainslie; Murdoch McKenzie (2), St Ann's; D.H. McKenzie (1), St Ann's; Hugh McKenzie (4), St Ann's; William McKenzie (4), Big Harbour; Archie McLennan (1), Broad Cove; Donald McLeod (8), St Ann's, Big Glen; Hugh McLeod (5), St Ann's; John McLeod (8), St Ann's; Murdoch McLeod (8), St Ann's; Murdoch McLeod (1), St Ann's; Angus McMillan (4), St Ann's; Archibald McMillan (4), St Ann's; Donald McMillan (3), St Ann's; Neil McPhee (4), St Ann's, Big Glen; Roderick McRae (3), Middle River; Kenneth Matheson (8), St Ann's; Widow Munro (3), St Ann's; John Munro (4), St Ann's; John Munro (3), St Ann's; John McKenzie (5), Big Harbour; Kenneth McKenzie (4), — ; Angus McLean (4), St Ann's, Big Glen; Donald McLean (2), St Ann's, Big Glen; John McLean (4), St Ann's, Big Glen; Hugh McKinnon (1) — .

* Remained at Adelaide; ‡ Died at Adelaide; † Returned to Nova Scotia; § Lost at sea.

Appendix 2

Marriages of Migrants

Preparation of this list, a huge task, was originally undertaken by J.J. Finlayson and first appeared in N.R. McKenzie's *The Gael Fares Forth*, published in 1935. Since then, more information has come to hand. Betty Powell and an enthusiastic group centred on the House of Memories at Waipu has revised both sections, which now provide even more hard facts for those seeking information about their families. We owe warm thanks to Betty and her helpers for the work they have done.

Note. 'Family on Boat' includes parents. The figure 2 indicates a couple without children. To aid identification, nicknames are included in quotation marks and other information, such as the locality with which the person was associated (e.g. Heads) is given in brackets. A ? indicates an unknown name, and a — indicates either no offspring or an unknown number of children.

Barque *MARGARET*
Married before Migrating

Home/Head of Family			Family on Boat	Born in NZ
WAIPU				
Donald Campbell	*married*	Mary McLeod	9	–
John Fraser	*married*	Mary McLeod	8	–
John McGregor (Centre)	*married*	Elizabeth Matheson	8	–
Roderick McGregor	*married*	Mary McGregor	2	6
James McGregor	*married*	?	3	–
John McKay ("Ruadh")	*married*	Ann McRae	14	–
Roderick McKay ("Og")	*married*	Jessie McRae	4	6
Roderick McKay ("Seann")	*married*	Margaret Matheson	12	–
WHANGAREI HEADS				
Donald McGregor	*married*	Christina McRae	8	–
Donald McLeod	*married*	Helen Munro	9	–
John D. McLeod	*married*	Mary McGregor	10	–
George McLeod	*married*	Ann McGregor	3	–

WAIPU

Rev. Norman McLeod	*married*	Mary McLeod	8	–
Roderick Ross	*married*	Mary McLeod	7	5
Hector Sutherland	*married*	Jessie Ferguson	9	–

MELBOURNE AND AUCKLAND

Donald Ross	*married*	Sarah E. Hendry	10	–

Barque *M A R G A R E T*
Married in New Zealand

Home/Name			*Children*

WAIPU

Donald, son of John Fraser	*married*	Christina McKenzie	5
Hugh, son of John Fraser	*married*	Margaret McKay	9
Martha McRae	*married*	John Dingwall	2
Jessie, daughter of John Fraser	*married*	Capt. John Jacob	–

NEW PLYMOUTH

Murdoch, son of John Fraser	*married*	Eleanor Macrae	7

WHANGAREI HEADS

Kenneth, son of Donald McGregor	*married*	Ann McLean	6
Donald, son of Donald McGregor	*married*	Mary McRae	11

WAIPU

Donald, son of John McGregor	*married*	Catherine McLeod	9
Murdoch, son of John McGregor	*married*	Jessie McDonald	2
Donald, son of John McKay	*married*	Arabella McRae	6
Roderick, son of John McKay	*married*	Christina McDonald	7
Alex., son of John McKay	*married*	Mary McRae	12
John, son of John McKay	*married*	Alexandrina Stewart	12
Philip, son of John McKay	*married*	Jessie McLean	–
Norman, son of John McKay	*married*	Barbara McGregor	5
Alex., son of Roderick McKay ("Seann")	*married*	Margaret Sutherland	3
Donald, son of Roderick McKay ("Seann")	*married*	Isabella McKay	6
John M., son of Roderick McKay ("Seann")	*married*	Winifred McLennan	8

WHANGAREI HEADS

Donald J., son of John D. McLeod	*married*	Margaret McDonald	3
John, son of John D. McLeod	*married*	Frances Wykes	4
Lexy, daughter of John D. McLeod	*married*	Alex. Ross	11
Jessie, daughter of John D. McLeod	*married*	George Ross	7
John G., son of Rev. N. McLeod	*married*	Mary McGregor	3
Roderick, son of Don. McLeod	*married*	Annie McDonald	–
George, son of Geo. McLeod	*married*	Matilda Drewitt	6

WAIPU

Murdoch, son of Rev. N. McLeod	*married*	Margaret Finlayson	2
John, son of Hector Sutherland	*married*	Mrs Mary Mort (*née* Breen)	5

CLEVEDON

Hugh, son of Hector Sutherland	*married*	Ann Campbell	13
Janet, daughter of H. Sutherland	*married*	George Munro	11
Mary, daughter of H. Sutherland	*married*	Thos. Hyde	1

AUCKLAND

Margaret, daughter of Hector Sutherland	*married*	James George	8
Jessie, daughter of H. Sutherland	*married*	Thomas Shove	6

WANGANUI

Ann, daughter of H. Sutherland	*married*	John Cameron	5

AUCKLAND

Hugh F. Anderson	*married*	Margaret McLeod	4

WAIPU

Robert Campbell, son of Donald	*married*	Isabella McKay	10
Donald Finlayson	*married*	Christina Matheson	2
Alex. McInnes	*married*	Ann Campbell	3
Angus McInnes	*married*	Jessie McKenzie	–
John McLeod (McAllister)	*married*	Annabella Matheson	5

Barque *MARGARET*
Married in Australia

MELBOURNE

Donald, son of Rev. N. McLeod	*married*	Caroline Hillier	–

ADELAIDE

Ewen McInnes	*married*	Mary McBain	5

HIGHLAND LASS
Married before Migrating

Home/Head of Family			Family on Boat	Born in NZ
WAIPU				
John Finlayson	*married*	Mary McLean	3	7
Roderick Finlayson	*married*	Catherine McLean	4	8
Donald McDonald	*married*	Margaret McKenzie	11	3
Neil McGregor	*married*	Catherine McKenzie	2	5
Duncan Kennedy McKay	*married*	Elizabeth McKay	5	4
Duncan McKay ("Ban")	*married*	Mary McRae	12	–
Capt Dun. McKenzie	*married*	Jessie McKenzie	7	4
Hector McKenzie	*married*	(1) Mary Campbell	4	–
		(2) Christina McKay*	–	4
William McKenzie ("Beag") son of Murdoch and Arabella	*married*	Annabella McKenzie	3	6
Capt. Mur. McKenzie	*married*	Elizabeth Campbell	7	3
Donald McLean	*married*	Catherine McGregor	10	–
John McLennan	*married*	Christina McKenzie	7	4
Murdoch McKenzie died in Australia	*married*	Arabella McKenzie	5	–
WHANGAREI HEADS				
Kenneth Stuart	*married*	Margaret McGregor	10	–
AUCKLAND				
Donald McKenzie	*married*	Jessie McKenzie	5	–

* married in New Zealand

HIGHLAND LASS
Married in New Zealand

Home/Name			Children
WAIPU			
Murdoch, son of Donald McDonald	*married* (1)	Margaret Cameron	4

		(2) Catherine McGregor – (from Nova Scotia c. 1878)	
Kenneth, son of Don. McDonald	*married*	Mary McAulay	11
William, son of Don. McDonald	*married*	Isabella Fraser	8

OHAUPO

Norman, son of Don. McDonald	*married*	Margaret Morrison	9

WAIPU

Donald, son of Duncan "Ban" McKay	*married*	Flora Stewart	7

NAPIER

John, son of Duncan "Ban" McKay	*married*	Isabella McKenzie	8

AUCKLAND

Roderick, son of Duncan "Ban" McKay	*married*	Elizabeth Murchie	6

WAIPU

Alex., son of Duncan "Ban" McKay	*married*	Maria Ross	9
Duncan, son of Duncan "Ban" McKay	*married*	Mary Campbell	8

AUCKLAND

Kenneth, son of Capt D. McKenzie	*married*	Elizabeth Smith	4
John, son of Capt. D. McKenzie	*married*	Mary Smith	5
John, son of Capt. M. McKenzie	*married*	Jane Smith	4

WAIPU

Norman, son of Capt. D. McKenzie	*married*	Mary Campbell	8
Murdoch, son of Donald McLean	*married*	Mary McLeod	6
Donald, son of Donald McLean	*married*	Margaret McLeod	2
John, son of Donald McLean	*married*	Dolina McLeod	9
John McQuarrie	*married*	?	–

CAMBRIDGE

Margaret, daughter of Capt. D. McKenzie	*married*	Jas. Anderson	9

WHANGAREI HEADS

Capt. Donald, son of Kenneth Stuart	*married*	Ann McLeod	7
Duncan, son of Kenneth Stuart	*married*	Isabella Urquhart	7

MAUNU

Kenneth, son of Kenneth Stuart	*married*	Jane McMillan	3

WAIPU

Kenneth McLennan, son of John	*married*	Isabella McAulay	1
Duncan H. McKenzie, son of Hector	*married*	Mary McKenzie	–
Jonathan McKay	*married*	Catherine McDonald	2
Alexander Finlayson	*married*	Margaret McInnes	8

G E R T R U D E
Married before Migrating

Home/Head of Family			Family on Boat	Born in NZ
KAURI				
Alex. Buchanan	*married*	Jessie Munro	8	–
WAIPU				
Donald Campbell	*married*	Ann Matheson	10	–
Neil Campbell	*married*	Catherine McLeod	8	2
Roderick Campbell ("Buchan")	*married*	Catherine McKay	10	–
AUCKLAND				
John Gillanders	*married*	Mary McRae	11	–
WAIPU				
Robert Haswell	*married*	Christina Gunn	9	–
WHANGAREI HEADS				
Robert McDonald	*married*	Margaret McMillan	2	–
WHAU VALLEY				
Roderick McDonald	*married*	Mary Matheson	10	–
Kenneth McLeod	*married*	(1) Barbara McLeod*	2	–
		(2) Ann McDonald	9	–

KAURI

William McDonald	*married*	Catherine McKenzie	10	–

WAIPU

Donald McGregor (Cove)	*married*	Catherine McGregor	2	3
John McGregor	*married*	Ann Morrison	2	–
Murdoch McGregor	*married*	Christina McGregor	5	2
John McInnes	*married*	Catherine Nicholson*	6	–

WHANGAREI

George McKay	*married*	(1) Sarah McInnes	6	–
		(2) Johanna Maitland†		–

WAIPU

Alex. McKenzie (Shoemaker)	*married*	Jessie Campbell	3	4
Alex. McKenzie ("Thung")	*married*	Annabella McKenzie	5	4
John McLennan	*married*	Mary Campbell	5	4
Donald McLeod ("McAllister")	*married*	Barbara Munro	10	–
Alex. McLeod ("McAllister")	*married*	Jessie McLeod‡	3	2
John Campbell	*married*	Henrietta McRae*	1	–

KAURI

William McLeod	*married*	Barbara McKenzie	4	4

WAIPU

Ebenezer McMillan	*married*	Barbara Haswell	2	11
John McMillan	*married*	Elizabeth Campbell	8	2

AUCKLAND

Norman McMillan	*married*	Margaret Haswell	2	8

WAIPU

John Morrison	*married*	Isabella McKay	9	–
Aeneas Morrison	*married*	Jane McKay	2	–

WHANGAREI HEADS

John Munro (Owner)	*married*	Isabella McKenzie	8	–

OKAIHAU
Angus Nicholson   *married*   Mary McInnes   8   3

WAIPU
Neil McLeod   *married*   Christina Munro   3   –

* died in Cape Breton; † married in New Zealand; ‡ later Mrs David Hay

GERTRUDE
Married in New Zealand

Home/Name			Children
WAIPU			
John G., son of Neil Campbell	*married*	Marion Fraser*	4
Neil J., son of Neil Campbell	*married*	Margaret Campbell	5
NAPIER			
Charles, son of Neil Campbell	*married*	Mary Greenwood	4
WAIPU			
Alexander P., son of Rodk. Campbell	*married*	Annie McKay	8
JORDAN			
Donald, son of Donald McLeod ("McAllister")	*married*	(1) Jessie Fraser	1
		(2) Margaret McLean	8
WAIPU			
John A., son of Don. McLeod ("McAllister")	*married*	Margaret McKenzie	3
Donald Munro	*married*	Ann McLeod	–
KAURI			
John, son of John McMillan	*married*	Flora McKenzie	5
KAMO			
Donald, son of John McMillan	*married*	Mary McKenzie	2
John Campbell, son of Donald	*married*	Annie McDonald	5
Norman Campbell, son of Donald	*married*	Annie Lang	10
KAURI			
Kenneth McDonald, son of William	*married*	Mary Stewart	4

WAIPU
Donald McGregor, son of Murdoch	*married*	Margaret Kelly	7
Thomas McLennan, son of John	*married*	Ann McKenzie	7

AUCKLAND
Henry Haswell, son of Robert	*married*	Elizabeth Lang	12

WAIPU
Alex. McLeod ("Eiric")	*married*	Mary McLean	6
Alex. Nicholson, son of Angus	*married*	Susan Howe	9
James Nicholson, son of Angus	*married*	Annabella McKenzie	8
Don. C., son of F. McLennan	*married*	Margaret McGregor	6
John Nicholson, son of Angus	*married*	Isabella McKenzie	–

KAURI
John McLeod, son of William	*married*	Maria McPhee	6
Alex. M. McLeod, son of William	*married*	Jemima Simpson	1

* from the South Island

GERTRUDE
Married in Australia

John W. MacKay, son of George	*married*	Katrine J. Bilson	2
Donald Gillanders, son of John	*married*	Christina McKay	5

SPRAY
Married before Migrating

Home/Head of Family			Family on Boat	Born in NZ
KAIWAKA				
Alex. Cameron	*married*	(1) Margaret McIntyre	–	–
		(2) Catherine McLean	6	–
WAIPU				
Donald McKenzie	*married*	Arabella Matheson	8	–
Hugh McKenzie	*married*	Mary Fraser	5	5
ONEHUNGA				
Alex. McKenzie	*married*	Isabella Stuart	4	4

WAIPU				
Ewen McLean*	*married*	Sarah McLeod	3	5
Farquhar McLennan*	*married*	Flora Campbell	5	3

KAURI				
Alex. MacKenzie	*married*	Margaret Matheson	6	–

WHANGAREI HEADS				
Alex. McKenzie ("Ban")	*married*	Ann Stuart	5	4

AUCKLAND				
Robert McNab	*married*	Jessie Matheson†	2	–

HAKARU				
William McMillan	*married*	Isabella Stewart	2	6
Archibald Stewart	*married*	Margaret Ross	3	8
James Stewart	*married*	Margaret McLeod	8	2

OMAHA				
Angus Matheson	*married*	Jessie Matheson	3	10

WHANGAREI HEADS				
Alex. Stewart	*married*	Flora Stuart	3	–

OMAHA				
Kenneth McKenzie	*married*	Margaret McKenzie	6	–

* family by *Gertrude*. Hence some confusion in records. † later Mrs Sealey

SPRAY
Married in New Zealand

Home/Name			*Children*

WAIPU			
Alex. J. Finlayson	*married*	Flora McKay	6
Roderick McKenzie, son of Donald	*married*	Jane Fraser	–
Murdoch W. McKenzie	*married*	Jessie McGregor	10
John B. McKenzie, son of Hugh	*married*	May Kidd	3

OMAHA			
Alex. Matheson, son of Angus	*married*	Mary Haskell	7
Duncan Matheson	*married*	Catherine Finlayson	4

Alex. McKenzie	*married*	Catherine Kempt	1

KAURI

John MacKenzie*	*married*	Flora McInnes	5
Alex. G. MacKenzie*	*married*	(1) Flora McInnes	4
		(2) Barbara McInnes	4
Norman MacKenzie*	*married*	Jessie McKenzie	–

WHANGAREI HEADS

Kenneth Stewart, son of Alexr	*married*	Jessie Sutherland	7

AUCKLAND

Dan Ewen McLean, son of Ewen	*married*	Helen Guinea	6

HAKARU

Kenneth Stewart, son of Archibald	*married*	Frances Rouse	1

WAIPU

John P. Cameron, son of Alexr	*married*	Maria McLennan	5
Kenneth Campbell	*married*	(1) Mary McKenzie	1
		(2) Rose Archibald	–

CAMBRIDGE

Margaret Matheson, niece of Donald McKenzie	*married*	Wm. Riley	5

ONEHUNGA

Alex. McKenzie Jr., son of Alexr	*married*	Elizabeth Geard	3

* sons of Alexander

BREADALBANE
Married before Migrating

Home/Head of Family			Family on Boat	Born in NZ
WAIPU				
Roderick Fraser ('Miller')	*married*	Marcella McLennan	11	–
WHANGAREI HEADS				
Roderick Fraser	*married*	Dolina McLeod	2	–

WAIPU

Kenneth Ferguson	*married*	Margaret McDonald	2	–
Alex. McAulay	*married*	Arabella McKenzie	4	10
Colin McDonald	*married*	Mary Fraser	12	–

WHANGAREI HEADS

John McDonald	*married*	Margaret McLeod	11	–

WAIPU

Norman McDonald ("Mhor")	*married*	Ann McKenzie	3	–

KAURI

John McInnes	*married*	Mary McLeod	2	–
Donald McInnes*	*married*	(1) Flora McKenzie	3	5
		(2) Jessie McLeod	–	–
Malcolm McInnes*	*married*	Ann McLeod	2	8
Roderick McInnes*	*married*	Mary McLeod	4	8

WAIPU

Alex. McKenzie ("Mhor")	*married*	Ann Fraser	8	–

OKAIHAU

James McKenzie	*married*	Jessie McDonald	3	12

WAIPU

Murdoch T. McKenzie	*married*	Margaret Sutherland	6	4
William McKenzie ("Alester Mohr")	*married*	Annabella Sutherland	2	9

OTAGO

Roderick McKenzie	*married*	Barbara McLeod	5	–

WAIPU

Donald McLean ("Pa")	*married*	Ann Morrison	5	4
Roderick McLean ("Bhui")	*married*	Margaret McKenzie	8	3
Murdoch McLennan	*married*	Hannah Fraser	4	–

WHANGAREI HEADS

Alex. McLeod (Mason)	*married*	Margaret McLeod	10	–

WAIPU

Donald Morrison (Cave)	*married*	Catherine McAskill	8	–

WHANGAREI HEADS

Coan Stewart	*married*	?	2	–

WAIPU

James Sutherland	*married*	(1) Margaret Fraser	–	–
		(2) Christina McDonald	5	–
Hugh Sutherland, son of James	*married*	Margaret McDonald	2	7

˙ sons of John

B R E A D A L B A N E
Married in New Zealand

Home/Name			*Children*

WAIPU

Rev. J. Murdoch, son of Rodk. Fraser	*married*	Ada Brooks	–
John, son of Roderick Fraser	*married*	Catherine McLean	6

OKAIHAU

Johanna McAulay, daughter of Alexr	*married*	Jas. White	8
Hector, son of Roderick Fraser	*married*	Dolina McLean	19

MARTON

Murdoch McDonald	*married*	Pauline Fenner	2

KAURI

Norman McInnes, son of Rodk.	*married*	Jean Henry	7

PARUA BAY

Alex. McDonald, son of John	*married*	Dolina McLeod	4

WAIPU

Murdoch, son of Colin McDonald	*married*	(1) Sarah Campbell	7
		(2) Ann McMillan	–
Donald, son of Colin McDonald	*married*	Catherine McRae	–

WHANGAREI

John D. McKenzie, son of Murdoch T.	*married*	Flora McInnes	5

WAIPU

John, son of Donald McLean	*married*	Mary Morrison (Cave)	10

WHANGAREI

Neil, son of Donald McLean	*married*	Isabella McDonald	10

WAIPU

Duncan, son of Roderick McLean	*married*	Mary Urquhart	4
John, son of Roderick McLean	*married*	Elizabeth McGregor	5

AUCKLAND

Capt. Murdoch, son of James Sutherland	*married*	Henrietta McKenzie*	3

WAIPU

John D., son of James Sutherland	*married*	Mary Ann McKay	7

OHAUPO

Kenneth Morrison (Cave), son of Donald	*married*	Harriet Temperly	4

WAIPU

John Morrison (Cave), son of Donald	*married*	Bessie Scott	5
Charles Lewis	*married*	Christina Morrison	9
Kenneth McAulay, son of Alexr	*married*	Jessie McRae	5

AUCKLAND

Donald McInnes[†]	*married*	Mary Haswell	2
Norman McInnes[†]	*married*	Christina McInnes	5

* later Mrs Wm. Bruce; † sons of Widow McInnes (Flora Shaw)

ELLEN LEWIS
Married before Migrating

Home/Head of Family			Family on Boat	Born in NZ
Alex. Campbell	*married*	Jane Moore*	6	–
Donald Campbell	*married*	(1) Sarah McLeod	3	2
		(2) Catherine Campbell	–	3
WAIPU				
James Fraser	*married*	(1) Catherine Fraser	3	–
		(2) Margaret McDonald	4	2
WAIHEKE				
John Fraser	*married*	Mary Kempt	6	–
AUCKLAND				
Peter Fraser	*married*	Jessie Fraser	9	–
WAIPU				
Hugh Fraser, son of James	*married*	Mary Collins	2	1
OMAHA				
Alex. Kempt	*married*	Annabella Fraser	6	–
Duncan Kempt	*married*	Mary Morrison	5	–
Gregor Kempt	*married*	Mary McGregor	9	–
Alexr Kempt, son of Alex.	*married*	Margaret E. Robertson	–	–
WAIPU				
John Kempt, son of Duncan	*married*	Ann McPherson	2	–
Donald McAulay	*married*	Margaret McGregor	6	3
KAURI				
John McBeth	*married*	Ann McLennan	4	4
WHAU VALLEY				
John McDonald	*married*	Flora McKenzie	4	6

KAMO
Ewen McGregor	*married*	Catherine Matheson	9	–

THAMES
Alexander McIsaac	*married*	Mary Beaton †	11	–

MERCURY BAY
Hector McKay	*married*	Mary McLean	5	–

WAIPU
Murdoch McKenzie ("Ban")	*married*	Christina McAulay	2	6

KAURI
Hugh McKenzie	*married*	Jessie McInnes	4	3

AUCKLAND
Angus McLean	*married*	Mary McKay	5	7
John McLean ("Big John")	*married*	Mary McLean	5	3

DEVONPORT
Donald McLean	*married*	Isabella McLean	3	7

WAIPU
Hugh McLeod	*married*	Catherine McAulay	4	7
Ewen Campbell	*married*	Ann McKinnon	7	–
Donald McLeod ("Bear")	*married*	Ann Morrison	8	–

HIKURANGI
John McLeod	*married*	Mary McDonald	12	–

AUCKLAND
Murdoch McLeod‡	*married*	Isabella McDonald‡	9	–

WAIPU
Angus McMillan	*married*	Mary McLeod	5	7
Archibald McMillan	*married*	Ann Campbell	4	1
Donald Mc Millan ("Gow")	*married*	Christina McLeod	5	8
Roderick McRae	*married*	Jane Fraser	3	7

KAURI

Neil McPhee	*married*	Henrietta McLeod	4	5

HIKURANGI

Kenneth Matheson	*married*	Flora McKenzie	11	–

KAMO

John Munro	*married*	Catherine Matheson	4	9

MARSDEN POINT

John Munro	*married*	Leah Thompson	4	3

WAIPU

Kenneth McKenzie ("Ruadh")	*married*	Ann Kempt	4	5

OTAHUHU

Dr Jos. Elmsley	*married*	Lydia Ingraham	7	4

* later Mrs Semaderi; † died at Cape Breton; ‡ died shortly after arrival

ELLEN LEWIS
Married in New Zealand

Home/Name			*Children*

WAIPU

Andrew, son of Hugh McLeod	*married*	Ann McMillan	10
John McLeod, son of Donald ("Bear")	*married*	(1) Margaret Campbell	8
		(2) Mary McLean	–
		(3) Kate McPherson	–
William McLeod, son of Donald	*married*	Isabella McKay	14

NAPIER

Donald, son of Donald McLeod ("Bear")	*married*	Isabella Coghill	2

WAIPU

Neil H. Campbell, son of Ewen	*married*	Catherine McInnes	7
Alex. D. Kempt, son of Gregor	*married*	Jessie McDonald	7
Don. M. McLeod, son of Murdoch ("Danny Mohr")	*married*	Maria Campbell	8

GISBORNE

Malcolm McLeod, son of Murdoch	*married*	(1) Louisa Brown	2
		(2) Alice Phillips	
		(*née* Brown)	–

WAIPU

Murdoch McLeod ("Neil")	*married*	Annabella Matheson	2

KAURI

Dan. McKenzie, son of Hugh	*married*	Margaret Whitelaw	1
John McKenzie, son of Hugh	*married*	Catherine Archibald	4
Murdoch McPhee, son of Neil	*married*	Jeannie Whitelaw	3
Malcolm McPhee, son of Neil	*married*	Flora McInnes	3
Kenneth Matheson, son of Kenneth	*married*	Elizabeth Henry	6

HIKURANGI

Alex. McLeod*	*married*	(1) Kate Davis	1
		(2) Edith Murphy	–
Donald McLeod*	*married*	Catherine McLeod	5

KAIMAMAKU

Donald ("Dan") Matheson, son of Kenneth	*married*	Antonie Heyber	10

AUCKLAND

Capt. D.H. McKenzie	*married*	Margaret Smith	4

WAIPU

Murdoch McAulay	*married*	Isabella McLean	4
Roderick McGregor	*married*	Jean Kempt	2

WHAU VALLEY, WHANGAREI

Malcolm McDonald†	*married*	Beatrice Dando	9
Don. McDonald†	*married*	Jessie McKenzie	7

AUCKLAND

Murdoch McLean‡	*married*	Isabella Ratcliffe	10

WELLINGTON

Neil McLean‡	*married*	Hannah Ratcliffe	4

TUTUKAKA

Hugh Ferguson	*married*	Isabella McLean	9

WHANGAROA

Hugh McKinnon	*married*	Jessie McLeod	7

WAIPU

Don ("Dan"), son of Arch. McMillan	*married*	Ann McGregor	1
Norman, son of Arch. McMillan	*married*	Mary Beasley	14

MERCURY BAY

James, son of Hector McKay	*married*	Isabella Cameron	7

THAMES

Allan Gillies	*married*	Anne McIsaac	7
Francis McIsaac§	*married*	Charlotte Copeland	3
Joseph McIsaac§	*married*	Catherine Peterson	6

* sons of John; † sons of John; ‡ sons of "Big John"; § sons of Alex

PIONEERS BY OTHER SHIPS
From Scotland Direct

Pioneer Family

WAIPU

Duncan Allison	*married*	Catherine McLean	9
John Durham, son of Christina	*married*	Mary McLennan, daughter of John	13
William Lang	*married*	Ann McGregor, daughter of John	5
Hector McDonald	*married*	Ann McKenzie	7
Duncan McLean, brother of Rodk "Rory Bhui" McLean, *Breadalbane*	*married*	Rebecca Watson	6
John McLean	*married*	Mary McRae	2
Murdoch McKay	*married*	Jessie McRae	5
Norman Matheson	*married*	Ann McDonald	10
J. Duncan Morrison	*married*	(1) ? (2) Lily Lamont	2 or 3 –
Kenneth Morrison	*married*	(1) Margaret Matheson (2) Margaret McGregor, daughter of John	2 3
Finlay Urquhart	*married*	Christina McLean	4
Alex. Kenny	*married*	Mary Mills	2

John McFarlane	*married*	Ann McMillan	10

WHANGAREI
Simon Fraser	*married*	Margaret McKenzie	6

KAIWAKA
David Balderston	*married*	Margaret Logan	3
John Cameron, son of Alex., *Spray*	*married*	Mary McPherson	4
James Hastie	*married*	Jane Cameron	5
William Leslie	*married*	Ann Bairnson	5
James Morrison	*married*	?	–
Robt. S. Ross	*married*	Christina Munro	9

WHANGAREI
John Hector McDonald	*married*	Mary Louisa Smith	6

WHANGAREI HEADS
Murdoch McRae	*married*	Ann Urquhart	8
Donald Urquhart	*married*	Catherine McAskill	5

From Prince Edward Island

KAIWAKA
Angus Stewart	*married*	Margaret Stewart	6

From Nova Scotia via Melbourne

AUCKLAND
Capt. Alex McGregor	*married*	Charlotte Matheson	–

MARRIAGES OF MIGRANT WOMEN
List compiled by Mrs C.J. Lang

This list, which is probably not quite complete, contains the names of women whose husbands were not Nova Scotian Gaels. The names of others may be found in the foregoing list.

MARGARET

Dolina, daughter of Donald McGregor (Heads)	*married*	Richard Harnett
Martha, daughter of Don. McGregor	*married*	John Urquhart
Mary, daughter of John McKay ("Ruadh")	*married*	Thos. Fenton

251

Mary, daughter of Donald Campbell   *married*   James Findlay
Sarah, daughter of Rodk. McKay
  ("Seann")   *married*   Christopher McLennan
Margaret, daughter of Donald McLeod
  (Heads)   *married*   — Paul
Henrietta, daughter of Donald McLeod
  (Heads)   *married*   James McLeod
                                    (Scotland to Bay of Islands)

HIGHLAND LASS

Margaret, daughter of Capt. M. McKenzie *married*   Roderick McLeod
Mary, daughter of Duncan McKay   *married*   Joseph Webster
Annie, daughter of Murdoch McKenzie   *married*   And. Anderson
Mary McKenzie*   *married*   Robt. Shedden
Jessie McKenzie*   *married*   William Miller
Flora McKenzie*   *married*   William Adair
Catherine, daughter of Rodk. Finlayson   *married*   Rev. Wm. Macrae
Mary, daughter of Donald McDonald   *married*   Richard Hoe
Mary, daughter of Neil McGregor   *married*   Herbert Carter
Mary, daughter of Kenneth Stuart   *married*   Henry Murphy
Margaret, daughter of Kenneth Stuart   *married*   John Faulkner
Alexandrina, daughter of Kenneth Stuart *married*   Saml. Ruddle

* daughters of Donald McKenzie

GERTRUDE

Isabella, daughter of William McDonald   *married*   Norman McLennan
Kate, daughter of Norman McMillan   *married*   Fred. Dibble
Margaret, daughter of Donald Campbell   *married*   Henry Gill
Annie, daughter of Donald Campbell   *married*   John Urquhart
Catherine, daughter of Donald Campbell *married*   Capt. James Smith
Christina, daughter of Rodk Campbell   *married*   Duncan McQuarrie
Christina, daughter of Robt Haswell   *married*   Thos P. Williams
Johanna, daughter of John Munro   *married*   James I. Wilson
Catherine, daughter of John Munro   *married*   Henry S. Wilson
Catherine, daughter of Wm McDonald   *married*   Peter Sinclair
Margaret, daughter of Neil Campbell   *married*   Richard Byrne
Anne, daughter of John Morrison   *married*   W. McNeil
Katherine, daughter of Alex Buchanan   *married*   James Murchie
Mary, daughter of John Gillanders   *married*   — Blaikie
Annabella, daughter of Alex McKenzie   *married*   William Friar

Jane, daughter of Donald McLeod	*married*	Bartlett Stevens
Margaret, daughter of Donald McLeod	*married*	Robert Davidson
Ann, daughter of Kenneth McLeod	*married*	Hector McQuarrie
Henrietta, daughter of Mrs John McRae (widow)	*married*	William Walker
Johanna, daughter of Mrs John McRae (widow)	*married*	Robert Hill

SPRAY

Catherine, daughter of James Stewart	*married*	Leslie Vickers
Margaret, daughter of Alex. Cameron	*married*	Geo. Bailey
Margaret, daughter of Alex. McKenzie (Onehunga)	*married*	Fred. Moore
Annie, daughter of Ewen McLean	*married*	Albert Brookes
Christina, daughter of Alex. MacKenzie (Kauri)	*married*	Andrew Dreaver
Isabella, daughter of Angus Matheson	*married*	Wm. Young
Johanna, daughter of Mrs Margaret Matheson ("Widow")	*married*	(1) Henry Maitland (2) George McKay

BREADALBANE

Christina McKenzie*	*married*	Thos. Gell
Jessie McKenzie*	*married*	Richard Fleet
Johanna McKenzie*	*married*	James Longbottom
Annie McKenzie†	*married*	Josiah Wykes
Margaret McKenzie†	*married*	Simon Fraser
Johanna McKenzie†	*married*	John McRae
Margaret, daughter of Rodk. Fraser ("Miller")	*married*	George Carter
Margaret, daughter of Donald Morrison	*married*	George Thornton
Mary, daughter of Murdoch McLennan	*married*	Chas. Bishop
Annie Macleod‡	*married*	Andrew Munro
Jessie Macleod‡	*married*	Capt. Angus Kerr
Ann Macleod‡	*married*	Capt. Donald Kerr
Flora Macleod‡	*married*	James W. Kerr
Margaret, daughter of John McDonald (Heads)	*married*	Robert Howie
Jessie, daughter of John McDonald (Heads)	*married*	Joseph Strong

253

Flora, daughter of John McDonald
(Heads)   *married*   Hugh Caven

Ann, daughter of Mrs John McInnes
(widow)   *married*   Alex Sutherland

Ann, daughter of Roderick McKenzie
(Otago)   *married*   John McRae

* daughters of Alex McKenzie ("Mhor"); † daughters of Murdoch T. McKenzie;
‡ daughters of Alex. Macleod

ELLEN LEWIS

Annie, daughter of Donald McLeod ("Bear")	*married*	Oscar Bryan
Annie, daughter of Hugh McLeod	*married*	Neil Campbell
Johanna, daughter of Hugh McLeod	*married*	Malcolm McLeod
Mary, daughter of Donald Campbell	*married*	John Lozell
Christina, daughter of Donald Campbell	*married*	(1) Rodk Urquhart (2) Herman Johansen
Annie, daughter of Donald Macaulay	*married*	James Cobb
Mary, daughter of Donald Macaulay	*married*	Wm. Hill
Catherine, daughter of Donald Macaulay	*married*	Arthur Hill
Jessie, daughter of Donald Macaulay	*married*	Patrick Gribbon
Flora, daughter of Neil McPhee	*married*	Richard Weaver
Jane, daughter of Alex. Campbell	*married*	Clive Rose
Eliza, daughter of Alex. Campbell	*married*	Alfred Carter
Margaret, daughter of James Fraser	*married*	Matthew McDonald
Mary, daughter of James Fraser	*married*	Thomas Kelsey
Nora, daughter of James Fraser	*married*	Ebenezer Morris
Catherine, daughter of James Fraser	*married*	William Lister
Jessie, daughter of James Fraser	*married*	Richard Dunne
Janet, daughter of James Fraser	*married*	Richard Farrar
Jessie, daughter of Gregor Kempt	*married*	Robert Hodge
Johanna, daughter of Gregor Kempt	*married*	James Wallace
Catherine, daughter of John McBeth	*married*	John Cork
Elizabeth, daughter of John McBeth	*married*	Nicholas Murphy
Catherine, daughter of Angus McMillan	*married*	Andrew Craig
Catherine, daughter of Donald McMillan	*married*	Alex. McKenzie
Jane Matheson*	*married*	John Burden
Johanna Matheson*	*married*	(1) John McKay (2) Donald Matheson
Willina Munro†	*married*	George Ross

Isabella Munro[†]	*married*	George Sutherland
Flora, daughter of John Munro (Marsden Pt)	*married*	James Witt
Flora McLeod[‡]	*married*	Jos. Simcock
Anne McLeod[‡]	*married*	Chas. Simcock
Mary McLeod[‡]	*married*	John Sinclair
Dolina McLeod[‡]	*married*	Wm. Paton
Christina McLeod[‡]	*married*	Ken. McKenzie
Ann McLeod[§]	*married*	Wm. Abraham
Johanna McLeod[§]	*married*	Henry Meurant
Catherine, daughter of Hector McKay	*married*	Capt. Norris
Mary Fraser[ʃ]	*married*	Wm. Whitmarsh
Betsy Fraser[ʃ]	*married*	— Colson
Margaret Kempt[**]	*married*	Thos. Knaggs
Isabella Kempt[**]	*married*	Geo. Knaggs

From Scotland direct

Christina Urquhart (Heads)	*married*	Horace T.E. Rowlands

[*] daughters of Kenneth Matheson; [†] daughters of John Munro (Kamo);
[‡] daughters of John McLeod (Hikurangi); [§] daughters of Murdoch McLeod;
[ʃ] daughters of Peter Fraser; [**] daughters of Duncan Kempt

WIDOWS WHO ACCOMPANIED THEIR SONS

HIGHLAND LASS

Ann (McDonald), widow of John McKenzie and mother of Capts Duncan and Murdoch McKenzie. Died 8 January, 1871, aged 93.

GERTRUDE

Henrietta (McLeod), widow of Neil McLeod and mother of Alex. McLeod, who was drowned in the *Thistle*. Died March 1865, aged 70.

SPRAY

Christina (Cameron), widow of John Finlayson and grandmother of J.J. and Norman Finlayson. Died 18 November, 1875, aged 85.

Isabella (Cameron), widow of Ewen Matheson and mother of Capts Duncan and Angus Matheson, owners of the *Spray*. Died 19 January, 1891, aged 90.

BREADALBANE

Catherine (McGregor), widow of Roderick McDonald and mother of Murdoch and Colin McDonald. Died at Marton, 24 December, 1877, aged 76.

Flora (Shaw), widow of John McInnes, died in Auckland.

ELLEN LEWIS

The widow of Donald Munro, Senior, died at the Braigh, Waipu. She was born in Assynt, Sutherlandshire, and was one of the early settlers of St Ann's. She was the mother of John Munro (Kamo).

Bibliography

Ainslie, Kenneth, *Pacific Ordeal*

Butler, Dick. *This Valley in the Hills*, 1963

Collins, G.N.M. *The Days of the Years of my Pilgrimage*, 1991

Delaney, Frank. *A Walk to the Western Isles*, 1994

Gillis, James D. *The Cape Breton Giant*, 1993

Gunn, Neil. *Butcher's Broom*

Haldane, A.R.B. *The Drove Roads of Scotland*, 1952

MacDonald, Gordon. *The Highlanders of Waipu*, 1928

MacGregor, Alisdair A. *Over the Sea to Skye*, 1934

MacInnes, Hamish. *West Highland Walks: Two*, 1979

MacKay, Donald. *Scotland Farewell: The People of the* Hector, 1980

MacLean, Norman. *The Former Days*, 1945

McKenzie, N.R. *The Gael Fares Forth*, 1935, 1942

MacLeod, Ian G. *A History of the Church in St Ann's*, 1970

McPherson, Flora. *Watchman Against the World*, 1962, 1993

Molloy, Maureen. *Those Who Speak to the Heart*, 1991

Markham, A.H. *Cruise of the* Rosario: *Kidnapping in the South Seas*, 1873

Nicholson, John A. *et al. Middle River: A Cape Breton Community*, 1985

Prebble, John. *The Highland Clearances*, 1963

Robinson, Neil. *Lion of Scotland*, 1952, 1974

Smout, T.C. and Wood, Sydney. *Scottish Voices 1745–1960*, 1990

Stanley, Laurie. *The Well-Watered Garden: The Presbyterian Church in Cape Breton, 1798–1860*, 1983

Index